Fundamentals of

Pharmaceutical Inorganic Chemistry

Fundamentals of Pharmaceutical Inorganic Chemistry

Dr. Rati Kailash Prasad Tripathi
Assistant Professor (Pharmaceutical Chemistry)
Department of Pharmaceutical Science
Sushruta School of Medical and Paramedical Sciences
Assam University (A Central University), Silchar
Assam, India

I.K. International Pvt. Ltd.
NEW DELHI

Published by
I.K. International Pvt. Ltd.
4435-36/7, Ansari Road, Daryaganj
New Delhi-110 002 (India)
E-mail: info@ikinternational.com
Website: www.ikbooks.com

ISBN 978-93-90620-23-4

Published by Krishan Makhijani for I.K. International Pvt. Ltd., 4435-36/7, Ansari Road, Daryaganj, New Delhi–110 002 and Printed by Rekha Printers Pvt. Ltd., Okhla Industrial Area, Phase II, New Delhi–110 020.

Preface

Fundamentals of Pharmaceutical Inorganic Chemistry is meant for **Bachelor of Pharmacy** students. The book follows the revised syllabi framed by the Pharmacy Council of India under Regulation 6, 7 & 8 of the Bachelor of Pharmacy (B. Pharm) course regulations 2014, which came into effect from the Academic Year 2016–17.

Pharmaceutical Inorganic Chemistry is a discipline of pharmacy incorporating the study of various pharmaceutical inorganic compounds used as drugs or intermediates in the preparation of drugs. Inorganic compounds also occur in abundance in the biological systems wherein they play a vital role in the smooth functioning of almost all physiological processes pertaining to life.

The idea of writing this book was an ever-growing research and daily addition of newer and novel information on developing new drug entities to benefit the human beings and making students aware about them.

In the present book, subject matter has been organized into different classes of inorganic compounds including their pharmaceutical standards, methods of preparation, physical and chemical properties, assays, identification tests, incompatibilities, storage conditions and medicinal and pharmaceutical applications. It has been compiled in a unit-wise format as per the prescribed syllabi. It includes five units. Each unit has been written in a simplified manner with the objective to enable easy grasp of the subject matter.

Unit 1 introduces the students to the basics of pharmaceutical chemistry and pharmaceutical inorganic chemistry. It also presents information on various types of Pharmacopoeias including Indian Pharmacopoeia, sources and types of impurities in pharmaceuticals and various tests to identify and control them, viz., limit tests as per Indian Pharmacopoeia 2014. This has been followed by **Unit 2** containing information on pharmaceutical inorganic compounds belonging to categories like acids, bases and buffers; and dental products. Additionally, major intra- and extracellular electrolytes have been dealt with to familiarize the students regarding the importance of various electrolytes for the proper functioning of human physiological processes. **Unit 3**

provides information on gastrointestinal agents (viz., acidifiers, antacids, cathartics, and antimicrobial agents). **Unit 4** comprises detailed description of various inorganic compounds of pharmaceutical importance and includes various miscellaneous classes like expectorants, emetics, haematinics, poison and antidotes, and astringents. Besides, various aspects of radio pharmaceuticals that are gaining recognition in pharmaceutical, medical and research fields are presented in **Unit 5**.

The concluding part includes appendices, viz., the methods of various reagent preparations **(Appendix 1)**, buffers solutions used in pharmacy and research **(Appendix 2)**, as per Indian Pharmacopoeia; and some important definitions **(Appendix 3)**.

All these units and appendices have been systematically well-written and put together in a comprehensive manner with the aid of neat and labelled figures, tables and reactions such that the subject is made easy to understand and remember by the students.

I sincerely hope that this book will be immensely helpful to the teachers of Bachelor of Pharmacy as well as the students and research scholars to gain fundamental knowledge of the subject and to succeed in various examinations.

Constructive suggestions for the betterment of this book are gladly accepted and will be appreciatively recognized.

"Best wishes for the first step towards success ..."

Dr. Rati Kailash Prasad Tripathi

Contents

1
Pharmaceutical Chemistry

1.1 INTRODUCTION

- Pharmaceutical chemistry is a branch of science that makes use of general laws of chemistry to study medicinal and pharmaceutical substances, including their synthesis, isolation, identification of chemical nature and composition, structural elucidation and structural modification, biochemical changes after drug administration, evaluation of their pharmacological effects and investigation of structure-activity relationship studies.
- It also includes the study of physical and chemical properties of drugs, the methods of quality control, quality assurance and conditions of their usage in addition to their delivery, pharmacokinetics and pharmacodynamics.
- Pharmaceutical chemistry depends on various other chemical disciplines, such as inorganic, organic, analytical, physical and colloid chemistry, and medico-biological disciplines such as pharmacology, physiology, biological chemistry, etc., to study therapeutic pharmaceutical substances, also called drugs.

1.1.1 Prospects of Pharmaceutical Chemistry

The various panoramas of pharmaceutical chemistry include:

- Procedures for isolation, purification and characterization of medicinally active agents and substances from natural sources like mineral, vegetable, animal or microbiological origin which finds use in treatment of diseases and in compounding prescriptions.
- Synthetic methods by which natural substances are converted into products possessing more favourable therapeutic or pharmaceutical properties.
- Determination of medicinal substances which results in optimum medicinal activity with good stability and elegant dispensing.
- Determination of chemical and biological incompatibilities amongst various ingredients of a prescription.

- Establishment of safe and pragmatic standards with respect to both dosage and quality, to maintain uniform and therapeutic measures for all forms of medication.

1.1.2 Inorganic Pharmaceutical Chemistry

- Inorganic pharmaceutical chemistry is a branch of science that makes use of the laws of chemistry to study inorganic substances as drugs, viz., their preparation, chemical nature, composition, structure, standards of purity, tests for identification, limit tests for quality determination, extent of purity, storage conditions, influence on an organism, therapeutic uses, etc.
- It includes the study of the entire elements and their compounds, except carbon and its compounds (which basically are studied in organic chemistry).
- The principal source of inorganic drugs is the natural sources, such as minerals. However, several of these substances have been established to be malicious but still are employed cautiously by some physicians in sufficiently low quantities (e.g., arsenic, antimony and mercury).
- The various branches of inorganic chemistry include bioinorganic chemistry, co-ordination chemistry, organometallic chemistry, synthetic inorganic chemistry, etc.
- Inorganic compounds have wide range of applications in pharmaceutical field, including catalysis, surfactants, pigments and agriculture.
- The term 'pharmaceutical' relates to any chemical substance that finds use in the preparation of medicament for internal administration of the human beings.

1.1.3 Importance of Inorganic Pharmaceuticals

The inorganic pharmaceuticals exhibit a variety of applications such as:

- In pharmaceutical analysis, e.g., potassium permanganate ($KMnO_4$) and ethylenediamine tetra acetic acid (EDTA), etc.
- As pharmaceutical aids, e.g., talc, bentonite, etc.
- For therapeutic purposes, e.g., antimicrobials, antacids, etc.
- As replenishers, e.g., sodium chloride (NaCl), potassium chloride (KCl), etc.
- As reagents to carry out reactions, e.g., reducing agents like lithium aluminium hydride ($LiAlH_4$), catalysts like palladium, nickel, etc.

1.2 INTRODUCTION TO PHARMACOPOEIA

- Every country has its legislation on pharmaceutical preparations that sets criteria and obligatory quality indices for medicaments, raw materials, and preparations employed in the manufacturing of drugs.
- These regulations are presented as separate articles, general and specific, related to individual drugs and are published in the form of a book called 'Pharmacopoeia'.

- The word 'pharmacopoeia' derives from the Greek words, '*pharmakon*', which means 'a drug or medicine' and '*poeia*', which means 'to make'.
- Thus, pharmacopoeia, meaning 'drug-making', in the modern technical sense, is a book comprising of instructions for the identification of compound medicines and published by the authority of a government or a medical or pharmaceutical society of the respective countries.

1.2.1 Classification of Compendia

- The drug compendia are classified as (a) Official compendia, and (b) Non-official compendia.

(a) Official Compendia

- Official compendia are the compilations of drugs and other related substances which are recognized as legal standards for purity, quality and strength by the government of the respective countries of their origin.
- Examples include:
  - British Pharmacopoeia (BP)
  - British Pharmaceutical Codex (BPC)
  - Indian Pharmacopoeia (IP)
  - United States Pharmacopoeia (USP)
  - National Formulary (NF)
  - The State Pharmacopoeia of USSR
  - Pharmacopoeias of other countries

(b) Non-Official Compendia

- Non-official compendia are the books other than official drug compendia which are used as secondary reference sources for drugs and other related substances.
- Examples include:
  - Extra pharmacopoeia (Martindale)
  - United States Dispensatory
  - Merck Index

1.2.2 History of Pharmacopoeia

- The term 'Pharmacopoeia' was first used in 1580 in a book on drug standards printed in Bergamo, Italy.
- Later, a number of national pharmacopoeias were published by various European Pharmacopoeias - the London, the Edinburgh and the Dublin Pharmacopoeias were official throughout the kingdom.
- Each pharmacopoeia described different strengths and methods of preparation for the same formulation, causing a lot of confusion.

- To overcome this difficulty, the first British Pharmacopoeia (BP) came into existence in 1864. It included monographs on benzoic acid, camphor, gallic acid, lactose, sucrose, tartaric acid, tannic acid and seven alkaloids along with their salts.
- Besides, the first United States Pharmacopoeia (USP) was published in December 1820, both in English and Latin.

1.2.3 Indian Pharmacopoeia

- Indian Pharmacopoeia (IP) is an official document meant for overall quality control and assurance of pharmaceutical products marketed in India by way of contributing on their safety, efficacy and affordability.
- IP is published by the Indian Pharmacopoeia Commission (IPC) on behalf of the Ministry of Health & Family Welfare, Government of India, to promote public health in India by bringing out authoritative and officially accepted standards for quality of drugs, including active pharmaceutical ingredients (APIs), excipients and dosage forms, used by health professionals, patients and consumers.
- IP contains a collection of authoritative procedures of analysis and specifications for drugs.
- The IP, or any part of it, has got legal status under the Second Schedule of the Drugs & Cosmetics Act, 1940 and Rules 1945 thereunder.
- It prescribes standards for identity, purity and strength of drugs essentially required from health care perspectives of human beings and animals.
- IP standards are authoritative in nature. They are enforced by the regulatory authorities for quality control of medicines in India.
- During quality assurance and at the time of dispute in the court of law, the IP standards are legally acceptable.

1.2.3.1 History of Indian Pharmacopoeia

- The history of the IP began in the year 1833 when a committee of the East Indian Company's Dispensary recommended the publication of a pharmacopoeia and thereby, Bengal Pharmacopoeia and General Conspectus of Medicinal Plants were published in 1844, which mainly listed most of the commonly used indigenous remedies.
- This was followed by IP 1868, which covered both the drugs of British Pharmacopoeia (BP) 1867 and indigenous drugs used in India, with a supplement published in 1869 incorporating the vernacular names of indigenous drugs and plants.
- However, from 1885, the BP was made official in India.
- Later in 1927, a Drugs Enquiry Committee appointed by the Government of India, recommended the publication of National Pharmacopoeia.

- After independence, the Indian Pharmacopoeia Committee was constituted in 1948 for publication of IP as its primary function and also, maintaining it up-to-date.
- Further, revisions were made to pharmacopoeia and published periodically in the form of supplements to keep the pharmacopoeia up-to-date with respect to matters pertaining to the drug quality.

Table 1.1: Publication history of the Indian Pharmacopoeia

Edition	Year	Addendum/supplement
1st	1955	Supplement 1960
2nd	1966	Supplement 1975
3rd	1985	Addendum 1989
		Addendum 1991
4th	1996	Addendum 2000
		Vet supplement 2000
		Addendum 2002
		Addendum 2005
5th	2007	Addendum 2008
6th	2010	Addendum 2012
7th	2014	Addendum 2015
		Addendum 2016
8th	2018	Addendum 2019

- The first edition of IP was published in 1955, followed by a Supplement in 1960.
- It contained both western and traditional system drugs commonly used in India and the same policy continued while preparing the pharmacopoeia of India 1966 and its Supplement in 1975.
- There had been a phenomenal growth and development of the Indian Pharma Industry since independence, especially from early 1970, both in the range of APIs (Active Pharmaceutical Ingredients) and the dosage forms produced.
- This totally transformed the profile of the Indian Pharmaceuticals market and the Indian pharma industry emerged as one of the important global suppliers of pharmaceutical products, both to the developed and developing countries.
- In view of these rapid advances, it was decided to publish a new edition of the pharmacopoeia and its Addenda at regular and shorter intervals, for which the Indian Pharmacopoeia Committee was reconstituted in 1978.
- In the IP 1985, its Addenda 1989 and 1991, inclusion of traditional system of drugs was limited. However, most of the new drugs manufactured and/or marketed were included, while only those herbal drugs which had definitive quality control standards had got place in it.

1.2.3.2 Specific Features of the First Edition of IP (1955)

- Covered 986 monographs.
- Titles of monographs in Latin language.
- Weight and measures in metric system.
- Doses were expressed in both metric and English system.
- Abbreviated titles were used.
- List of preparations was given at the end of some of the monographs.
- Descriptive terms were used for solubility instead of exact solubility.

1.2.3.3 Specific Features of the Second Edition of IP (1966)

- Published in 1966 and its supplements in 1966 and 1975.
- Titles of monographs changed from Latin to English.
- Name of the drug comes first in title.
- Solubility expressed in parts of solvent per unit part of solute.
- 93 new monographs were added.
- New analytical techniques were included.
- Test for sterility was modified to detect fungi.
- 'Usual strength' was used as heading to represent the strength of tablet.
- 214 monographs from IP 1955 were deleted.

1.2.3.4 Role of CIPL in IP Work

- Central Indian Pharmacopoeia Laboratory (CIPL) was established in 1965 under Directorate General of Health Services, M/o H&FW as subordinate office/ laboratory of CDSCO/DCG (I) (i.e., Central Drugs Standard Control Organization/ Drug Controller General of India).
- Drugs Controller was the Member Secretary, and Director, CIPL was the member of IP Committee.
- CIPL played an active role in publication of IP 1985, IP 1996 and its subsequent Addendum in 2000 and 2002, along with other regulatory and zonal testing of drug samples from North Zone of India.

1.2.3.5 Specific Features of the Third Edition of IP (1985)

- Published in 1985 with two volumes and nine appendices.
- 260 new monographs were added and 450 were amended.
- ew analytical techniques like flame photometry, fluorometry, electrophoresis, gas liquid chromatography, etc. were introduced.
- Dissolution was introduced.
- Microbial limit tests were prescribed for liquid preparations.
- Determination of viscosity was modified and involved the use of Ostwald viscometer.

- New appendix "Water for Pharmaceutical Use" was introduced.
- Drugs were renamed and some drugs were omitted.
- Addendum I to IP 1985 was published in 1989, wherein 46 new monographs were added and 126 amended.
- Addendum II to IP 1985 was published in 1991, wherein 62 new monographs were added and 110 amended.

1.2.3.6 Development in IP for 21st Century

- In view of the continuing rapid increase in the range of drugs produced in India, the IP 1996, its Addendum 2000, Supplement 2000 for veterinary products and Addendum 2002 were published.
- For the first time, emphasis was given to veterinary products in veterinary Supplement 2000 to IP 1996.
- First time the monographs on anti-retroviral drugs were introduced in the Addendum 2002.
- Moreover, the IP Committee deleted the obsolete or less used product monographs and added monographs based on the therapeutic merit, medical need and extent of use of such articles in the country.

1.2.3.7 Specific Features of the Fourth Edition of IP (1996)

- Published in 1996 and its Addendums in 2000, 2002 and 2005.
- Contained 1149 monographs and 123 appendices in two volumes.
- Computer-generated structural formulae were used.
- Infrared (IR) and ultraviolet (UV) absorption spectrophotometric tests for identification of drug were added.
- Included 294 new monographs and 110 were deleted.
- High performance liquid chromatography, used as analytical method, was added.
- Bacterial endotoxin tests were introduced.
- Quantitative method for determination of particulate matter in injectable preparation was replaced by qualitative method.
- Monographs of oral rehydration salt (ORS), ORS-bicarbonate was omitted and ORS-citrate formula was added.
- Specific biological assays and tests were transferred to individual monographs.
- The veterinary supplement of IP 1996 contained 208 monographs and four appendices.

1.2.3.8 Role of IPC in Frequent Publication of IP

- The IPC was established in 2005, after dissolving the existing IP Committee and started working in existing CIPL with its Director as Member Secretary.

- The Addendum 2005 was published by IPC which included a large number of anti-retroviral drugs and raw plants commonly used in making medicinal products not covered by any other pharmacopoeias, which attracted much global attention.
- It provided systematic approach and practices for publication of IP 2007.
- Ministry of Health and Family Welfare, Govt. of India, submerged the existing CIPL along with IPC as a fully financed autonomous body from 1st Jan, 2009, located at NCR (National Capital Region) in Ghaziabad.
- The IPC Secretariat and Indian Pharmacopoeia Laboratory (IPL) staff, with the support of different advisory experts committee and expert members of the scientific body examined the suitability of the standards for the 6th edition IP 2010.

1.2.3.9 Specific Features of the Fifth Edition of IP (2007)

- Published in 2007 (three volumes) followed by its addendum in 2008.
- Volume one contained general notices, structure of IPC and acknowledgements.
- Volume two and three contained general monographs on dosage forms, drug substances and pharmaceutical aids.
- It contained 271 new monographs with focus on those drugs and formulation that covered the National Health Care Programmes and the National Essential Medicines.
- Addendum 2008 to IP 2007 contained 72 new monographs and an amendment was published in the year 2008.

1.2.3.10 Specific Features of the Sixth Edition of IP (2010)

- Published in 2010 (three volumes) followed by its Addendum in 2012. In addition, DVD of IP 2010 was also available.
- Volume one contained notices, preface, structure of IPC and general chapters.
- Volume two contained general monographs on dosage form, drug and pharmaceutical aid (A to M).
- Volume three contained general monographs on dosage form, drug and pharmaceutical aid (N to Z).
- It contained monographs on anti-retroviral, anti-cancer, anti-tuberculosis and herbal drugs.
- It further emphasized on biological monographs such as vaccines, immunosera for human use, blood products, biotechnological and veterinary (biological and non-biological) preparations.
- Standards for new drug under NHP (Natural Health Products) were added.
- Microbial contamination chapter was updated.
- Chapter on Nuclear Magnetic Resonance Spectra was incorporated in appendices section.

- New chapter on liposomal products was also added.
- Addendum 2012 to the IP 2010 was published which had taken care of the amendments to IP 2010 along with 52 new monographs.

1.2.3.11 Publication of IP 2014

- The 7th edition, IP 2014 was published (4th Nov, 2013) in accordance with the principles and designed plan decided by the Scientific Body of the IPC.
- The standards prescribed in this edition were encouraged to adhere with the concept of harmonization, keeping in view the technological status for manufacture and analysis of drugs and pharmaceuticals in the country, without compromising with the quality of the products.
- 577 new monographs were added in this edition.
- Number of monographs and appendices were expanded further to incorporate the latest technological advancements and regulatory compliance and to bring them in line with the International Standards.

1.2.3.12 Specific Features of the Seventh Edition of IP (2014)

- For the first time, IP 2014 was included with DVD-ROM.
- Out of 577 new monographs, 134 API monographs, 161 formulations monographs, 18 excipient monographs, 43 NDS (New Drug Submission) monographs, 10 antibiotic monographs, 19 anti-cancer monographs and 11 anti-viral monographs were included in this edition.
- Also, 31 herbal monographs, 5 monographs on vaccine & immunosera for human use, 6 monographs on insulin products and 7 monographs on biotechnology products were included.
- 19 new general chapters and about 200 new IR spectra's were also added.
- For the first time, 19 new radiopharmaceutical monographs with one general chapter on radiopharmaceutical preparations were introduced.
- In addition, a separate volume of veterinary products was also introduced for easy access.
- 143 monographs on veterinary products along with 16 Appendices/general chapter on veterinary products were also introduced.
- Use of chromatographic methods was greatly extended.
- More specific IR and UV spectrophotometer tests were introduced and chemical tests for identification of articles were eliminated.
- Tests for pyrogens were almost eliminated.
- Obsolete monographs were also omitted.
- Additionally, it included several new monographs not included in any other major pharmacopoeias of the world.

- Thus, total number of IP standards reached almost 3000, which was almost at par with other international pharmacopoeias and comprised different categories of drugs and appendices as mentioned in **Table 1.2.**

Table 1.2: Total standards in IP 2014

S. No.	Particulars	Number of monographs	Total new monographs
1.	General monograph on dosage forms	37	
2.	Monographs on drug substances, dosage forms and pharmaceutical aids (A to Z)		
	APIs	850	2013
	Formulations	1035	
	Excipients	128	
3.	Monographs on vaccines and immunosera for human use	63	245
4.	Monographs on herbs and herbal product	123	
5.	Monographs on blood and blood-related products	29	
6.	Monographs on biotechnology products	11	
7.	Monographs on radiopharmaceuticals	19	
8.	Monographs on veterinary products		
	Non-biological	208	290
	Biological	56	
	Diagnostics	14	
	Immunosera	05	
	Surgical	07	
Total monographs		2585 + 82 = 2667	
Appendices		197	
Total standards		2782 + 82 = 2864	

1.2.3.13 *New Chapters Added in IP 2014*

These included:

(a) Biological methods
(b) Chemical methods
(c) Physical and physicochemical methods
(d) Pharmaceutical methods

(a) Biological Methods

(i) DNA-based authentication techniques
(ii) Transfusion and infusion assemblies and similar medical devices or sterile assemblies and medical devices
(iii) Amino acid analysis

(b) Chemical Methods

(i) 2-Ethylhexanoic acid
(ii) Assay of folic acid
(iii) Ammonium
(iv) Assay of Alpha tocopherol
(v) Fluorides

(c) Physical and Physicochemical Methods

(i) Bulk density and tapped density of powders
(ii) Completeness of solution
(iii) Crystallinity
(iv) Specific surface area
(v) Mass spectrometry
(vi) Ethylene oxide and dioxin
(vii) Acetic acid in peptides
(viii) Inductively coupled plasma - mass spectrometry
(ix) Characterization of crystalline and partially crystalline solids by X-ray powder diffraction
(x) Flash point

(d) Pharmaceutical Methods

(i) Polymorphism

1.2.3.14 IP Addendum 2015 and 2016 to IP 2014

- General chemical tests for identification of an article were almost eliminated and the more specific IR and UV spectrophotometric tests were given emphasis.
- The use of chromatographic methods were greatly extended to cope with the need for more specificity in assays and particularly, in accessing the nature and extent of impurities in ingredients and products.
- Most of the existing assays and related substances tests were upgraded by liquid chromatographic methods in view to harmonize with other international pharmacopoeias.
- General chapters on volumetric glasses, peptide mapping, sterility testing, conductivity, solubility, dissolution test, bulk density and tapped density of powders were revised for monitoring the quality of drug.
- For controlling the microbial quality of all medicinal products, general chapters on microbial contamination in non-sterile products and test for colony forming units were revised.

- **Table 1.3** enlists the new additions to IP 2014 in the form of Addendum 2015.
- Further, IP Addendum 2016 comprised inclusion of various categories of drugs such as antiviral, anticancer, antibacterial, antihypertensive, antidepressant and analgesic, etc. Addendum 2016 to IP 2014 incorporated 89 New Monographs consisting of 64 Chemical Monographs, 14 Herbal Monographs, 3 Vaccines and Immunosera for human use, 3 Radiopharmaceuticals Monographs, 1 Blood Related products, 4 Biotechnology Products Monographs and 2 General Chapters.

Table 1.3: New additions to IP 2014 (IP Addendum 2015)

S. No.	Particulars	Number of items	Total number of items
1.	Monographs on drug substances, dosage forms and pharmaceutical aids (A to Z)		
	APIs	43	57
	Formulations	14	
2.	Other monographs		
	Herbal monographs	13	25
	Vaccines & immunosera for human use	02	
	Radiopharmaceutical preparations	10	
3.	Revised monographs	06	
4.	Revised tests	29	
5.	New IR spectras	20	

1.2.3.15 IP 2018

- The latest edition of Indian Pharmacopoeia, IP 2018, was released on 29th September, 2017.
- IP 2018 has been brought out in four volumes incorporating 220 new monographs (chemical monographs - 170, herbal monographs - 15, monographs on blood and blood-related products - 10, vaccines and immunosera for human use monographs - 02, radiopharmaceutical monographs - 03, biotechnology-derived therapeutic products - 06, veterinary monographs - 14), 366 revised monographs and 07 omissions.

1.2.3.16 Specific features of Eighth Edition IP (2018) and its Addendum (2019)

The following steps have been taken for monitoring drug standards:

- General chemical tests & thin layer chromatography for identification of an article have been almost eliminated and more specific IR, UV spectrophotometer and high performance liquid chromatography tests have been given emphasis. The concept of relying on published IR spectra as a basis for identification has been continued.
- The use of chromatographic methods has been greatly extended to cope with the need for more specificity in assays and in particular, in assessing the nature and extent of impurities in ingredients and products.

- Most of the existing assays and related substances test methods are upgraded by liquid chromatography in view to harmonize with other international pharmacopoeia.
- Pyrogen tests have been replaced by bacterial endotoxin tests in parenteral preparations and other monographs.
- For ease of access to make pharmacopoeia more user-friendly, Index has been incorporated in Volume I along with that already existing in Volume IV of IP.
- 53 new Fixed Dose Combination (FDC) monographs have been included, out of which 25 FDC monographs are not available in any pharmacopoeia.
- General chapters on volumetric glassware, conductivity, dissolution test, disintegration test, dimensions of hard gelatine capsule shells, etc. have been revised.
- For controlling the microbial quality of the entire medicinal products, general chapter on maintenance, identification, preservation and disposal of microorganisms have been revised.
- Besides this, index is also added to Volume I of IP 2018.
- Volume IV of IP 2018 contains veterinary monographs and index separately.
- IP Addendum 2019 to IP 2018 contains 66 new monographs including those of chemicals (61) (viz., Monographs on Dosage Forms - 33, APIs - 26, and Fixed Dose Combination - 2), herbs and herbal products (3), and radiopharmaceuticals preparations (2). One general monograph on lotion has also been included in this Addendum. Special emphasis has been given to the dosage forms of API whose dosage forms were not in the IP 2018. General chemical tests for identification of an article have been almost eliminated and more specific infrared, ultraviolet spectrophotometric, HPLC (High Performance Liquid Chromatography) and HPTLC (High Performance Thin Layer Chromatography) tests have been given emphasis. Special emphasis has been given to include/ upgrade dissolution test in the existing monographs. Most of the existing assays and tests on related substances have been upgraded to liquid chromatography method.

1.2.4 Pharmacopoeial Description

Most of the pharmacopoeias, including Indian Pharmacopoeia, consist of three major sections, namely:

(a) Introduction including general notices
(b) Monographs of the official drugs
(c) Appendices and index

1.2.4.1 Introduction Including General Notices

- It is a useful pointer to pharmaceutical progress since last edition.
- It summarizes the different changes, including additions/deletions in the current edition as compared to the last edition.

- To avoid misinterpretation and misunderstanding of later parts of the text, attention should be paid to general notices at the outset.

1.2.4.2 Monograph

- In pharmacopoeias, each pharmaceutical has been described under a monograph.
- **Monograph** is a document which defines pharmaceutical substances and provides information for its proper identification.
- In a broader sense, it is the reference work for pharmaceutical drug specifications.
- The pharmacopoeial monographs have been organized as described below:
  - (a) Title
  - (b) Chemical formulae
  - (c) Atomic and molecular weight
  - (d) Category
  - (e) Doses
  - (f) Statement of content or standards
  - (g) Description
  - (h) Solubility
  - (i) Identification
  - (j) pH
  - (k) Limit for impurities
  - (l) Assay
  - (m) Storage
  - (n) Storage containers
  - (o) Labelling

(a) Title

- The main title for a drug substance is the International Non-proprietary Name (INN) approved by the World Health Organization (WHO).
- Subsidiary names and synonyms are also given in some cases; where included, they have the same significance as the main title.
- Synonyms drawn from the full non-proprietary name of the active ingredient or ingredients are also given.
- For example, *calcium carbonate* can also be called *precipitated chalk.*

(b) Chemical Formulae

- The title is followed by the chemical formulae of the pure compound.
- It refers to the chemically pure substance and is not to be regarded as an indication of the purity of the official material.

- Where the absolute stereochemical configuration is specified, the International Union or Pure and Applied Chemistry (IUPAC) *R/S* and *E/Z* systems of designation are used.
- If the substance is an enantiomer of unknown absolute stereochemistry, the sign of the optical rotation, as determined in the solvent and under the conditions specified in the monograph, is attached to the systematic name.
- For example, potassium permanganate has the formula $KMnO_4$.

(c) Atomic and Molecular Weights

- The atomic weight or molecular weight of the substance is shown as and when appropriate at the top right-hand corner of the monograph.
- The atomic and molecular weights and graphic formulae do not constitute analytical standards for the substances described.
- For example, potassium permanganate has the Mol. wt. 158.03.

(d) Category

- This describes the therapeutical or pharmacological or pharmaceutical application of the compound.
- Some of the main categories for inorganic pharmaceuticals mentioned in the include antacid, astringent, laxative, cathartic, etc.

(e) Doses

- It represents the quantities for guidance of the prescriber or the physician to achieve desired therapeutic effects in human beings.
- For example, $CaCO_3$ dose of 1 to 5 g.
- However, this is omitted for substances not used for internal administration.

(f) Statement of Content or Standards

- The limits of content stated are those determined by the method described under assay.
- In other words, it specifies the quantitative purity of the title compound, where the compound is of definite composition. For example, potassium bromide contains not less than 98 per cent of KBr, calculated with reference to the dried substance.
- However, if the composition is not definite, the standards are vaguely defined. For example, bentonite is a natural, colloidal, hydrated aluminium silicate.

(g) Description

- This gives the physical description of the substance, viz., the crystalline or amorphous nature of the substance, its colour, odour, taste, etc.

  For example, $CaCO_3$ – fine, white coloured microcrystalline powder, odourless, tasteless.

- The statements are not to be interpreted in a strict sense and are not to be regarded as official requirements.

(h) Solubility

- Statements on solubility are intended as information on the approximate solubility at a temperature between 15° and 30°, unless otherwise stated and are not to be considered official requirement.
- However, a test for solubility stated under the quantitative solubility test constitutes part of the standards for the substance, that is, the subject of that monograph.
- This is usually given in water, sometimes in hot or boiling water, alcohol, glycerol, solvent ether, other organic solvents, acids or alkalis, etc.
- If the exact solubility of the substance is not known, a descriptive term is used to indicate its solubility.
- The various descriptive terms associated with solubility are expressed in **Table 1.4**.

Table 1.4: Descriptive terms associated with solubility

Descriptive terms	Relative quantities of solvent for 1 part of solute
Very soluble	Less than 1 part
Freely soluble	From 1 to 10 parts
Soluble	From 10 to 30 parts
Sparingly soluble	From 30 to 100 parts
Slightly soluble	From 100 to 1000 parts
Very slightly soluble	From 1000 to 10,000 parts
Practically insoluble or Insoluble	More than 10,000 parts

(i) Identification

- This involves specific chemical test for the identification of the substance.
- The tests provide a means of verifying that the identity of the material under examination is in accordance with the label on the container.
- However, these tests are not necessarily sufficient to establish absolute proof of identity.
- For example, phenol when reacts with $FeCl_3$, gives violet colour.

(j) pH

- This information provides the manufacturing pharmacist to develop various dosage forms and to avoid physiological complications.
- For example, 2% w/v solution of calcium amino salicylate gives pH of 6.0 to 8.0.

(k) Limit for Impurities

- Different limit tests have been included in the monograph for different pharmaceutical substances.
- It also provides information regarding the amount of such impurities permitted in the pharmaceutical.
- The various tests include: acidity or alkalinity, pH, specific impurities (viz. phosphates, magnesium, sulphides, barium, etc.), chloride, sulphate, iron, heavy metals, arsenic, etc.
- Limit tests for impurities are approximate values, generally represented in parts per million (ppm), weight or as a percentage.

(l) Assay

- It represents a step-by-step description of chemical analytical method for the active substance.
- It is an official method upon which the standards of the pharmacopoeia depend.

(m) Storage

- This is the last item under the monograph and constitutes a non-mandatory advice.
- The pharmacopoeia indicates the measures to be taken to protect the article from contamination and deterioration during its entire shelf life in relation to the effects of the atmosphere, moisture, heat and light, whichever is appropriate.
- Specific directions are given in some monographs with respect to the temperatures at which pharmacopoeial articles should be stored, where it is considered that usage at a lower or higher temperature may produce undesirable results.
- The storage conditions with respect to the temperatures are defined by the following terms:
  - (i) Store in a dry, well-ventilated place at a temperature not exceeding 30°.
  - (ii) Store in a refrigerator (2° to 8°). Do not freeze.
  - (iii) Store in a freezer (-2° to -18°).
  - (iv) Store in a deep freezer (below -18°).
- Storage conditions not related to temperature are indicated by the following terms:
  - (i) Store protected from light.
  - (ii) Store protected from light and moisture.
- When no specific storage directions or limitations are given in the monograph or by the manufacturer, it is to be understood that the storage conditions include protection from moisture, freezing and excessive heat (any temperature above 40°).

(n) Storage Containers

- A container should be designed so that the contents may be removed in a manner suitable for the intended use of the article in it. It should also provide an adequate degree of protection, minimise the loss of constituents and should not interact physically or chemically with the contents in a way that alters their quality to an extent beyond the limits given in the individual monograph or present a risk of toxicity.
- The closure is a part of the container.
- Containers must be chosen with utmost care and after taking into account the nature of the articles and the likely effects of transportation and storage, even for short periods of time.
- For inorganic pharmaceuticals, the pharmacopoeia uses the following terms:
  (i) Airtight container
  (ii) Hermetically sealed container
  (iii) Light-resistant container
  (iv) Multi-dose container
  (v) Sealed container
  (vi) Single-dose container
  (vii) Tamper-evident container
  (viii) Tightly-closed container
  (ix) Well-closed container

(i) *Airtight Container*

- It refers to the container that is impermeable to solids, liquids and gases under ordinary conditions of handling, storage and transport.
- If the container is intended to be opened more than once, it must be so designed that it remains airtight after re-closure.

(ii) *Hermetically Sealed Container*

- It refers to the container that is impervious to air or any other gas under normal conditions of handling, shipment, storage and distribution, e.g., sealed glass ampoule, gas cylinder, etc.
- A hermetically sealed container may be used for a single dose of an article.

(iii) *Light-resistant Container*

- It refers to the container that protects the contents from the effects of actinic light by virtue of the specific properties of the material of which it is made.
- Alternatively, a clear and colourless or a translucent container may be made light-resistant by means of an opaque (light-resistant) covering and/or stored in a dark place; in such cases, the label on the container should bear a statement that the opaque covering or storage in dark place is needed until the contents have been used up.

(iv) ***Multi-dose Container***

- It refers to the container that holds a quantity of the preparation suitable for two or more doses.

(v) ***Sealed Container***

- It refers to the container closed by fusion of the material of the container.

(vi) ***Single-dose container***

- It refers to the container that holds a quantity of the preparation intended for total or partial use as a single administration.

(vii) ***Tamper-evident Container***

- It refers to the container fitted with a device or mechanism that reveals irreversibly whether the container has been opened.

(viii) ***Tightly-closed Container***

- It refers to the container that protects the contents from contamination by extraneous liquids, solids or vapours, from loss or deterioration of the article from effervescence, deliquescence or evaporation under normal conditions of handling, shipment, storage and distribution.
- A tightly-closed container must be capable of being tightly reclosed after use. For example, a gas cylinder may be considered to be a metallic, tightly-closed container designed to hold gas under pressure.

(ix) ***Well-closed Container***

- It refers to the container that protects the contents from extraneous solids and liquids and from loss of the article under normal conditions of handling, shipment, storage and distribution.

(o) Labelling

- The statements under this heading are, in general, not comprehensive.
- Only those that are necessary to demonstrate compliance or otherwise with the monograph are given and they are mandatory.
- For example, in the monograph on Betamethasone Sodium Tablets, the labelling statement is "The label states the strength in terms of the equivalent amount of betamethasone". Any other statements are included as recommendations.
- The labelling of drugs and pharmaceuticals is governed by the Drugs and Cosmetics Rules, 1945.

1.2.4.3 Appendices and Index

- The pharmacopoeia contains a comprehensive section of appendices followed by general notices and monographs.

- The appendix includes the apparatus needed for various pharmacopoeial tests and assays apart from that included in appendices. These consist of:
  - IR spectra of drugs
  - Apparatus for tests and assays
  - Biological tests and determination
  - Chemical tests and assays
  - Chromatography and electrophoresis
  - Spectrophotometry
  - Clarity and colour of solutions
  - Disintegration and dissolution tests
  - Physical tests and determinations
  - Microbiological assays and tests
  - Limit tests of particulate matter
  - Other tests and determination
  - General information
  - Reagents and solutions
  - Reference substances
  - Tables
- IP contents and amendments are published by The Controller of Publications, Delhi, on behalf of the Government of India, Ministry of Health and Family Welfare.
- For the preparation of pharmacopoeia of India, the pharmacopoeias of other countries such as United Kingdom, United States, Europe, USSR, Japan, the National Formulary and Merck Index were consulted. The candidates working in pharmaceutical industry, drug control laboratories, research and teaching institutions also participated actively.
- Under the Drugs and Cosmetics Act, 1940, the Indian Pharmacopoeia is an official book that contains the standards for drugs and other related substances included in the pharmacopoeia. The drugs and other related substances prepared by the pharmaceutical manufacturers must comply with these standards.

1.2.5 British Pharmacopoeia (BP)

- British Pharmacopoeia (BP) was published by the health ministers of the United Kingdom.
- The first BP was published in 1864 and was an outcome of the combination of three older and reputed pharmacopoeias, namely, Pharmacopoeia Londinensis (1618), Edinburgh Pharmacopoeia (1699), and Dublin Pharmacopoeia (1807).

- It consisted of two separate parts, viz., "Materia Medica" and "Preparations and Compounds".
- New editions and Addendums followed in quick succession, with second edition released in 1867, its Addendum in 1874; third edition in 1885, its addendum in 1890; and the fourth edition published in 1898.
- The various publications of BP were released in the subsequent years and are summarized in **Table 1.5**.
- The latest edition of BP has been published in 2018.
- BP is used in about 100 countries worldwide. Australia and Canada are the two countries that have adopted BP as their national standard.
- In other countries, like South Korea, BP is recognized as an acceptable reference standard.

Table 1.5: Publication history and development of British Pharmacopoeia

Publication year	Development, amendment and features
1864	1st edition was published.
1867	2nd edition was published. The contents had been arranged alphabetically.
1874	Addendum to BP 1867 was published.
1885	3rd edition was published.
1890	Addendum to BP 1885 was published.
1898	4th edition was published.
1914	5th edition was published. Drug specifications were increased.
1928	6th edition was published.
1932	Addendum to BP 1928 was published. A range of diagnostic materials and standards and tests for antitoxins and insulin were included.
1948	7th edition was published. Generic names were provided for substances newly introduced into medicine. Methods of analysis, disintegration tests for tablets and sterilization methods got expanded. Many new monographs related to penicillins and sex hormones were included.
1953	8th edition was published. The titles of drugs and preparations were given in English instead of Latin. Abbreviated Latin title was retained as a synonym. Capsules constituted a new group of formulation. The implant methods for sex hormones and their standards were described.
1958	9th edition was published. It contained 160 new monographs. Tranquilizing drugs and spectrophotometric analysis were added.
1963	10th edition was published.
1968	11th edition was published.
1970	British Pharmacopoeia Commission was constituted in Medicines Order 1970.
1970	12th edition was published.

(Contd...)

1980	The first edition of BP that was prepared strictly under the provisions of Medicines Act was the 13th edition. It was published in two volumes due to the expansion of drug information. Volume I dealt with medicinal and pharmaceutical substances. It also included the IR reference spectra needed for the identification of many of the materials. Volume II contained sections on formulated preparations, blood products, immunological products, radio-pharmaceutical preparations and surgical materials.
1988	14th edition was published.
1989, 1990, 1991 and 1992	Four Addendums to 14th edition of BP 1988 were published. These incorporated the monographs of the European Pharmacopoeia for the convenience of the user.
1993	The BP 1993 provided authoritative standard for the quality of many substances, preparations and articles used in medicine and pharmacy for some 130 years.
	The first Addendum to BP 1993 was published. It included monographs for a substantial number of substances and preparations for the first time. Several new European Pharmacopoeia monographs, revisions to monographs, edited texts relevant to the human medicine that had been published fascicule 17 of the 2nd edition of the European Pharmacopoeia replaced the limit test for particulate matter. An indication of the approximate levels of impurities controlled by chromatographic tests, wherever appropriate, was indicated. A new supplementary section containing auxiliary material of relevance to users of the pharmacopoeia was also introduced.
2013	This edition was in six volumes. It contained nearly 3000 monographs for drug substances, excipients and formulated preparation, together with supporting general notices, appendices (which included test methods, reagents, etc.), and reference spectra used in the practice of medicine.
2014	This edition of BP 2014 was in five volumes and one volume of the BP (Veterinary) 2014. 40 new monographs were included and 272 monographs were amended. Three new Supplementary Chapters, four new BP (Veterinary) monographs and one new BP (Veterinary) Supplementary Chapter were introduced. Free in-year updates were introduced in April and July to harmonize with the European Pharmacopoeia.
2018	This edition of BP 2018 was in six volumes, containing nearly 3000 monographs for drug substances, excipients, and formulated preparations, together with supporting general notices, appendices, and reference spectra used in practice of medicine. Items used exclusively in veterinary medicine in the UK are included in BP (Veterinary). Volumes I and II (Medicinal Substances). Volume III (Formulated Preparations, Blood-Related Preparations, Immunological Products, Radiopharmaceutical Preparations, Surgical Materials, and Homeopathic Preparations). Volume IV (Appendices, IR Reference Spectra, Index). Volume V (British Pharmacopoeia (Veterinary)). Volume VI (CD-ROM Version, British Pharmacopoeia, British Pharmacopoeia (Veterinary) and British Approved Names).

1.2.6 European Pharmacopoeia

- It is an official book of standards adopted by Germany, France, Italy the, Netherlands, Switzerland and Belgium.
- An order was issued in July 1964 by the Council of Europe to form European Pharmacopoeial Commission for compiling European Pharmacopoeia.
- The first edition of European Pharmacopoeia appeared in 1969 and its official standards became applicable within the respective member countries.
- It was an official standard book for medicinal substances and other drugs.
- The second edition of European Pharmacopoeia was published in a series of volumes.
- Later, it was revised time to time to keep the information up-to-date.

1.2.7 United States Pharmacopoeia

- The first edition of United States Pharmacopoeia (USP) was compiled, edited and published on 15th December, 1820, under the authority of United States Pharmacopoeial Convention.
- It contained 217 drugs in about 272 pages.
- Subsequent editions of USP appeared after the gap of ten years.
- The 9th edition of USP was published in 1905. However, it was given the title of USP VIII, to show that it was eighth revision.
- USP considered 25°C as the standard temperature for specific gravity and solubility statements.
- Later, the 1940 convention directed that the pharmacopoeia must be revised every 5 years.

1.2.8 National Formulary

- The National Formulary (NF) was published in 1888 under the guidance of American Pharmaceutical Association.
- Later in 1974, the NF was purchased by the United States Pharmacopoeial Convention and unification of the USP and NF was announced.
- From 1980 onwards, the subsequent editions consolidated USP and NF into a single volume under the heading "The United States Pharmacopoeia and The National Formulary (USP-NF)".
- All the drug substances and drug products were covered in USP, while NF included all pharmaceutical ingredients exclusively.

1.2.9 USP-NF

- In January 1990, the XXII edition of USP combined with XVII edition of NF was published.

- The current version of USP-NF standards deemed official by USP are enforceable by the United States Food and Drug Administration (US-FDA) for medicines manufactured and marketed in US.
- It contains standards for medicines, dosage forms, drug substances, excipients, biologics, compounded preparations, medical devices, dietary supplements and other therapeutics.
- The USP 41 – NF 36 became official on May 1, 2018.
- The latest edition, USP 42 – NF 37, was published on November 1, 2018 in English and shall come into force on May 1, 2019.

1.2.9.1 Specific Features of USP 41 – NF 36

- It comprises 5 volumes and two supplements.
- It contains more than 4900 monographs with specifications for identity, strength, quality, purity, packaging, and labelling for substances and dosage forms.
- It also comprises more than 350 general chapters, providing clear, step-by-step guidance for assays, tests and procedures.
- It also focuses on specific charts and a combined index which help the users to easily find the information.
- It also contains helpful sections on reagents, indicators and solutions, plus reference tables.
- It also includes new General Chapter of Hazardous Drugs (about 800) and their handling in healthcare settings.

1.2.10 The International Pharmacopoeia (Pharmacopoeia Internationalis)

- The International Pharmacopoeia is published by the WHO and is particularly used in developing countries.
- It is prepared by the WHO Expert Advisory Panel on the International Pharmacopoeia and Pharmaceutical Preparation.
- It has been developed to provide a uniform list which would avoid confusion caused by different national standards, strengths and names.
- The latest, eighth edition of the International Pharmacopoeia was published in 2018.
- It includes a collection of recommended procedures for analysis and specifications for the determination of pharmaceutical substances (APIs), excipients, and dosage forms (general texts and individual finished pharmaceutical products) that is intended to serve as source material for reference or adaptation by any WHO Member State wishing to establish pharmaceutical requirements.
- Although the International Pharmacopoeia cannot be imposed legally on any country, the pharmacopoeial authorities of all countries are expected to give due consideration to its standards for achieving uniformity of standards as far as practicable.

Table 1.6: Publication history of the International Pharmacopoeia

Publication year	Development and amendment	Salient features
1951	Volume I of 1st edition was published.	344 monographs on drug substances.
1952	Volume II of 1st edition was published.	183 monographs on dosage forms (capsules, injections, tablets and tinctures). 84 tests, methods and general requirements.
1959	Supplement to 1st edition was published.	
1967	2nd edition was published as specification for the Quality Control of Pharmaceutical Preparations.	New analytical techniques involving IR spectroscopy, chromatography (column, paper and thin-layer), non-aqueous titration and radioactivity were introduced. 162 new pharmaceutical preparations were added. 114 monographs were deleted.
1975	Volume I of 3rd edition was published. Included general methods of analysis.	Emphasized on the classical chemical techniques available in the developing world. Incorporated drugs used all over the world by various WHO programs. Included drugs that degrade or are difficult to manufacture. Also included drugs from *WHO Model List of Essential Drugs*, and their updates.
1981	Volume II of 3rd edition was published. Contains the quality specifications of essential drug substances in the WHO Model List of Essential Drugs.	
1982	Volume III of 3rd edition was published. Contains the quality specifications of essential drug substances in the WHO Model List of Essential Drugs.	
1988	Volume IV of 3rd edition was published. Includes tests, methods, and general requirements in addition to quality specifications for pharmaceutical substances, excipients and dosage forms.	
2003	Volume V of 3rd edition was published. Contains tests and general requirements for dosage forms and quality specifications for pharmaceutical substances and tablets, and a section on anti-malarial drugs and their most widely used dosage forms.	
2006	Volumes I and II of 4th edition were published. Volume I contained the general notices and many of the monographs for pharmaceutical substances. Volume II contained the remaining monographs for pharmaceutical substances together with those for dosage forms and radiopharmaceutical preparations, methods of analysis and the reagents section and index.	The main volumes of this edition consolidated and updated the texts of the five separate volumes of the third edition and included new monographs for antiretroviral substances.

(Contd...)

2015	The 5th edition was published in CD-ROM and online formats.	New and revised texts were introduced for 8 monographs on pharmaceutical substances, 24 monographs on dosage forms, 1 general monograph, 2 methods of analysis and 1 text for the section on "Supplementary Information". A list of these texts has been provided as an annexure. 4 additional spectra of emtricitabine, iopanoic acid, salbutamol and tenofovir disoproxil fumarate were added to the IR reference spectra.
2016	The 6th edition was published.	New and revised texts were introduced for 12 monographs on pharmaceutical substances, 12 monographs on dosage forms, 1 method of analysis and 3 texts for the section on "Supplementary Information". A list of these texts has been provided as an annexure. 18 texts from 5th edition were omitted following a decision at the 50th meeting of the WHO Expert Committee on Specifications for Pharmaceutical Preparations (ECSPP).
2017	The 7th edition was published in CD-ROM and online formats	New and revised texts were introduced for 6 monographs on pharmaceutical substances, 7 monographs on dosage forms, 3 methods of analysis and 2 texts for the section on "Supplementary Information". A list of these texts has been provided as an annexure. 80 texts from 6th edition were omitted following a decision at the 51st meeting of the ECSPP.
2018	8th edition of The International Pharmacopoeia was published.	New and revised texts were introduced for 40 monographs on pharmaceutical substances, 13 monographs on dosage forms and one method of analysis.

1.2.11 Pharmaceutical Index

- The new Codex provides a reference source on all aspects of pharmaceutical science and technology that are relevant to the development and provision of medicine.
- Part I covers the multidisciplinary nature of pharmaceutics and demonstrate how quality is built into medicines from conception and development to production and use.

- The chapters broadly encompass the pharmaceutics content of the syllabus for pharmacy undergraduates and also provide direction and support for the continuing education of graduates, with special emphasis on the requirements of those associated with product development and innovation.
- Part II includes an extensive collection of pharmaceutical data arranged in monograph form.
- The Codex is edited by the staff of the Royal Pharmaceutical Society, using known experts to write individual chapters.

1.2.12 Extra Pharmacopoeia (Martindale: The Complete Drug Reference)

- The Extra Pharmacopoeia was first published in 1883 by William Martindale, a practising pharmacist and is thus called 'Martindale'.
- It is produced by The Royal Pharmaceutical Society of the United Kingdom with the objective to provide physicians and pharmacists with practical and up-to-date information concerning drugs and gelenicals to supplement that was included in the British Pharmacopoeia.
- It contains information about drugs and medicines, selected investigational and veterinary drugs, herbal medicines, pharmaceutical excipients, vitamins and nutritional agents, vaccines, radiopharmaceuticals, contrast media and diagnostic agents, medicinal gases, drugs of abuse and recreational drugs, toxic substances, disinfectants and insecticides.
- Monograph headings consist of definitions and descriptions, pharmacokinetics, adverse effects and treatments, uses, precautions, administration, interactions, trade names of preparations, etc.
- Sources of information include journal and periodicals, licensed product literature, WHO publications, government reports and legislation and other official and standard publications.
- The 24th edition of Volume I was published in 1958 and 23rd edition of Volume II in 1955. A Supplement was published in 1961. The 25th edition appeared in February 1967 while the 26th edition was released in July 1972.
- The 30th edition, Martindale 1993, contained up-to-date authorative information on drugs and medicines in use throughout the world. This new edition of Martindale has been markedly changed in order to meet the requirements of users. The modifications included a massive increase in the formation on proprietary medicines, a significant shift to a more clinical emphasis, an increase in the number of referenced reviews and shortening of the usual period between the editions, to meet the need for up-to-date information.
- The 38th edition, Martindale June 2014, is arranged into two main parts followed by three extensive indices.

- It included monographs on drugs and ancillary substances, listing over 6000 monographs arranged in 49 chapters with the corresponding disease treatment reviews. Monographs summarize the nomenclature, properties and actions of each substance. A chapter on supplementary drugs and other substances covered some 1190 monographs on new drugs, those not easily classified, herbals and drugs no longer clinically used but still of interest. Monographs of some toxic substances were also included.
- It also includes preparations with over 180,000 items from 43 countries and regions including China; directory of manufacturers listing some 20,000 entries; pharmaceutical terms in various languages; and general index prepared from 175,000 entries containing approved names, synonyms and chemical names.
- Its digital versions included an additional 1000 drug monographs, 60,000 preparation names and 5000 manufacturers.
- The latest 39th edition of Martindale: The Complete Drug Reference was published in June 2017.

1.2.13 British Pharmaceutical Codex

- British Pharmaceutical Codex (BPC) was prepared as a reference book for the use of medical practitioners and dispensing pharmacists.
- In 1903, the Pharmaceutical Society of Great Britain came up with BPC.
- The first edition of the BPC was published in 1907.
- The subsequent editions were published in 1911, 1923, 1934, 1949, 1954, 1959, 1963, 1968 and 1973.
- From 11th edition 1979 onwards, BPC was regarded as Pharmaceutical Codex only.
- It included general monographs of drugs and also provided standards of medicaments and materials that are not included in BP and British National Formulary (BNF).
- The current edition is the 12th, published in 1994.

1.3 SOURCES AND TYPES OF IMPURITIES IN PHARMACEUTICAL SUBSTANCES

- The substances employed in the pharmaceutical field must be almost pure, so that they can be used safely.
- However, absolutely pure chemical compounds are rarely met with in commerce.
- Even analytically pure samples of most compounds possess minute traces of impurities.
- Purification of chemicals is an expensive process; hence a substance should not be purified more than required, as it brings about waste of time, material and money.

1.3.1 Impurity

- **Impurity** is the unwanted matters that are present along with APIs and are developed either during the formulation or upon ageing of API or drug products. These may or may not be toxic.
- The presence of these unwanted chemicals even in minute or trace amounts may influence the potency and safety of pharmaceutical substances.
- As a result, the check on these impurities is a critical issue.

1.3.1.1 Impure Chemical Compound

- A compound is said to be **impure** if it has the presence of foreign matter, i.e., impurities.

1.3.1.2 Pure Chemical Compound

- **Pure chemical compound** refers to that compound which is free from foreign matter, i.e., impurities.

1.3.2 Classification of Impurities

- The International Conference on Harmonization (ICH) has formulated guidelines regarding the control of impurities.
- According to ICH, an impurity in a drug substance is defined as "any component of the new drug substance that is not the chemical identity defined as the new drug substance".
- Impurities have been classified differently as follows.
- As per the ICH guidelines, impurities associated with APIs are classified into the following categories:
  - (a) Organic impurities (process and drug-related)
  - (b) Inorganic impurities
  - (c) Residual solvents
- As per the United States Pharmacopoeia, impurities are classified into the following categories:
  - (a) Impurities in official articles
  - (b) Ordinary impurities
  - (c) Organic volatile impurities

(a) Organic Impurities

- These may arise during the manufacturing process and/or storage of the drug substance which includes starting material, by-products, intermediates, degradation products, reagents, ligands, catalysts and enantiomeric impurity.
- These are the actual and potential impurities most likely to arise during the synthesis, purification and storage of the drug substance.
- Raw material may contribute to the impurity profile of a drug substance.

(b) Inorganic Impurities

- Inorganic impurities involve reagents, catalysts, ligands, heavy metals or other residual metals, inorganic salts, charcoal, filter-aids, etc.
- These impurities may also derive from the manufacturing processes used for bulk drugs.

(c) Residual Solvents

- These are organic volatile chemicals used during the manufacturing process or generated during the production.
- Although it is very difficult to remove these solvents completely by the work-up process, efforts should be taken to meet the safety data.
- Residual solvents are further classified into three classes:
  - **Class I solvents:** Examples include benzene (limit 1-2 ppm) and carbon tetrachloride (limit 1-4 ppm). These are avoided because of their toxic and carcinogenic effect.
  - **Class II solvents:** Examples include methanol (3000 ppm), methylene chloride (600 ppm), toluene (890 ppm), N,N-dimethylformamide (880 ppm), acetonitrile (410 ppm), pyridine (200 ppm). These are the most common solvents used pharmaceutically.
  - **Class III solvents:** Examples include acetic acid, acetone, butanol, ethanol, isopropyl alcohol, ethyl acetate, etc. These are permitted to be used in the daily exposure of 50 mg or less.

1.3.3 Types of Impurities Found in Pharmaceutical Preparations

The impurities usually found in pharmaceutical preparations may be of the following types:

- The impurities having a toxic effect and bring about unpleasant reactions when present beyond limits. For example, lead and arsenic salts.
- The impurities which, though otherwise harmless, occur in such proportions that the active strength of the substance gets lowered and does not have the same therapeutic activity as the pure substance. For example, hard soap having much water is uneconomical.
- The impurities which are able to reduce the keeping properties (shelf life) of the substances.
- The impurities which make the substance incompatible with other substances.
- The impurities causing technical difficulties during manufacturing. For example, picking or sticking defects occurring during tablet manufacturing.
- The impurities affecting taste, odour, colour or appearance, thereby making the substance unaesthetic or unhygienic. For example, sodium chloride becomes damp because of the presence of traces of magnesium salts.

- Impurities, even when present in trace amounts, may show a cumulative toxic effect after a certain period.

1.3.4 Sources of Impurities

The type and amount of impurity present in the chemicals or pharmaceutical substances depend upon several factors, some of which are depicted below.

1. *Raw Materials Employed in Manufacture of Pharmaceutical Substances*

- Since most of the pharmaceutical substances are either obtained from natural sources (viz., minerals, plants, animals, microbes, etc.) or synthesized from chemical starting materials, it becomes necessary to verify the identity and quality of the raw materials which, if not removed, may contaminate the final product.
- For example, impurities such as arsenic, lead, heavy metals, etc., are present in raw materials and hence, found in the final product as impurities.
- Rock salt utilised for the preparation of sodium chloride contains small amounts of calcium sulphate and magnesium chloride; as a result sodium chloride prepared from this source will almost certainly contain traces of impurities of calcium and magnesium.

2. *Method or the Process Used in Manufacture*

The process or method used in the manufacture may introduce new impurities in the final product. These include:

(a) Impurities incorporated into the materials during the manufacturing process.

(b) Impurities present in the intermediates.

(c) Impurities of the product side reactions.

(a) Impurities Incorporated into the Materials During the Manufacturing Process

Various chemicals and drugs are manufactured using different raw materials by different methods or processes. However, the type and amount of impurity present in the chemicals or drugs vary.

(b) Impurities Present in the Intermediates

Certain drugs are manufactured by multi-step synthetic procedures which produce intermediate compounds. The impurities, if any, present in the intermediates get incorporated into the final product.

For example, reaction between sodium hydroxide and slight excess of bromine results in the formation of sodium bromate as an intermediate which is reduced to sodium bromide by treatment with charcoal.

$$\underset{\text{Sodium hydroxide}}{6NaOH} + 3Br_2 \longrightarrow \underset{\text{Sodium bromate}}{NaBrO_3} + 5NaBr + 3H_2O$$

$$\underset{\text{Sodium bromate}}{NaBrO_3} + 3C \longrightarrow \underset{\text{Sodium bromide}}{NaBr} + 3CO$$

(c) Impurities of the Product Side Reactions

Usually side reactions occur during the synthesis and act as impurities to the main product.

3. Reagents and Solvents

These impurities include contamination by:

(a) Reagents employed in the process
(b) Reagents added to remove other impurities
(c) Solvents
(d) Reaction vessels

(a) Reagents Employed in the Process

Calcium carbonate is obtained by interaction of a soluble calcium salt (e.g., $CaCl_2$) and a soluble carbonate (e.g., Na_2CO_3) and hence, the product obtained on reaction between these is liable to contain traces of soluble alkali as impurity, which cannot be removed by washing.

$$\underset{\substack{\text{Sodium}\\\text{carbonate}}}{Na_2CO_3} + \underset{\substack{\text{Calcium}\\\text{chloride}}}{CaCl_2} \longrightarrow \underset{\substack{\text{Calcium}\\\text{carbonate}}}{CaCO_3\downarrow} + \underset{\substack{\text{Sodium}\\\text{chloride}}}{2NaCl}$$

(b) Reagents Added to Remove Other Impurities

The preparation of potassium bromide uses barium in order to remove sulphate, which arises from the bromine used in the process; hence, it is likely that potassium bromide obtained may be contaminated by traces of barium impurities.

(c) Solvents

Traces of solvents used in the preparation and purification of reaction intermediates or the final product may also result in the contamination of the pharmaceutical substances. Water has been the cheapest solvent used frequently in the manufacture of inorganic pharmaceutical substances and can be the major source of impurities, since it contains different types and amounts of impurities which leads to contamination of the final product, even after several washings.

For example, tap water contains impurities of Ca^{2+}, Mg^{2+}, Na^+, Cl^-, CO_3^{2-}, SO_4^{2-}, etc. Softened water is almost free from divalent cations like Ca^{2+}, Mg^{2+} but contains excess amount of Na^+, Cl^- as impurities. Demineralised water is prepared by ion-exchange methods and is free from impurities of Ca^{2+}, Mg^{2+}, Na^+, Cl^-, CO_3^{2-}, SO_4^{2-}, etc. However, it may have pyrogens, bacteria and other organic impurities. Thus, even though it is a better solvent than tap water or softened water but the economic factors discourage its use on large scale. Distilled water is free from all kinds of inorganic and organic impurities and is therefore, the best solvent but it is quite expensive.

(d) Reaction Vessels

The impurities which arise from the reaction vessels may act as a source of impurity and may be transferred to the product material, thereby contaminating it. The reaction vessels utilised during the manufacturing process may be metallic, like copper, iron, silver, aluminium, nickel, zinc, lead, cast iron, galvanized iron, stainless steel, etc. The action of solvents may corrode these metallic vessels, thereby resulting in the leaching of traces of metal ions which may pass into the solution and may contaminate the product. Similarly, glass vessels may give rise to traces of alkali, which may percolate in the solvent, though this is less likely to occur in case of hard glass. In addition, lead may be found as impurity in the commercial sulphuric acid manufactured by lead chamber process. Further, in some cases, the substances prepared by electrolytic process may contain electrode material as an undesirable impurity. For example, bismuth, antimony, etc.

4. Chemical Processes Used in the Manufacture

- The synthesis of drugs requires the use of various chemical reactions like nitration, halogenation, oxidation, reduction, hydrolysis, etc., where by-products are formed during the reaction and result in contamination.
- For example, potassium iodide is manufactured from iodine, which is obtained from 'kelp', a sea weed. Cyanides are formed when nitrogenous organic matter is burnt with alkalis, which results in contamination.

5. Atmospheric Contamination

- Widespread atmospheric pollution may bring about considerable risk of contamination by dust (silica, sulphur, soot, aluminium oxide, etc.), sulphur dioxide, hydrogen sulphide, arsenic, in addition to carbon dioxide and water vapour.
- For example, calcium hydroxide solutions can absorb carbon dioxide from the atmosphere to form calcium carbonate.

$$\underset{\text{Calcium hydroxide}}{Ca(OH)_2} + CO_2 \longrightarrow \underset{\text{Calcium carbonate}}{CaCO_3\downarrow} + H_2O$$

6. Manufacturing Hazards

Certain hazards exist even in a well-run manufacturing house, which can give rise to contamination at various stages of manufacturing. These include:

(a) Contamination from Particulate Matter

- This type of contamination may stem from either bulk materials used during the formulation process or from the use of improperly cleaned equipment or containers and also due to wear and tear of equipment.
- For example, accidental inclusion of dust, dirt, pieces of glass, porcelain, metallic and plastic fragments from sieves, granulating, tableting and filling machines or even product containers.
- It may also arise from the bulk materials used in the formulation or from dirty or improperly maintained equipment.

(b) Process Errors

- Gross errors arising from the incomplete reactions during processing may be readily detected by the normal analytical control procedures.
- Failure to acknowledge the limits of mechanical efficiency of mixing, filling, tableting, sterilising and other equipment can result in minor variation and very occasionally gross error, in the content of both active ingredient and formulatory adjuncts in compounded products.

(c) Cross-contamination of the Products

- The handling of powders, granules and tablets in large bulk, frequently results in the production of considerable amount of air-borne dust, which if not controlled, may lead to cross-contamination of other products.
- For example, manufacture of penicillin and cephalosporin preparations.

(d) Microbial contamination

- Various pharmaceutical products like parenteral, ophthalmic preparations, liquid preparations and creams are liable to contamination due to bacterial mould and fungi from the atmosphere **(Table 1.7)**.
- Hence, sterility testing is carried out for parenteral and ophthalmic preparations.
- Moreover, suitable antimicrobial and antifungal agents are added to control the microbial contamination.

Table 1.7: Recommended control of microbial contamination in natural pharmaceutical substances

Microbes	Natural pharmaceutical substances
Freedom from *Salmonellae*	Acacia, senna, tragacanth
Freedom from *Salmonellae* & *Escherichia coli*	Digitalis, gelatine, starch, pancreatin
Freedom from *Pseudomonads*	Aluminium hydroxide gel, dried aluminium hydroxide gel, aluminium phosphate gel

(e) Packing Errors

- The products of similar appearance, such as tablets of the same size, colour and shape, packed in similar containers can constitute a potential source of danger through mislabelling of either or both.
- Adequate care should be taken to avoid the handling of such products in the close proximity.

7. Storage

- Various types of materials are used for storage purpose. These include plastic, polythene, iron vessels, stainless steel, aluminium, copper, etc.
- Inadequate storage conditions and their effects include:

(a) Filth

- Stored products may become contaminated with dust, insect bodies and even animals and insect excreta.

(b) Chemical Instability

- Pharmaceutical substances undergo chemical decomposition when stored under non-ideal conditions.
- The nature of decomposition may be catalysed by light, traces of acid or alkali, air oxidation, water vapour, carbon dioxide, traces of metallic ions, etc.
- This can be avoided by adopting suitable storage procedures and conditions.

(c) Reaction with Container Materials

- The possibility of reaction between container and contents constitutes a hazard which cannot be ignored.
- Creams and ointments are liable to react with metal surfaces.
- All glass containers for injectable preparations must comply with the test for hydrolytic resistance.
- Plastic containers and closures require careful evaluation because of the tendency to yield undesirable additives, such as plasticisers.
- Rubber closures, widely used in the packing of multi-dose injections, are more prone to absorb medicaments including antioxidants and bactericides, if present, from solution, unless pre-treated by immersion in solutions of the compounds concerned.

(d) Physical Changes

- Changes in crystal size and form, agglomeration and even caking of suspended particles, which are not always preventable, may lead to changes in the efficiency of the product.

(e) Temperature Effects

- The rate at which chemical and physical changes occur in the stored products is conditioned by the temperature.
- Labile products may have temperature storage requirements assigned to them to guard against unnecessary decomposition.
- Products required for tropical use must be capable of withstanding effects of change to tropical temperatures.
- The high humidity is yet another hazard encountered in tropical countries that is conductive to mould contamination of the product.

8. Decomposition of the Product During Storage

- Decomposition and loss of potency through insufficient attention to chemical stability of pharmaceutical chemicals or additives under the conditions of manufacture represent a further source of impurity.
- Decomposition becomes greater in the presence of light-air or oxygen.
- Additionally, substances which contain water of crystallisation lose it on being kept open, while deliquescent substances absorb water from the atmosphere and get liquefied.

9. Accidental Substitution or Deliberate Adulteration with Spurious or Useless Materials

- The cheap substances are added in pure substances as a substitute and therefore, added substances act as impurity in pure substances. For example, sodium bromide, if added, acts as impurity in potassium bromide as the sodium salt is cheaper.

1.3.5 Effect of Impurities

The impurities present in the pharmaceutical substances may exert the following effects:

(a) Impurities may produce toxic effect when present above certain limits.

(b) Impurities, even in traces, may exert a cumulative toxic effect after a certain period.

(c) Impurities, if present in higher concentration than the strength of active ingredient, the therapeutic effect of active ingredient gets decreased.

(d) Impurities may change physical and chemical properties of substance, thereby rendering it medically useless.

(e) Impurities may cause technical difficulties in the formulations.

(f) Impurities may cause incompatibility with other substances.

(g) Impurities may decrease the shelf life of the substance.

(h) Impurities may cause changes in colour, odour, taste, appearance, etc., and thus, can make the substance unhygienic.

1.3.6 Purification Methods

Inorganic pharmaceutical substances may be purified by the following procedures:

(a) Washing
(b) Drying
(c) Recrystallisation
(d) Sublimation

(a) Washing: This method is used especially when water soluble substances are to be washed away and a water insoluble substance is needed.

(b) Drying: Inorganic chemicals are generally dried in air; however, special precautions are to be taken to exclude dust. Whereas using anhydrous or expensive chemicals, drying is usually performed under vacuum.

(c) Recrystallisation: It is the most common method of purifying soluble salts. A saturated solution of the salt is obtained at a higher temperature and the solution is allowed to cool slowly after which crystals of greater purity could be obtained.

(d) Sublimation: This method is used to purify very few inorganic substances. For example, iodine, arsenic trioxide, mercurous chloride and sublimed sulphur.

1.3.7 Tests for Purity

- The pharmacopoeias of various countries prescribe "tests for purity" for pharmaceutical substances in order to ensure their reasonable freedom from the undesirable impurities.
- The "tests for purity" have been, in fact, the tests for the presence of impurities and to fix the limits of tolerance for these impurities.

Certain tests are performed on the pharmaceutical substances which include:

1. Colour, Odour and Taste

- When other tests for purity are not available, these are employed. Though these have limited value, they are useful in determining whether the substance is reasonably pure, hygienic, etc., or not.

2. Physicochemical Constants

- These include the determination of solubility of substances in different solvents, determination of melting and boiling points for organic substances, optical rotation for optically active substances and refractive index for liquids, which can reveal the purity of the substances.
- For vegetable oils, determination of the acid value, iodine value, saponification value, acetyl value, ester value, etc., signify the presence of impurities.
- A very low concentration of impurities may fail to alter these constants and thereby, remain undetected, unless tested specifically by special tests.

3. Acidity, Alkalinity and pH

- Determination of acidity or alkalinity or pH constitutes an important test for ascertaining the purity of medicinal and pharmaceutical substances. Substances prepared from chemical reactions which involve acids and alkalis, often contain considerable amounts of acid or alkali as impurity.
- Further, presence of impurity may cause a change in pH and is needed to be detected.

4. Humidity

- Estimation of moisture or humidity content of some crude drugs may provide valuable information about the conditions of their storage and, in turn, about their therapeutic potency.

5. Identification Tests

- It includes various chemical tests to verify the identity of the substance. These are not absolute proof of identity.
- Tests for anions such as chloride, sulphate, etc., are usually carried out especially in testing synthetic organic compounds.
- Similarly, tests for cations like sodium, ammonium ions, etc., are usually carried out to detect the impurities in organic compounds.
- Tests for heavy metals, such as lead, iron, copper, and mercury, are also carried out because these are very common impurities in substances.

6. Tests for Purity, Including Limit Tests

- Different limits for impurities are prescribed for different substances.
- Tests for purity are tests for the presence of impurities in the substance.
- Such tests fix the limits of tolerance for undesirable impurities.

7. Insoluble Constituents or Residue

- A substance in pure state gives a clear solution, whereas presence of insoluble impurities produces a turbid solution.
- The turbidity may be attributed either to insoluble ingredients or other particles from filtering materials, wrappings, etc.
- The measurement of opalescence helps to indicate the extent of impurities and thus, provides a good check on the purity of soluble substances.

8. Ash, Water Insoluble Ash

- Determination of ash in crude vegetable drugs, organic compounds and some inorganic compounds serves as a good indication about the extent of impurities of heavy metals or minerals in nature.

9. *Organic Impurities*

- Various tests are carried out to know the impurities in the process of production for those substances which have been either significant in the use of the medicinal compound or which serve as a criteria for its freedom from other impurities.

10. *Arsenic*

- The arsenic content is expressed in ppm.
- Monographs on many substances do not include any test for arsenic because of the advanced method in preparing acids.
- It is included only for those substances where experience has shown that commercial articles may get contaminated with arsenic.

11. *Loss on Drying (LOD)*

- LOD is the classic laboratory method of measuring high level moisture in solid or semi-solid materials.
- In this technique, a sample of material is weighed, heated in an oven for an appropriate period, cooled in the dry atmosphere of a desiccator and then reweighed.

12. *Loss on Ignition (LOI)*

- LOI is a test used in inorganic analytical chemistry, particularly in the analysis of minerals.
- It involves strongly heating (igniting) a sample of material at a specified temperature, allowing volatile substances to escape, until its mass ceases to change.

13. *Assay*

- It describes the step-by-step method for the quantitative determination of the active ingredient of the pharmaceutical substance and its preparation.

1.4 LIMIT TESTS

- Limit tests are quantitative or semi-quantitative tests designed to identify and control small quantities of impurities, which are likely to be present in the substance.
- The quantity of any one impurity in an official substance is often small and consequently, the visible reaction response to any test for that impurity is also small.
- The design of individual tests is, therefore, important if errors are to be avoided in the hands of different operators.

- This depends on a number of factors like:
  - (a) Specificity of the tests
  - (b) Sensitivity of the tests

(a) Specificity of the tests

- Any test used as a limit test must, of necessity, give some form of selective reaction with the trace impurity.
- Many tests used for the detection of inorganic impurities in official inorganic chemicals are based upon the separations involved in inorganic qualitative analysis.

(b) Sensitivity of the tests

- The degree of sensitivity required in a limit test varies enormously according to the standard of purity demanded by the monograph.
- The sensitivity of most of the tests depends upon a number of variable factors, all capable of strict definition and all favourable towards the production of reproducible results.
- Precipitation of an insoluble substance from solution is governed by factors like concentration of the solute of precipitating reagent, reaction temperature, duration of reaction, nature and concentration of other substances unavoidably present in the solution.
- In general, cold dilute solutions give light precipitates, while more granular ones are obtained from hot concentrated solutions.
- Many of the limit tests, however, are concerned with very dilute solutions which are often slow to react and hence, the sensitivity of the reaction can often be increased by extending the duration of the reaction or by raising the reaction temperature.
- Similar considerations apply in the design of colour and other tests employed as limit tests.
- With suitable control of the factors described, the same degree of reproductivity can be guaranteed in all cases.

1.4.1 Importance of Limit Tests

- To find out the harmful amount of impurities.
- To find out permissible/impermissible amount of impurities.

Note: All the reagents and solutions used in limit tests and their method of preparations are enlisted in **Appendix 1.**

1.4.2 Limit Test for Chlorides as per IP 2014

The limit test for chlorides is designed to determine the allowable limit of chloride contained in the pharmaceutical sample.

1.4.2.1 Principle

- The limit test for chloride **(Table 1.8)** is based on the simple reaction between silver nitrate and the soluble chlorides to obtain silver chloride, which is insoluble in dilute nitric acid.
- The silver chloride produced in the presence of dilute nitric acid makes the test solution turbid.
- The extent of turbidity depends upon the amount of chloride present in the substance, which is then compared with the turbidity of the standard solution.
- If the turbidity of the sample solution is less than that of the standard solution, then sample passes the limit test and vice versa.

1.4.2.2 Reaction

$$Cl^- + AgNO_3 \xrightarrow{\text{dil. } HNO_3} \underset{\text{White curdy ppt. or white turbidity}}{AgCl\downarrow} + NO_3^-$$

$$NaCl + AgNO_3 \xrightarrow{\text{dil. } HNO_3} \underset{\text{White curdy ppt. or white turbidity}}{AgCl\downarrow} + NaNO_3$$

1.4.2.3 Procedure

Table 1.8: Limit test for chloride

Test solution	Standard solution	Explanations
Weigh and dissolve the substance under examination in water or prepare a solution as directed in individual monograph and transfer to a Nessler cylinder.	Take 10 mL of chloride standard solution (25 ppm chloride) in a Nessler cylinder.	The aqueous solution will leach out all the chloride ions present in the sample and make them ready to react with silver nitrate.
Add 10 mL of dilute HNO_3.	Add 10 mL of dilute HNO_3.	Dilute HNO_3 is added to make the solution acidic and help AgCl precipitate, to make solution turbid at the end process.
Dilute the solution up to 50 mL with water.	Dilute the solution up to 50 mL with water.	Equal volume of the solutions is taken to compare the opalescence.
Add 1.0 mL of 0.1 M $AgNO_3$ solution.	Add 1.0 mL of 0.1 M $AgNO_3$ solution.	The Ag^+ ions will react with the Cl^- ions to form the opalescence of silver chloride. $Ag^+ + Cl^- \rightarrow AgCl$

(Contd...)

Stir immediately with a glass rod and set aside for 5 minutes.	Stir immediately with a glass rod and set aside for 5 minutes.	
Observe turbidity and compare with that of the standard.	Observe turbidity.	

Remarks

- If turbidity produced in the test solution is less than that in the standard solution, the sample passes the limit test for chloride and vice versa.

Note

- Purified water is used for dilution and should be free from dissolved gases and impurities.
- Standard solution is prepared as it gives maximum permissible limit for comparison.
- Dilute HNO_3 is used as it avoids the reaction of acidic radicals other than chloride with that of $AgNO_3$.
- The opalescence is directly proportional to the amount of chloride impurity present in the substance.
- If the test substance is coloured (e.g., $KMnO_4$), then it is decolourised first and then followed for limit test.

1.4.3 Modified Limit Test for Chloride

- With reference to the International Pharmacopoeia, 6th edition 2016, the limit test for chloride has been modified in the context of the standard solution preparation.
- Earlier the standard solution of chloride was prepared by dissolving NaCl (known as Cl^- impurity), but now it has been modified by using HCl instead of NaCl.

1.4.4 Limit Test for Sulphates as per IP 2014

1.4.4.1 Principle

- The limit test for sulphate **(Table 1.9)** is based on the reaction between barium chloride and the soluble sulphates in the presence of dilute hydrochloric acid, which makes the test solution turbid.
- The extent of turbidity depends upon the amount of sulphate present in the substance, which is then compared with the turbidity of the standard solution.
- If the turbidity of the sample solution is less than that of the standard solution, then sample passes the limit test and vice versa.

1.4.4.2 Reaction

$$SO_4^{2-} + BaCl_2 \xrightarrow{\text{Dil HCl}} BaSO_4 + 2Cl^-$$

1.4.4.3 Procedure

Table 1.9: Limit test for sulphate

Test solution	Standard solution	Explanations
Take 1.0 mL of 25.0% w/v solution of barium chloride in a Nessler cylinder.	Take 1.0 mL of 25.0% w/v solution of barium chloride in a Nessler cylinder.	The barium ion produced reacts with SO_4^{2-} to form opalescence of barium sulphate. $BaCl_2 + SO_4^{2-} \rightarrow BaSO_4 + 2Cl^-$
Add 1.5 mL of ethanolic sulphate standard solution (10 ppm sulphate), mix and allow it to stand for 1 minute.	Add 1.5 mL of ethanolic sulphate standard solution (10 ppm sulphate), mix and allow it to stand for 1 minute.	The ethanolic solution of potassium sulphate increases the sensitivity of the test and alcohol prevents the super-saturation of barium sulphate precipitates.
Add 15 mL of the solution prepared as directed in the monograph or a solution of the specified quantity of the substance under examination in 15 mL of water.	Add 15 mL of the sulphate standard solution.	It gives sulphate ion present in sample and standard.
Add 0.15 mL of 5 M acetic acid.	Add 0.15 mL of 5 M acetic acid.	Acetic acid prevents precipitation of various anions, such as borate, oxalate, phosphate, etc.
Dilute the solution up to 50 mL with water.	Dilute the solution up to 50 mL with water.	Equal volumes of opalescence are easily compared by viewing in black background.
Stir immediately with a glass rod and set aside for 5 minutes.	Stir immediately with a glass rod and set aside for 5 minutes.	
Observe turbidity and compare with that of the standard.	Observe turbidity.	

Remark

- If turbidity produced in the test solution is less than that of the standard solution, the sample passes the limit test for sulphate and vice versa.

Note

- Purified water is used for dilution and should be free from dissolved gases and impurities.
- Standard solution is prepared as it gives maximum permissible limit for comparison.
- Dilute HCl is used as it avoids the reaction of acidic radicals other than sulphate with that of $BaCl_2$.

- The opalescence is directly proportional to the amount of sulphate impurity present in the substance.
- If the test substance is coloured (e.g., $KMnO_4$), then it is decolourised first and then followed for limit test.
- **Potassium sulphate** is added to increase the sensitivity of the test.
- **Alcohol** helps prevent supersaturation and thus, produces a more uniform opalescence.
- The very small amount of **barium sulphate** present in the reagent acts as a seeding agent for precipitation of barium sulphate, if sulphate is present in the substance under test, results in increase in the solubility product.

1.4.5 Modified Limit Test for Sulphate

- From IP 1996 onwards, the limit test for sulphate has been modified to a great extent.
- The barium chloride test solution in the IP 1985 has been replaced by **barium sulphate reagent**, which consists of barium chloride, sulphate-free alcohol and potassium sulphate to produce comparable turbidity.

1.4.6 Limit Test for Iron as per IP 2014

1.4.6.1 Principle

- The limit test for iron **(Table 1.10)** is based on the reaction of iron in ammoniacal solution in the presence of citric acid with thioglycollic acid and a pale pink to deep reddish purple colour is formed due to ferrous compounds.
- The colour produced from a specified amount of substance from the test is compared with that from the standard (ferric ammonium sulphate).
- If the colour of the sample solution is less than that of the standard solution, then sample passes the limit test and vice versa.

1.4.6.2 Reaction

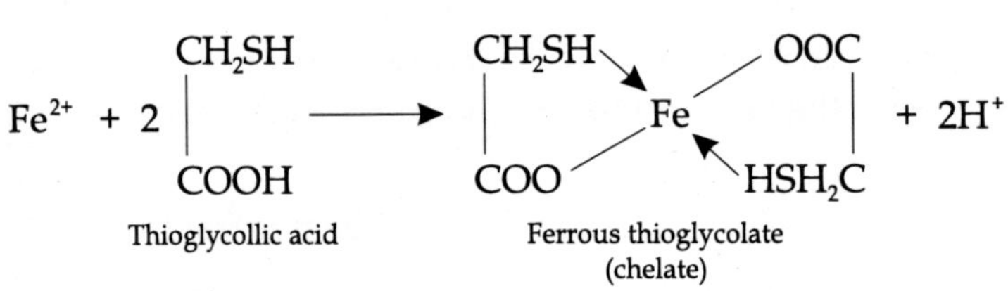

1.4.6.3 Procedure

Table 1.10: Limit test for iron

Test solution	Standard solution	Explanations
Weigh and dissolve the substance under examination in water or prepare a solution as directed in individual monograph and transfer to a Nessler cylinder.	Take 2.0 mL of iron standard solution (20 ppm iron) in a Nessler cylinder.	The aqueous solution will leach out all the iron present in the sample.
Add 2.0 mL of 20% w/v solution of iron-free citric acid.	Add 2.0 mL of 20% w/v solution of iron-free citric acid.	Citric acid prevents the precipitation of iron with ammonia and keeps iron in solution, even in the presence of ammonia, by forming complex with iron as iron citrate. $2Fe + 10NH_3 \rightarrow 2Fe(NH_2)_5 + 5H_2$ $C_6H_8O_4 + Fe \rightarrow Fe(C_6H_6O)_2 + 2H_2$
Add 0.1 mL of thioglycollic acid.	Add 0.1 mL of thioglycollic acid.	Thioglycollic acid converts ferric ions to ferrous ions. $2HSCH_2COOH + Fe^{3+} \rightarrow Fe^{2+} + 2H^+ + HSCH_2COO^-$ Thioglycollic acid further reacts with ferrous ions to form ferrous thioglycolate. $2HSCH_2COOH + Fe^{2+} \rightarrow 2H^+ + (HSCH_2COO)_2Fe$
Mix the solution and make it alkaline with iron-free ammonia solution.	Mix the solution and make it alkaline with iron-free ammonia solution.	The ferrous thioglycolate formed is colourless in medium but in alkaline medium, it gives purple colour.
Dilute the solution up to 50 mL with water.	Dilute the solution up to 50 mL with water.	Equal volumes of test and standard are compared easily.
Stir immediately with a glass rod and set aside for 5 minutes.	Stir immediately with a glass rod and set aside for 5 minutes.	
Observe the intensity of colour and compare with that of the standard.	Observe the intensity of colour.	

Remark

- If purple colour obtained in the test solution is less than the standard solution, the sample passes the limit test for iron and vice versa.

Note

- Purified water is used for dilution and should be free from dissolved gases and impurities.

- Standard solution is prepared as it gives maximum permissible limit for comparison.
- **Ammoniacal alkaline medium** is necessary for reaction of thioglycollic acid with iron impurity.
- **Citric acid** prevents precipitation of iron by ammonia. Also, interference of other metal cations is eliminated by making use of 20% citric acid, which forms a complex with other metal cations.
- **Thioglycollic acid** is used because it reacts with ferrous form of iron and converts it into ferric form. Thus, it forms purple colour.
- Earlier, **ammonium thiocyanate reagent** was used for the limit test of iron. Since, **thioglycollic acid** is a more sensitive reagent for iron; it has replaced ammonium thiocyanate in the test.
- All the reagents used in the limit test for iron should be iron-free.

1.4.7 Limit Test for Arsenic as per IP 2014

- Arsenic is a well-known undesirable and harmful impurity, which is present in medicinal substances.
- The pharmacopoeial method is based on the **Gutzeit test**.

1.4.7.1 Principle

- The pharmacopoeial test **(Table 1.11)** is based on the fact that arsenic in the arsenious state (H_3AsO_3 +3 state) can be easily reduced to arsine gas (AsH_3).
- When this gas is passed over mercuric chloride paper, it produces a stain, which ranges in colour from yellow to brown, the intensity and length of which are proportional to the amount of arsenic.
- If the colour from the sample solution is less than that of the standard solution, then sample passes the limit test and vice versa.

1.4.7.2 Reactions

(a) When the sample is dissolved in acid (e.g., HCl), the arsenic present in the sample is converted into arsenic acid.

$$\underset{\text{(in sample)}}{\underset{\text{Arsenic}}{As^{3+}}} \xrightarrow{\text{HCl}} \underset{\text{Arsenic acid}}{H_3AsO_4}$$

(b) The arsenic acid formed then gets reduced by reducing agents (like Zn, HCl, KI, stannous chloride, etc.) to arsenious acid.

$$\underset{\text{Arsenic acid}}{H_3AsO_4} \xrightarrow[\text{KI/SnCl}_2]{\text{Reduction}} \underset{\text{Arsenious acid}}{H_3AsO_3}$$

(c) The nascent hydrogen formed during the reaction, further reduces arsenious acid to arsine gas, which reacts with mercuric chloride paper; giving a yellow stain.

$$\underset{\text{Arsenious acid}}{H_3AsO_3} + 3H_2 \longrightarrow \underset{\text{Arsine}}{AsH_3} + 3H_2O$$

(d) The depth of yellow stain on mercuric chloride paper depends upon the quantity of arsenic present in the sample.

$$\underset{\text{Arsine}}{2AsH_3} + HgCl_2 \longrightarrow \underset{\substack{\text{Mercuric arsenide} \\ \text{Yellow stain}}}{Hg(AsH_2)_2} + 2HCl$$

1.4.7.3 Apparatus

- The apparatus consists of a 100 mL conical flask or glass bottle closed with a rubber or ground glass stopper through which passes a glass tube (about 20 cm × 5 mm) **(Figure 1.1)**.
- The lower part of the tube drawn to an internal diameter of 1 mm and 15 mm from its bottom is a lateral orifice 2 to 3 mm in diameter.
- When the tube is in position in the stopper, the lateral orifice should be at least 3 mm below the lower surface of the stopper.

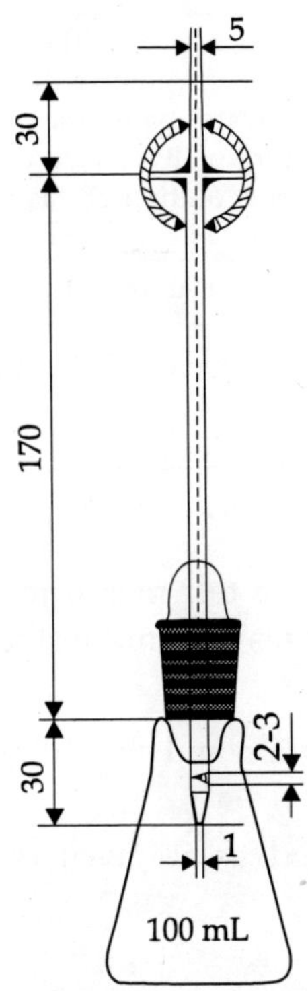

Figure 1.1: Gutzeit apparatus for limit test for arsenic (dimensions are shown in mm)

- The upper end of the tube has a perfectly flat surface at right angles to the axis of the tube.
- A second glass tube of the same internal diameter and 30 mm long with a similar flat surface is placed in contact with the first and is held in position by two spiral springs or clips.
- Into the lower tube, insert 50 to 60 mg of lead acetate cotton, loosely packed, or a small plug of cotton and a rolled piece of lead acetate paper weighing 50 to 60 mg.
- Between the flat surfaces of the tubes, place a disc or a small square of mercuric chloride paper large enough to cover the orifice of the tube (15 mm × 15 mm).

1.4.7.4 Procedure

Table 1.11: Limit test for arsenic

Test solution	Standard solution	Explanations
Into the bottle or conical flask, introduce the test solution prepared as directed in the individual monograph; add 5.0 mL of 1 M potassium iodide and 10 g zinc AsT.	Into the bottle or conical flask, introduce 1.0 mL of arsenic standard solution (10 ppm arsenic) diluted to 50 mL with water; add 5.0 mL of 1 M potassium iodide and 10 g zinc AsT.	Suspected sample is taken which might have an impurity of heavy metal and make its solution. Zinc, potassium iodide and stannous chloride are used as reducing agents.
Immediately assemble the apparatus and immerse the flask in a water bath at a temperature of 40°C such that a uniform evolution of gas is maintained.	Immediately assemble the apparatus and immerse the flask in a water bath at a temperature of 40°C such that a uniform evolution of gas is maintained.	Uniform evolution of arsine gas is maintained at 40°C.
Keep aside for 40 minutes and observe the colour and intensity on mercuric chloride paper and compare with that of the standard.	Keep aside for 40 minutes and observe the colour and intensity on mercuric chloride paper.	Arsine gas reacts with mercuric chloride paper and makes a yellow stain. Compare the intensity of yellow colour in both.

Remark

- If yellow colour obtained in the test mercuric chloride paper is less than the standard stain, the sample passes the limit test for arsenic and vice versa.

Note

- Purified water is used for dilution and should be free from dissolved gases and impurities.
- Standard solution is prepared as it gives maximum permissible limit for comparison.

- **Lead acetate cotton plug** is used to avoid the interaction of hydrogen sulphide gas with mercuric chloride.
- **Stannated zinc** is used for slow and steady evolution of nascent hydrogen.
- Time required for the preparation is more and therefore, this test should be observed after 40 minutes.
- All the reagents used in the limit test for arsenic should be free from arsenic and are designated as 'AsT' grade reagents.

1.4.8 Limit Test for Lead as per IP 2014

1.4.8.1 Principle

- The limit test for lead **(Table 1.12)** is based on the reaction of lead and diphenylthiocarbazone (dithizone) in alkaline solution to form lead dithizonate complex, which is violet in colour.
- Nessler cylinders are not used to perform this test. But instead, the test is performed by extraction using separating funnel.
- The original colour of dithizone in chloroform is green while the lead dithizonate complex is violet in colour.
- The intensity of the violet colour of the complex depends upon the amount of lead present in the substance, which is then compared with the standard colour produced by treating standard solution containing definite amount of lead in the similar manner.
- The intensity of this violet colour is compared in both the tests and standard solution in a chloroform solvent medium.
- If the intensity of the sample solution is less than that of the standard solution, then sample passes the limit test and vice versa.

1.4.8.2 Reaction

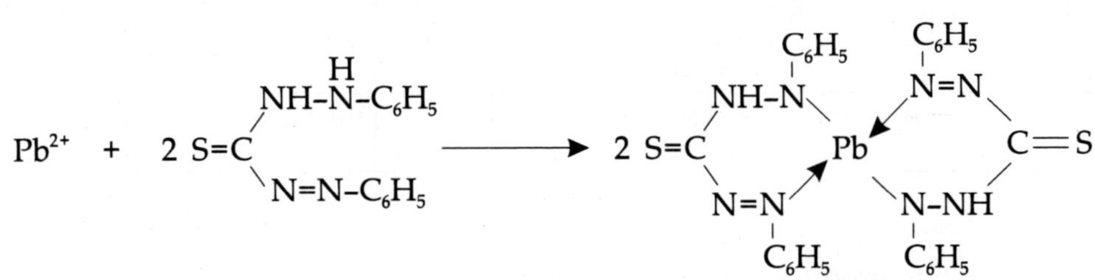

Lead ion | Dithizone (Green colour in chloroform) | Lead dithizonate (Violet colour)

1.4.8.3 Procedure

Table 1.12: Limit test for lead

Test solution	Standard solution	Explanations
Transfer a known quantity of sample solution in a separating funnel.	A standard lead solution is prepared equivalent to the amount of lead permitted in the sample under examination.	Suspected sample is taken, which might have an impurity of lead.
Add 6 mL of ammonium citrate.	Add 6 mL of ammonium citrate.	Ammonium citrate is added to maintain optimum pH and to prevent the formation of undesired impurities.
Add 2 mL of potassium cyanide and 2 mL of hydroxylamine hydrochloride.	Add 2 mL of potassium cyanide and 2 mL of hydroxylamine hydrochloride.	Cyanide forms complexes with all the interfering metals in the solution.
Add two drops of phenol red.	Add two drops of phenol red.	Used as an indicator to develop colour at the end of the process.
Make solution alkaline by adding ammonia solution.	Make solution alkaline by adding ammonia solution.	Ammonia provides basic conditions to develop red colour.
Extract with 5 mL of dithizone until it becomes green.	Extract with 5 mL of dithizone until it becomes green.	At least 2-3 extractions are done in separating funnel, mix all the extracts in the end.
Combined dithizone extracts are shaken for 30 minutes with 30 mL of nitric acid and the chloroform layer is discarded.	Combined dithizone extracts are shaken for 30 minutes with 30 mL of nitric acid and the chloroform layer is discarded.	Acidic layer (contains free lead Pb^{2+}) is separated from chloroform. Nitric acid makes lead free from chloroform layer.
To the acid solution, add 5 mL of standard dithizone solution.	To the acid solution, add 5 mL of standard dithizone solution.	Violet colour appears due to complex lead-dithizonate.
Add 4 mL of ammonium cyanide.	Add 4 mL of ammonium cyanide.	Maintains optimum pH.
Shake for 30 minutes and observe colour.	Shake for 30 minutes and observe colour.	Comparison of colour

Remark

- If the colour produced in the test solution is less than that in the standard solution, the sample passes the limit test for lead and vice versa.

Note

- All reagents and solutions used in the test must be free from lead.
- The reagents are used in the test to buffer the solution of the sample to the optimum pH for extraction of lead dithizonate and disallow interference with other metals which produce similar colours with dithizone.

1.4.9 Limit Test for Heavy Metals as per IP 2014

1.4.9.1 Principle

- The limit test for heavy metals is based on the reaction of heavy metals with hydrogen sulphide (H_2S) / sodium sulphide (Na_2S) in the presence of acidic/ alkaline medium, respectively.
- Colour reactions occur due to the formation of insoluble metal sulphides.
- The colour produced in the test solution is compared with the intensity of colour from the standard solution.
- The limits for heavy metal in individual sample are expressed in terms of ppm.

1.4.9.2 Reaction

$$M + H_2S \longrightarrow MS + 2H^+$$

$$\underset{\text{Metal}}{M} + Na_2S \longrightarrow \underset{\substack{\text{Metal sulphides} \\ \text{(Brown precipitation)}}}{MS} + 2Na^+$$

1.4.9.3 Procedure

Method A

Step 1: Preparation of standard solution

- Into a 50 mL Nessler cylinder, pipette 1.0 mL of lead standard solution (20 ppm lead) and dilute with water up to 25 mL.
- Adjust with dilute acetic acid or dilute ammonia solution to pH between 3.0 and 4.0, dilute with water to about 35 mL and mix.

Step 2: Preparation of test solution

- Into a 50 mL Nessler cylinder, place 25 mL of the solution prepared for the test as directed in the individual monograph or dissolve the specified quantity of the substance under examination in sufficient water to make 25 mL.
- Adjust with dilute acetic acid or dilute ammonia solution to pH between 3.0 and 4.0, dilute with water to about 35 mL and mix.

Step 3: Procedure

- To each of the cylinders containing the standard solution and test solution respectively, add 10 mL of freshly prepared hydrogen sulphide solution, mix, dilute to 50 mL with water and allow it to stand for 5 minutes.
- Observe the colour of test solution and compare with that of the standard.

Method B

Step 1: Preparation of standard solution

- Procedure same as that directed under Method A.

Step 2: Preparation of test solution

- Weigh in a suitable crucible the quantity of the substance specified in the individual monograph, add sufficient sulphuric acid to wet the sample and ignite carefully at a low temperature, until thoroughly charred.
- To the charred mass, add 2 mL of nitric acid and five drops of sulphuric acid and heat cautiously, until white fumes are no longer evolved.
- Ignite, preferably in a muffle furnace, at 500 to 600°C, until the carbon is completely burnt off.
- Cool, add 4.0 mL of HCl, cover, digest on a water bath for 15 minutes, uncover and slowly evaporate to dryness on a water bath.
- Moisten the residue with one drop of HCl, add 10 mL of hot water and digest for 2 minutes.
- Add ammonia solution drop wise until the solution is just alkaline to litmus paper, dilute to 25 mL with water and adjust with dilute acetic acid to pH between 3.0 and 4.0.
- Filter and if necessary, rinse the crucible and filter with 10 mL of water, combine the filtrate and washings in a 50 mL Nessler cylinder, dilute with water to about 35 mL and mix.

Step 3: Procedure

- Procedure same as that directed under Method A.

Method C

Step 1: Preparation of standard solution

- Into a 50 mL Nessler cylinder, pipette 1.0 mL of lead standard solution (20 ppm lead), add 5.0 mL of dilute sodium hydroxide solution, dilute with water to 50 mL and mix.

Step 2: Preparation of test solution

- In a 50 mL Nessler cylinder, place 25 mL of the solution prepared for the test as directed in the individual monograph or dissolve the specified quantity of the substance under examination in a mixture of 20 mL of water and 5.0 mL of dilute sodium hydroxide solution.
- Dilute with water to 50 mL and mix.

Step 3: Procedure

- To each of the cylinders containing the standard solution and test solution respectively, add five drops of sodium sulphide solution, mix, allow it to stand for 5 minutes and observe the colour.

Method D

Step 1: Preparation of standard solution

- Into a Nessler cylinder, pipette 10.0 mL of either lead standard solution (1 ppm lead) or lead standard solution (2 ppm lead).

Step 2: Preparation of test solution

- Prepare as directed in the individual monograph and pipette 12 mL into a Nessler cylinder.

Step 3: Procedure

- To a cylinder containing the standard solution, add 2.0 mL of the test solution and mix.
- To each of the cylinders, add 2.0 mL of acetate buffer pH 3.5, mix, add 1.2 mL of thioacetamide reagent, allow it to stand for 2 minutes and observe the colour.

Remark

- If brown colour obtained in the test solution is less than the standard solution, the sample passes the limit test for heavy metal and vice versa.

Note

- Purified water is used for dilution and should be free from dissolved gases and impurities.
- Standard solution is prepared as it gives maximum permissible limit for comparison.
- H_2S and Na_2S solutions are the reactants and require acidic/alkaline media for their reactions, respectively.
- Acidic medium is adjusted by ammonia or acetic acid while acidic medium is adjusted by NaOH.
- All the reagents used in the limit test for heavy metals should be free from lead and are designated as 'Sp' reagents.

MULTIPLE-CHOICE QUESTIONS

1. Which of the following reagents is used to increase the sensitivity of limit test of sulphate?
   (a) $AgNO_3$ (b) $BaCl_2$
   (c) K_2SO_4 (d) CH_3COOH
2. Which of the following reagents is used to prevent precipitation of iron by ammonia in limit test of iron?
   (a) Citric acid (b) Thioglycolic acid
   (c) Potassium sulphate (d) Ammonium thiocyanate
3. Which of the following is used to avoid the interaction of hydrogen sulphide gas with mercuric chloride in limit test of arsenic?
   (a) Stannated zinc (b) Ammonia
   (c) Lead acetate (d) Citric acid
4. Which of the following is used for slow and steady evolution of nascent hydrogen in limit test of arsenic?
   (a) Citric acid (b) Ammonia
   (c) Lead acetate (d) Stannated zinc

5. Which of the following limit tests are not performed using Nessler cylinder?
   (a) Iron (b) Lead
   (c) Sulphate (d) Arsenic
6. Which of the following is added to maintain optimum pH and to prevent the formation of undesired impurities in the limit test of lead?
   (a) Ammonium citrate (b) Citric acid
   (c) Ammonia (d) Lead acetate
7. Which of the following compounds may be used as reducing agent(s) in the limit test of arsenic?
   (a) Zinc (b) Potassium iodide
   (c) Stannous chloride (d) All of the above
8. What kind of tests are limit tests?
   (a) Quantitative (b) Semi-quantitative
   (c) Both (a) and (b) (d) None of the above
9. Inorganic pharmaceutical substances may be purified by which procedure(s)?
   (a) Drying (b) Recrystallisation
   (c) Sublimation (d) All of the above
10. The term used for the container that is impervious to air or any other gas under normal conditions of handling, shipment, storage and distribution is
    (a) Hermetically sealed container (b) Single-dose container
    (c) Light-resistant container (d) All of the above

FILL IN THE BLANKS

1. Limit tests are quantitative or .... tests to identify and control small quantities of impurities.
2. Limit test for chloride is based upon the reaction between .... and ....
3. Limit test for sulphate is based upon the precipitate of sulphate with .... in presence of ....
4. Limit test for iron ferrous thioglycolate has stable pink to reddish purple colour in .... medium.
5. In the limit test for iron, purple colour is due to the formation of ....
6. The apparatus used to perform limit test of arsenic is called ....
7. In the limit test for arsenic, ... is converted into arsenious acid/ arsine gas.
8. In the limit test for arsenic, the function of granulated zinc is ....
9. In the limit test for heavy metals, ... is used for clear colourless/ turbid coloured solution.

10. In the limit test, the change in .... is compared with fixed standard in the pharmacopoeia.
11. If the test solution's colour, turbidity or opalescence is less than that of the standard solution, it .... the limit test.

SHORT QUESTIONS

1. What is meant by pharmaceutical chemistry?
2. What is pharmaceutical inorganic chemistry?
3. Define impurity.
4. Define limit tests.
5. Why only distilled water or purified water is used in performing limit tests?
6. Why nitric acid is used in performing limit test for chloride?
7. Why HCl is used in the limit test of sulphate?
8. Is there any special apparatus or container required for performing limit tests?
9. Why barium chloride is used in the limit test of sulphate?
10. What is barium sulphate reagent?
11. What do you understand by the term 'ppm'?
12. Why granulated zinc is used in the limit test of arsenic instead of ordinary zinc?
13. Why ammonia is used in the limit test of iron?
14. Why citric acid is used in the limit test of iron?
15. Why ethanol is used in the limit test of sulphate?

LONG QUESTIONS

1. Discuss the important aspects of pharmaceutical chemistry.
2. Define pharmacopoeia. Describe the year-wise developments and amendments that took place in the history of Indian Pharmacopoeia.
3. Enumerate the salient features of IP 2018.
4. What do you mean by the term monograph? What are the contents of monograph?
5. Write a note on: (a) British Pharmacopoeia, (b) International Pharmacopoeia, (c) United States Pharmacopoeia, (d) European Pharmacopoeia, and (e) Martindale.
6. Discuss the types of storage containers used for storaging pharmaceutical substances.
7. Mention the type of storage conditions with respect to temperature.
8. Define and explain the following terms: (a) Assay, (b) Monograph, and (c) Pharmacopoeia

9. What is the difference between impure chemical compound and pure chemical compound?
10. Mention the types of impurities found in pharmaceutical preparations.
11. Write a note on the sources of impurities.
12. Enlist the effects of impurities present in the pharmaceutical substances.
13. Discuss various methods to purify inorganic substances.
14. Write a note on tests for purity.
15. Mention the principle behind the limit test for chlorides and sulphates.
16. What is the composition of barium sulphate reagent?
17. Write a note on the limit test for iron.
18. Write a note on the limit test for lead.
19. Discuss the principle and various methods to perform the limit test for heavy metals.
20. Mention the principle, the reactions involved and the procedure to perform the limit test for arsenic.
21. Discuss with a neat and labelled diagram the apparatus to perform the limit test for arsenic.
22. Enumerate the permissible limits of chloride, sulphate, iron, lead, heavy metal and arsenic impurities as per IP.

ANSWERS

Multiple-Choice Questions

1. (c) 2. (a) 3. (c) 4. (d) 5. (b) 6. (a) 7. (d) 8. (c)
9. (d) 10. (a)

Fill in the Blanks

1. Semi-quantitative
2. $AgNO_3$/soluble chloride
3. Barium chloride/hydrochloride
4. Thioglycolic acid
5. Alkaline
6. Gutziet apparatus
7. Arsine
8. Slow and prolonged evolution of nascent H_2 gas
9. Method A
10. Colour, turbidity
11. Passes

2

Acids, Bases and Buffers, Electrolytes and Dental Products

2.1 ACIDS AND BASES

The concept of acid and base has undergone a considerable change. Various theories have been proposed to explain the concept of acid and base, which are described as follows:

(a) Earlier theory of acid and base
(b) Arrhenius theory
(c) Lowry-Bronsted theory (proton-donor concept)
(d) Lewis theory (electron-donor-acceptor concept)

2.1.1 Theories of Acids and Bases

(a) Earlier Theory of Acid and Base

Acid

- An acid may be defined as a substance which has sour taste.
- Its aqueous solution turns blue litmus red.

Base

- A base may be defined as a substance which has bitter taste.
- Its aqueous solution turns red litmus blue.

(b) Arrhenius Theory

This theory was first introduced in 1887 by Swedish scientist, Svante Arrhenius.

The main idea in this theory was that when an electrolyte is dissolved in water, it dissociates into positively and negatively charged ions.

Based on this hypothesis, Arrhenius gave the definition of acid and base as follows:

Acid

- It may be defined as any compound which produces hydrogen (H^+) ions in aqueous solution.
- For example, substances containing hydrogen, like HCl, HNO_3, H_2SO_4, etc., when dissolved in water, dissociate completely into H^+ ions and negative ions, and act as strong acids.

$$HCl \overset{H_2O}{\rightleftharpoons} H^+ + Cl^-$$

$$HNO_3 \overset{H_2O}{\rightleftharpoons} H^+ + NO_3^-$$

- Substances like acetic acid (CH_3COOH), carbonic acid (H_2CO_3), phosphoric acid (H_3PO_4), etc., when dissolved in water, dissociate into ions to small extent and act as weak acids.

$$CH_3COOH \overset{H_2O}{\rightleftharpoons} H^+ + CH_3COO^-$$

$$H_3PO_3 \overset{H_2O}{\rightleftharpoons} 3H^+ + PO_4^{3-}$$

Base

- It may be defined as any compound which produces hydroxide (OH^-) ions in aqueous solution.
- For example, substances like NaOH, KOH, etc., when dissolved in water, dissociate completely into OH^- ions and act as strong bases.

$$NaOH \overset{H_2O}{\rightleftharpoons} Na^+ + OH^-$$

$$KOH \overset{H_2O}{\rightleftharpoons} K^+ + OH^-$$

- Substances like NH_4OH, $Ca(OH)_2$, etc., when dissolved in water, dissociate into ions to small extent and act as weak bases.

$$NH_4OH \overset{H_2O}{\rightleftharpoons} NH_4^- + OH^-$$

Limitations

- The definitions are only in terms of aqueous solutions and not in terms of substance.

- The theory does not explain acidic and basic properties of substances in non-aqueous solvents.
- The theory does not explain the neutralization of acid and base in the absence of solvent.
- The theory gives no explanation for those basic substances which do not produce hydroxide ion.
- The theory does not explain the acidic character of certain salts, like $AlCl_3$ in aqueous solution.

(c) Lowry-Bronsted Theory (Proton-Donor Concept)

This theory was introduced independently in 1923 by the Danish chemist, Johannes Nicolaus Bronsted in Copenhagen and the English chemist, Thomas Martin Lowry in London. Accordingly,

Acid

- An acid is the substance which donates the protons.
- For example, HCl is an acid.

$$HCl \rightleftharpoons H^+ + Cl^-$$

Base

- Base is the substance which accepts the protons.
- For example, ammonia is a base.

$$NH_3 + H^+ \rightleftharpoons NH_4^+$$

Conjugate Acid-Base Pairs

$$\underset{Acid_1}{HCl} + \underset{Base_2}{H_2O} \rightleftharpoons \underset{Acid_2}{H_3O^+} + \underset{Base_1}{Cl^-}$$

- In this reaction, HCl donates a proton to H_2O and hence, acts as acid, while water accepts a proton from HCl and is therefore, a base.
- In the reverse reaction, which at equilibrium proceeds at the same rate as the forward reaction, the H_3O^+ ion donates a proton to Cl^- ion and hence, H_3O^+ is an acid, while Cl^- ion which accepts a proton from H_3O^+ acts as base.
- Such acid-base pairs, the members of which can be formed from each other mutually by the gain or loss of proton are called conjugate acid-base pairs.
- In the above reaction, the acid HCl is labelled as $acid_1$, and its conjugate base, i.e., Cl^- as base; while if H_2O is designated as $base_2$, then its conjugate acid will be H_3O^+ ($acid_2$).

- Some other examples of conjugate acid-base pairs are as follows:

$$H_2SO_4 + H_2O \rightleftharpoons H_3O^+ + HSO_4^-$$

$$CH_3COOH + H_2O \rightleftharpoons H_3O^+ + CH_3COO^-$$

$$NH_4^+ + H_2O \rightleftharpoons H_3O^+ + NH_3$$

- Water has a dual character. It can accept or donate a proton. Thus, it may act as an acid as well as a base and hence, it is called amphoteric or amphiprotic. For example,

$$\underset{Acid_1}{HCl} + \underset{Base_2}{H_2O} \rightleftharpoons \underset{Acid_2}{H_3O^+} + \underset{Base_1}{Cl^-}$$

$$\underset{Acid_1}{H_2O} + \underset{Base_2}{NH_3} \rightleftharpoons \underset{Acid_2}{NH_4^+} + \underset{Base_1}{OH^-}$$

Note

- According to this concept, if two acids are mixed, the weaker acid will act as base with respect to the stronger acid. For example,

$$\underset{Acid_1}{HClO_4} + \underset{Base_2}{H_2SO_4} \rightleftharpoons \underset{Acid_2}{H_3SO_4^+} + \underset{Base_1}{ClO_4^+}$$

Thus, H_2SO_4 is amphoteric or amphiprotic in nature.

- Hence, from the above discussion, it can be concluded that all Arrhenius acids are also Bronsted acids, but all Arrhenius bases are not Bronsted bases.

Advantages of Lowry-Bronsted Concept over Arrhenius Concept

- Lowry-Bronsted concept is not limited to molecules; it also includes the ionic species to act as acids or bases.
- It can explain the basic character of substances like Na_2CO_3, NH_3, etc., on the basis that they are proton acceptors.
- It can explain the acid-base reaction in the non-aqueous medium or even in absence of solvent.

Limitations of Lowry-Bronsted Concept

- The theory does not explain those acids which are not protonic in nature.
- The theory does not explain those acid-base reactions in which no proton transfer takes place. For example,

$$\underset{Acid_1}{SO_2} + \underset{Base_2}{SO_2} \rightleftharpoons \underset{Acid_2}{SO^{2+}} + \underset{Base_1}{SO_3^{2-}}$$

- Protonic definition cannot be used to explain the reactions occurring in non-protonic solvents, like $COCl_2$, SO_2, N_2O_4, BF_3, $AlCl_3$, etc.

(d) Lewis Theory (Electron Donor-Acceptor Concept)

This theory was proposed by an American Chemist, G. N. Lewis in 1923, which was rather a broader concept for acids and bases compared to the other theories.

This concept eliminated the necessity of presence of hydrogen in an acid and includes many more substances as acids and bases. Accordingly,

Acid

- Acid may be defined as species (molecules, radical or ion) that can accept an electron pair to form a coordinate bond.
- Examples of Lewis acid: H^+, NH_4^+, Na^+, K^+, Cu^{2+}, Al^{3+}, etc.

Types of Lewis Acids

Lewis acids can be of four types:

(i) Molecules having a central atom with complete octet

For example: BF_3, $AlCl_3$, $FeCl_3$

(ii) Simple cations

- For example: Ag^+, Cu^{2+}, Fe^{3+}, etc.
- These ions can accept pairs of electrons and hence, are called Lewis acids.

$$Ag^+ + 2\ \ddot{N}H_3 \longrightarrow [H_3N \rightarrow Ag \leftarrow NH_3]$$

(iii) Molecules having central atoms with empty d-orbitals

- The central atoms in these molecules can expand their outer octet by taking up electrons in their empty d-orbitals.
- For example: $SnCl_4$, SiF_4, PF_5, etc. having central atom containing the empty d-orbitals.

$$SiF_4 + 2F^- \longrightarrow [SiF_6]^{2-}$$

(iv) Molecules containing multiple bonds between two atoms of different electronegativity

- For example, CO_2 contains a double bond between carbon and oxygen. Since oxygen is more electronegative than carbon, therefore carbon acquires a slight positive charge and thus, can accept a pair of electrons. Hence, CO_2 acts a Lewis acid.

$$O{=}C{=}OH + :OH^- \longrightarrow HCO_3^-$$

Base

- Base may be defined as species (molecules, radical or ion) that can donate an electron pair to form a coordinate bond.
- Examples of Lewis base: NH_3, H_2O, OH^-, Cl^-, CN^-, S^{2-}, etc.

Types of Lewis Bases

Lewis bases can be of two types:

(i) Neutral molecules like NH_3, $R\text{-}NH_2$, R-OH, H-O-H, etc., in which the atom has at least one lone pair of electrons.

(ii) All negative ions like F^-, Cl^-, Br^-, I^-, OH^-, Cl^-, CN^-, S^{2-}, etc.

Limitations of Lewis Concept

- Lewis concept is not able to explain the strength of acids and bases, whereas Arrhenius and Lowry-Bronsted concepts can explain that.
- Lewis concept is so general that it considers every reaction forming a coordinate bond to be acid-base reaction. This, however, may not always be true.
- The necessary requirement in Lewis concept is the formation of a coordinate bond to be acid and base. However, the well-known acids like HCl and H_2SO_4 do not form any coordinate bond and hence, should not be acids according to this concept. But this is not true.
- The catalytic activity of an acid is due to H^+ (aqueous solution). Since the presence of hydrogen is not an essential requirement for a Lewis acid, many Lewis acids do not have this property.
- As Lewis acid-base reactions involve electrons, they are expected to be very fast reactions. However, there are many Lewis acid-base reactions which are slow.

2.1.2 Types of Acids and Bases

On the basis of strength of dissociation, acids and bases are classified into:

(a) Strong acid

(b) Weak acid

(c) Strong base

(d) Weak base

(a) Strong Acid

- A strong acid is the one which is virtually 100% ionised in solution.

Examples include:

Hydrochloric acid (HCl)

Nitric acid (HNO_3)

Sulphuric acid (H_2SO_4)

Hydrobromic acid (HBr)
Hydroiodic acid (HI)
Perchloric acid ($HClO_4$)
Chloric acid ($HClO_3$)

(b) Weak Acid

- A weak acid is the one which does not ionise completely when dissolved in water.
- For example, HF dissociates into H^+ and F^- ions in water but some HF remains in solution, so it is not a strong acid.
- There are more weak acids than strong acids.
- Most organic acids are weak acids.

Examples include:

Oxalic acid ($C_2O_4H_2$)
Sulphurous acid (H_2SO_3)
Hydrogen sulphate ion (HSO_4^-)
Phosphoric acid (H_3PO_4)
Nitrous acid (HNO_2)
Hydrofluoric acid (HF)
Benzoic acid (C_6H_5COOH)
Acetic acid (CH_3COOH)
Formic acid (HCOOH)

(c) Strong Base

- Strong bases are those which completely dissociate in water into cation and hydroxyl ions (OH^-).

Examples include:

Lithium hydroxide (LiOH)
Sodium hydroxide (NaOH)
Potassium hydroxide (KOH)
Rubidium hydroxide (RuOH)
Cesium hydroxide (CsOH)
Barium hydroxide ($Ba(OH)_2$)
Calcium hydroxide ($Ca(OH)_2$)
Strontium hydroxide ($Sr(OH)_2$)

(d) Weak Base

- A weak base is the one which does not ionise completely when dissolved in water.

Examples include:

Alanine
Ammonia (NH_3)
Ammonium hydroxide (NH_4OH)
Methylamine (CH_3NH_2)
Phosphine (PH_3)
Hydrazine (NH_2NH_2)
Zinc hydroxide ($Zn(OH)_2$)

2.1.3 Relative Strengths of Acids and Bases

- Acids and bases can be identified as monoprotic or polyprotic depending upon the numbers of dissociable protons the acid contains or the number of protons with which the base can combine.
- Irrespective of whether a substance is monoprotic or polyprotic, the strength of an acid or base refers to the efficiency with which the substance demonstrates the properties of an acid or base.
- For an acid, this means the ease with which it donates protons; while for base, this means the ease with which it accepts protons.
- These properties of a substance are affected by its environment; it is easier for an acid to donate protons in a proton-accepting medium.
- The strength of an acid or base is most frequently determined by the dissociation constant, K.
- If B is a strong base, it will have a high affinity for H^+ and hence, BH^+ is a weak acid.
- Conversely, if B is a weak base, it will have low affinity for H^+ and so BH^+ is a strong conjugate acid.
- For this reason, the strength of a base is frequently expressed in terms of the acid dissociation constant of its conjugate acid BH^+.

$$K_2 = \frac{[B][H^+]}{[BH^+]}$$

- Thus, the strength of an acid is given by K_a and the strength of a base by K_b or K_a of its conjugate acid.

2.1.4 Pharmaceutical Importance of Acids and Bases

(a) Biological Importance

- Maintenance of levels of acid and bases in the body is an important aspect because body needs a neutral pH.

- Acids and bases find use as therapeutic agents in the control of and adjustment of the pH of gastrointestinal tract, body fluids and urine.
- The body maintains this neutral pH by controlling the amounts of acids and bases through various processes involving the blood, lungs and kidneys.
- Acids and bases are found in food, environment and even in chemicals, including pharmaceuticals. On higher intake of acidic foods, the body uses a buffering system to neutralize the positive ions released from the acids. Conversely, bases are also controlled to keep the body from becoming too alkaline.
- Further, changes in the body pH lead to physical changes. For example, when body contains too much carbon dioxide, the blood becomes too much acidic. Hence, breathing is slowed to increase the pH in the blood. Conversely, if pH in the body is too high (i.e., alkaline), it will hyperventilate in an attempt to lower the pH. This acid-base control is a significant part of biological homeostasis in humans.
- Besides, the body also has a buffer system that helps control the levels of acids and bases. pH levels are controlled by bicarbonate (HCO_3^-) ions. The metabolism in the body produces high amount of acids. For example, while doing workout or during muscle building, the muscle tissue produces lactic acid; this lactic acid is picked up and neutralized by the bicarbonate ions.

(b) Analytical Importance

- Acid-bases are used in analytical procedures, wherein they are used to carry out acid-base titrations.
- Acid-base neutralisation reactions find use in the preparative procedures for preparing suitable salts, and for conversion of certain salts into more suitable forms, specific acid-base system is used for preparing effervescent mixtures.
- The conjugate pairs of acids or bases are used as buffers. For example, buffer acid acts as a proton donor and buffer base acts as a proton acceptor.

2.1.5 Handling and Storage of Acids and Bases

- Due precautions have to be undertaken during handling and storage of acids and bases.
- Storage problems include inadequate closures or exposure to heat and light.
- Inadequate closures result in vaporisation and loss of gaseous components and exposure to moisture, oxygen and carbon dioxide.
- Oxygen may further cause oxidation of acids or bases. For example, hydroiodic acid is capable of getting oxidised in the presence of oxygen.
- Carbon dioxide can react with bases like sodium hydroxide, potassium hydroxide, sodalime and lime water.

- Moreover, some hygroscopic substances, like sodium hydroxide, are capable of absorbing moisture on exposure to air and become liquid, thus showing *deliquescent property*.
- Besides, dehydrating agents like concentrated sulphuric acid and quicklime are to be protected from air by storing them in air-tight containers.
- Crystalline hydrated acids and bases like sodium carbonate and citric acid (which possess higher vapour pressure than the relative humidity of the atmosphere) may lose varying portions of their water of crystallisation to the atmosphere, exhibiting *efflorescent property*. Such substances are to be stored in closed containers with tight closures.
- Additionally, at higher temperatures also, these substances lose water of crystallisation and hence, needed to be protected from heat as well.

Some pharmaceutically useful acids and bases are described as follows:

2.1.6 Boric Acid

Synonym : Boracic acid, orthoboric acid
Molecular formula : H_3BO_3
Molecular weight : 61.83 g/mol
Category : Local anti-infective

Standards

It contains not less than 99.5% and not more than 100.5% of H_3BO_3 with reference to dried substance.

Method of Preparation

- Boric acid is prepared from native borax and borates by reacting them with hydrochloric acid or sulphuric acid.

$$Na_2B_4O_7 + H_2SO_4 + 5H_2O \longrightarrow Na_2SO_4 + 4H_3BO_3$$

Physical Properties

Colour : Colourless or white
Odour : Odourless
Taste : Bitter and acidic
State : Crystalline powder, pearly scales or six-sided triclinic crystals
Solubility : (i) Soluble in water and alcohol
(ii) Freely soluble in boiling water and alcohol
Nature : Acidic in nature, unctuous, greasy or soapy to touch and stable in air

Chemical Property

- Boric acid on heating to 100°C loses one molecule of water to give metaboric acid HBO_2, which on further heating to 160°C results in loss of one molecule of water to give tetraboric acid $H_2B_4O_7$. Heating to still higher temperature results in the formation of anhydride of boric acid called boron trioxide, B_2O_3.

Storage

- It is stored in well-closed containers.
- It can be very dangerous if ingested. Therefore, its container should bear the warning "not for internal use".

Pharmaceutical Uses

- As a weak germicide.
- As local anti-infective.
- Its aqueous solutions are used as eye wash and mouth wash.
- Employed in dusting powder, ointments, lotions, local antiseptic creams, etc., meant for local application to mucous membrane, skin or eyes.

2.1.7 Hydrochloric Acid

It is an aqueous solution of hydrogen chloride in water.

Synonym : Spirit of salt
Molecular formula : HCl
Molecular weight : 36.46 g/mol
Category : Solvent and acidifier

Standards

It contains not less than 35.0% w/w and not more than 38.0% w/w of HCl.

Method of Preparation

- It is prepared by the action of sulphuric acid on sodium chloride.

$$NaCl + H_2SO_4 \longrightarrow HCl + NaHSO_4$$

Physical Properties

Colour : Colourless
Odour : Pungent
State : Fuming liquid
Solubility : Soluble in water and alcohol
Nature : Strong acid with specific gravity of 1.18

Chemical Property

- It attacks metals forming their hydrochlorides with the evolution of hydrogen gas.

Storage

- It is stored in well-closed containers.

Pharmaceutical Uses

- As a solvent.
- As a catalyst.
- As an acidifier.
- In the preparation of dilute hydrochloric acid.

2.1.8 Strong Ammonium Hydroxide

Synonym : Strong ammonia solution, liquor ammonia *fortis*
Molecular formula : NH_4OH
Molecular weight : 35.05 g/mol
Category : Antacid

Standards

It contains not less than 27.0% w/w and not more than 30.0% of w/w of NH_3.

Method of Preparation

- It is obtained by passing ammonia gas into cooled water until the water gets saturated with ammonia.

Physical Properties

Colour : Colourless
Odour : Characteristic, strong and pungent
Taste : Alkaline
State : Transparent liquid
Solubility : Soluble in water
Nature : Strongly alkaline

Chemical Property

- It reacts with metals to form nitrogen gas.

Storage

- It is stored in well-closed containers in cool place. It is generally kept in amber-coloured bottles having a rubber stopper.

Pharmaceutical Uses

- As antacid.
- As a source of ammonia.
- As counter-irritant and respiratory stimulant.
- As fertilizer.
- In the preparation of aromatic spirit of ammonia.
- As a laboratory reagent.

2.1.9 Calcium Hydroxide

Synonym : Slaked lime or hydrated lime
Molecular formula : $Ca(OH)_2$
Molecular weight : 74.10 g/mol
Category : Antacid and astringent

Standards

It contains not less than 90.0% of $Ca(OH)_2$.

Method of Preparation

- Calcium hydroxide may be prepared by spraying water on quicklime. This process is called slaking.

$$CaO + H_2O \longrightarrow Ca(OH)_2 + Heat$$

Physical Properties

Colour : White
Odour : Odourless
Taste : Slightly bitter
State : Soft powder
Solubility : (i) Soluble in water and alcohol
(ii) Less soluble in boiling water
Nature : (i) Alkaline to litmus
(ii) On exposure to air, it absorbs atmospheric CO_2 and forms $CaCO_3$

Chemical Property

- When calcium hydroxide is heated strongly, it loses water and is converted to CaO.

$$Ca(OH)_2 \xrightarrow{\Delta} CaO + H_2O$$

Incompatibility

- It is incompatible with CO_2.

Storage

- It is stored in well-closed containers protected from moisture and carbon dioxide.

Pharmaceutical Uses

- As an antacid.
- As an astringent in infantile diarrhoea and vomiting.
- Used topically as a protective in solution form.
- In the preparation of skin lotions.

2.1.10 Sodium Hydroxide

Synonym : Caustic soda
Molecular formula : NaOH
Molecular weight : 40 g/mol
Category : Strong alkali and disinfectant

Standards

It contains not less than 95.0% of total alkali calculated as NaOH and not more than 3.0% of Na_2CO_3.

Method of Preparation

- It is obtained by the soda-lime process, in which sodium carbonate is heated with milk of lime $Ca(OH)_2$ in large tanks.

$$Na_2CO_3 + Ca(OH)_2 \longrightarrow CaCO_3\downarrow + 2NaOH$$

Physical Properties

Colour : White
Odour : Odourless
State : Flakes, sticks or pellets
Solubility : Soluble in water, freely soluble in alcohol and glycerine
Nature : Deliquescent, strongly alkaline and corrosive

Chemical Properties

- It absorbs carbon dioxide and gets partially converted into sodium carbonate.

$$H_2O + CO_2 \longrightarrow H_2CO_3$$

$$2NaOH + H_2CO_3 \longrightarrow Na_2CO_3 + 2H_2O$$

Storage Condition

- It is stored in well-closed containers protected from moisture and carbon dioxide.

Pharmaceutical Uses

- As a laboratory reagent.
- In the preparation of soap.
- As a disinfectant for veterinary purposes.

2.2 BUFFER SOLUTIONS

- The solutions which resist the changes in pH values are known as **buffer solutions**.
- They consist of a mixture of weak acid and its salt or a weak base and its salt.

2.2.1 Types of Buffer Solutions

The buffer solutions are classified on the basis of chemical nature and use.

On the basis of chemical nature, they are of two types:

(a) Solutions of Single Substance

- Also called neutral buffer.
- It consists of a single substance showing the properties of buffer.
- For example, ammonium acetate (CH_3COONH_4) buffer.

(b) Solutions of Mixtures

Solutions of mixtures are further classified into two types:

(i) Acidic buffer

(ii) Basic buffer

(i) *Acidic buffer*

- The solution consisting of a mixture of weak acid (e.g., acetic acid) and its salt (e.g., sodium acetate) is called acidic buffer.

(ii) *Basic buffer*

- The solution consisting of a mixture of weak base (e.g., ammonia) and its salt (e.g., ammonium chloride) is called basic buffer.

2.2.2 Properties of Buffer Solutions

- The pH of buffer solution should remain constant.
- The pH of buffer solution should not change on dilution.
- The pH of buffer solution should not change even after the addition of small quantities of acids or bases.
- The pH of buffer solution should not change on keeping for long time.

2.2.3 Hydrogen Ion Concentration, pH and pOH

Pure water is considered to ionise to a small degree as per the following equation:

$$H_2O \rightleftharpoons H^+ + OH^-$$

$$K = \frac{[H^+][OH^-]}{[H_2O]}$$

$$K[H_2O] = [H^+]\ [OH^-]$$

$$K_w = [H^+]\ [OH^-]$$

where, K_w = Ion product constant

The ion product constant (K_w) is expressed by involving only the concentration of ionic species on right-hand side of the reaction and has a constant value at 25°C of 1×10^{-14}. It can be represented as:

$$[H^+]\ [OH^-] = 1 \times 10^{-14}$$

In pure water, the concentrations of both ions are equal, each having the value of 1×10^{-7}.

$$[H^+] = [OH^-] = 1 \times 10^{-7}$$

The hydrogen ion concentration is greater than hydroxide ion concentration when an acid or base is added to water. The value of hydrogen ion concentration is 10^{-7} g ion/litre.

In neutral solution, $[H^+] = [OH^-]$

In acidic solution, $[H^+] > [OH^-]$

In basic/alkaline solution, $[H^+] < [OH^-]$

2.2.4 pH Scale

Hydrogen ion concentration is usually expressed in terms of mole/litre or gram equivalent/litre. It is very inconvenient to write the exponential power of ten to the power minus of particular figure. Hence, Sorenson introduced a practical concept of expressing acidity, i.e., pH scale.

The term pH is defined as the negative logarithm (to the base 10) of hydrogen ion concentration.

It is represented by the expression:

$$pH = -\log [H^+]$$

In pure water,

$$[H^+] = 1 \times 10^{-7}$$
$$\text{or } pH = -\log [1 \times 10^{-7}] = 7$$

The pH scale covers from 0 to 14 of all the hydrogen ion concentration. It can be measured by using pH meter.

If $[H^+]$ is high, the solution is acidic and pH < 7.

If $[H^+]$ is low, the solution is basic or alkaline and pH > 7.

Further, pOH is defined as the negative logarithm of hydroxyl ion concentration.

$$pOH = -\log [OH^-]$$

2.2.5 Relationship Between pH and pOH

Ionic product of water is given by,

$$K_w = [H_3O^+]\ [OH^-]$$

Taking log on both sides,

$$\log K_w = \log ([H_3O^+]\ [OH^-])$$
$$\text{or } \log K_w = \log [H_3O^+] + \log [OH^-]$$

Taking negative on both sides,

$$-\log K_w = -\log [H_3O^+] - \log [OH^-]$$

But, $pH = -\log [H_3O^+]$ and $pOH = -\log [OH^-]$

Also, $pK_w = -\log K_w$

Thus, $pK_w = pH + pOH$

At $25°C, K_w = 10^{-14}\ mol\ L^{-2}$

Hence, $pK_w = 14$

Thus, $pH + pOH = 14$

2.2.6 Buffer Action of Acidic Buffer

The property of buffer solution to resist change in pH of any solution in which it is added is called buffer action.

Let us consider buffer action of acidic buffer containing CH_3COOH and CH_3COONa. Acetic acid dissociates into small extent while sodium acetate is completely dissociated in aqueous solution as follows:

$$CH_3COOH + H_2O \rightleftharpoons CH_3COO^- + H_3O^+$$

$$CH_3COOH \rightleftharpoons CH_3COO^- + Na^+$$

By 'common ion effect', the ionisation of CH_3COOH is further suppressed. Thus, in the solution, there is excess of acetate (CH_3COO^-) ions and small amount of hydronium ions (H_3O^+).

When a few drops of acid are added to the above mixture, the H_3O^+ ions given by the acid combine with CH_3COO^- ions to form weakly ionised molecules of CH_3COOH.

$$CH_3COO^- + H_3O^+ \rightleftharpoons CH_3COOH + H_2O$$

And when a few drops of base is added, the OH^- ions given by base combine with H_3O^+ ions already present to form weakly ionised molecules of H_2O.

$$H_3O^+ + OH^- \rightleftharpoons 2H_2O$$

As the H_3O^+ ions are consumed, the equilibrium shifts towards right (according to Le Chatelier's principle). Thus, more of CH_3COOH gets dissociated to make up the loss of H_3O^+ ions. Hence, H_3O^+ ion concentration or the pH of the solution does not change.

2.2.7 Buffer Equations

The pH of the buffer solution and the change in pH upon the addition of an acid or base can be calculated by using the buffer equation. This expression is developed by considering the effect of salt on the ionisation of weak acid when the salt and the acid have common ions.

Calculation of pH of a Buffer Mixture

For acidic buffer mixture (Henderson-Hasselbach Equation)

Consider the dissociation of weak acid HA and its salt BA as follows:

$$K_a = \frac{[A^-]\,[H_3O^+]}{[HA]}$$

or $$[H_3O^+] = K_a \frac{[HA]}{[A^-]}$$

But $$[A^-] = [BA]$$

∴ $$[H_3O^+] = K_a \frac{[HA]}{[BA]}$$

or $$[H_3O^+] = K_a \frac{[Acid]}{[Salt]} \qquad \text{... (i)}$$

Now $$pH = -\log [H_3O^+] \qquad \text{... (ii)}$$

∴ $$pH = -\log\left\{K_a \frac{[Acid]}{[Salt]}\right\}$$

$$\therefore \quad pH = -\log K_a - \log\frac{[Acid]}{[Salt]}$$

$$\therefore \quad pH = pK_a + \log\frac{[Salt]}{[Acid]} \quad \text{... (iii)}$$

or substituting the value of $[H_3O]^+$ from equation (i) in equation (iii), we get

$$pH = -\log K_a - \log\frac{[HA]}{[A^-]}$$

or

$$pH = pK_a + \log\frac{[A^-]}{[HA]}$$

or

$$pH = pK_a + \log\frac{[Conjugate\ base]}{[Acid]} \quad \text{...(iv)}$$

It is interesting to observe from equation (iv) that if [Salt] = [Acid] and pH = pKa. Further, if,

$$\frac{[Salt]}{[Acid]} = 10, \text{ then } pH = pK_a + 1$$

and if

$$\frac{[Acid]}{[Salt]} = 10, \text{ then } pH = pK_a - 1$$

Thus, if the ratio of the conjugate acid-base pair is changed by 10 times, pH changes by ± 1.

Besides,

$$pOH = pK_a + \log\frac{[Salt]}{[Base]} \quad \text{...(v)}$$

Now, as pH + pOH = 14, pH can be calculated.

Alternatively, the above equation can be expressed in a different form as follows:

$$pH + pOH = 14$$

or

$$pOH = 14 - OH$$

Also, $pK_a + pK_b = 14$ or $pK_a = 14 - pK_b$

Substituting these values in equation (v), we get

$$14 - pH = 14 - pKa + \log\frac{[Salt]}{[Base]}$$

or

$$pH = pK_a - \log\frac{[Salt]}{[Base]}$$

or

$$pH = pK_a + \log\frac{[Base]}{[Salt]} \quad \text{...(vi)}$$

where, K_a is the ionisation constant of the conjugate acid of the base.

Consider the buffer, $NH_4OH + NH_4Cl$, NH_4^+ is the conjugate acid of the base, NH_3 and K_a represents the ionisation constant of the reaction.

$$\underset{(aq)}{NH_4^+} + \underset{(l)}{H_2O} \rightleftharpoons \underset{(aq)}{NH_3} + \underset{(aq)}{H^+}$$

Thus, for this basic buffer, the above equation implies that

$$pH = pK_a + \log\frac{[NH_3]}{[NH_4^+]}$$

or

$$pH = pK_a + \log\frac{[Base]}{[Conjugate\ acid]} \quad (vii)$$

Applying the formula (iii) and (v), a buffer solution of required pH can be prepared knowing the value of K_a or K_b and suitably adjusting the ratio of [Salt]/[Acid] or [Salt]/[Base]. A mixture of acetic acid (CH_3COOH) and sodium acetate (CH_3COONa) acts as a buffer solution around pH 4.75 and a mixture of NH_4OH and NH_4Cl acts as a buffer around pH 9.25.

2.2.8 Buffer Capacity (β)

- This term was first introduced by van Slyke in 1922.
- The buffer action is quantitatively described by buffer action.
- The magnitude of resistance of a buffer to pH changes is referred to as buffer capacity (β).
- It is also known as buffer index or buffer efficiency or buffer value.
- It is defined as the amount of acid or base that must be added to the buffer to produce a unit change of pH.

$$\beta = \frac{d[B]}{dpH}$$

- Practically, it is defined as the number of moles of an acid or base required to be added to 1 litre of buffer solution so as to change its pH by 1 unit.

$$\text{Buffer capacity} = \frac{\text{No. of moles of acid or base added to 1 L of buffer}}{\text{Change in pH}} = \frac{d[B]}{dpH}$$

- Buffer capacity is maximum when concentration of weak acid and its salt or weak base and its salt are equal, i.e., when pH = pK_a or pOH = pK_b (refer Henderson-Hasselbach equation).
- A buffer capacity always has a positive value.
- However, since addition of base increases the pH and addition of acid decreases the pH, thus, d[B] and dpH always have the same sign.
- The value of β depends not only on the nature of the buffer but also on the pH, which is determined by relative concentration of acid and its conjugate base.

2.2.9 Correlation Between Buffer Action and Buffer Capacity

- The efficiency of a buffer depends upon its buffer action and buffer capacity.
- The greater the buffer capacity provided, the more will be the buffer action.
- On addition of small amount of acid and base, the pH of the buffer is maintained by its buffer capacity.
- Buffer capacity refers to the efficacy while buffer action refers to the resistant provided.
- The greater the efficacy of the buffer, the greater will be the resistance provided by the buffer to maintain constant pH.

2.2.10 Criteria for Buffer

- It should possess adequate buffer capacity in the required pH range.
- It should be available in high degree of purity.
- It should be enzymatically and hydrolytically stable.
- It should be water soluble.
- It should be impermeable to biological membranes.
- It should be non-toxic.
- It should possess a pH which is minimally influenced by their concentration, temperature, ionic composition or salt effect of the medium.
- It should be resistant towards oxidation.
- It should only form complexes with cations that are soluble.
- It should not absorb light in the visible or ultraviolet regions.
- It should not participate in any redox reaction.
- It should not form complexes with API (active pharmaceutical ingredient).
- It should not affect the solubility of other ingredients.
- It should be safe and should not interfere in the pharmacological actions of active ingredients.
- The buffer action should be good.

2.2.11 Buffers in Pharmaceutical Systems

On the basis of use, buffer solutions are of two types:

(A) Analytical buffers

(B) Pharmaceutical buffers

(A) Analytical Buffers

- These are the buffers used to provide a specific pH for analytical purposes.
- For example, metal buffers (which are used in the calibration of ion-sensitive electrodes in the low concentration range).

(B) Pharmaceutical Buffers

- Buffer solutions of different types are needed for maintaining the pH of drug preparations.
- These include (a) Standard buffer solutions (b) Special buffer solutions

(a) **Standard buffer solutions** are solutions of standard pH and are used for reference purposes in pH measurements and for carrying out many pharmacopoeial tests which require adjustments or maintenance of a specified pH.

Precautions to be taken while preparing standard buffer solutions

- All the crystalline reagents except boric acid should be dried at 110° to 120° for 1 hour before use.
- *Carbon dioxide-free water* should be used for preparing buffer solutions and wherever *water* is mentioned for preparation of such solutions, the use of *carbon dioxide-free water* is implied.
- The prepared solutions should be stored in chemically-resistant, glass-stoppered bottles of alkali-free glass and used within three months of preparation.
- Any solution which has become cloudy or shows any other evidence of deterioration should be discarded.

(b) **Special buffer solutions** are needed for specific microbiological and antibiotic assays.

- **Examples** include Feldman's borate buffer (acid and alkaline), Sorensen's modified phosphate buffer, etc.

Pharmaceutical buffers are further classified into two types:

(i) Physiological buffers
(ii) Actual pharmaceutical buffers

(i) Physiological Buffers

- These are the chemicals used by the body to prevent sudden, rapid changes in the pH of the body fluid.
- Four types of physiological buffers are found in the blood. These include bicarbonate, phosphate, haemoglobin and protein buffer systems.

(ii) Actual Pharmaceutical Buffers

- These are the chemicals which adjust the pH of the product for maximum stability and maintain pH within the optimum physiological range.
- Most pharmaceutical buffers are composed of the ingredients that are found in the body. For example, acetate, phosphate, citrate and borate.

- These include:
  (1) Phosphate buffer
  (2) Borate buffer

(1) *Phosphate Buffer System*

- It is composed of monohydrogen and dihydrogen phosphate.
- The acidic member of this buffer is dihydrogen phosphate while basic member is monohydrogen phosphate.
- The pK_a of acidic member is reasonably close to pH of blood, thereby indicating that it is one of the physiological buffers.
- pK_a of phosphate buffer is 7.2.

Advantages

- It is non-toxic, therefore, useful for ophthalmic and parenteral preparations.
- pK_a of dihydrogen phosphate is 7.2, i.e., close to pH of blood and lachrymal fluid (7.4).

Disadvantages

- Incompatible with Zn and Al salts because of insolubility of these cations in buffer. If taken internally, it precipitates calcium, iron and magnesium in the intestine.
- It can support mould growth at room temperature. Hence, preservatives like benzethonium chloride or benzalkonium chloride are needed.

Uses

- In the ophthalmic, parenteral and internal preparations.

(2) *Borate Buffer System*

- It consists of tetraborate ion and boric acid.
- pK_a of borate buffer is 9.2.

Advantages

- It is generally used for external preparations only.
- These buffers cover the pH range of 7 to 11.
- It possesses bacteriostatic and antimicrobial action in powder form only.
- It is used for ophthalmic, nasal and ear preparations.

Disadvantages

- It is toxic; hence its use is restricted in internal preparations and injectables.
- The pK_a of boric acid is 9.2, making this system inefficient at physiological pH.
- It is susceptible to microbial growth when stored at room temperature. Hence, preservative like benzalkonium chloride is needed.

Uses

- It is generally used for external preparations only.
- It is used for ophthalmic, nasal and ear preparations.

Precautions to be taken while Preparing Actual Pharmaceutical Buffer Solutions

- Volatile substances such as NH_3 or CO_2 should be avoided because if they escape from pharmaceutical preparations, they will alter pH and buffer capacity of the system.
- Precautions have to be taken so that the alkaline buffers should be protected from CO_2 absorption, which would otherwise cause a drop in pH.
- There are certain media which can serve as nutrient media for the growth of certain microorganisms, especially when pH is close to neutrality.
- In order to prevent this, such solutions are preserved with low concentrations of quaternary ammonium antimicrobial agents. For example, 0.002% benzalkonium chloride.

2.2.12 Some Officially Used Buffers

Standard buffer solutions for various ranges of pH values between 1.2 and 10.0 may be prepared by appropriate combinations of *0.2 M hydrochloric acid* or *0.2 M sodium hydroxide* and of solutions described below, used in the proportions shown in the accompanying tables. The standard pH values given in the tables and elsewhere in the Appendix are considered to be reproducible within ±0.02 Unit at 25°C.

1. **Boric acid and potassium chloride, 0.2 M:** Dissolve 12.366 g of boric acid and 14.911 g of potassium chloride in water and dilute with water to 1000 mL.
2. **Disodium hydrogen phosphate, 0.2 M:** Dissolve 71.630 g of disodium hydrogen phosphate in water and dilute with water to 1000 mL.
3. **Hydrochloric acid, 0.2 M:** Hydrochloric acid diluted with water to contain 7.292 g of HCl in 1000 mL. Standardise it before use.
4. **Potassium chloride, 0.2 M:** Dissolve 14.911 g of potassium chloride in water and dilute with water to 1000 mL.
5. **Potassium dihydrogen phosphate, 0.2 M:** Dissolve 27.218 g of potassium dihydrogen phosphate in water and dilute with water to 1000 mL.
6. **Potassium hydrogen phthalate, 0.2 M:** Dissolve 40.846 g of potassium hydrogen phthalate in water and dilute with water to 1000 mL.
7. **Sodium hydroxide, 0.2 M:** Dissolve sodium hydroxide in water to produce a 40 to 60% w/v solution and allow it to stand. Taking precautions to avoid absorption of carbon dioxide siphon off the clear supernatant liquid and dilute with *carbon dioxide-free water* a suitable volume of the liquid to contain 8.0 g of NaOH in 1000 mL. Standardise it before use.

   Note: *0.2 M Sodium hydroxide must not be used later than one month after preparation.*

2.2.13 Composition of Standard Buffer Solutions

1. **Hydrochloric acid buffer:** Place 50.0 mL of the *0.2 M potassium chloride* in a 200 mL volumetric flask, add the specified volume of *0.2 M hydrochloric acid* **(Table 2.1)** and then add *water* to volume.

Table 2.1: Hydrochloric acid buffer (pH 1.2 to 2.2)

pH	0.2 M HCl, mL	pH	0.2 M HCl, mL
1.2	85.0	1.8	20.4
1.3	67.2	1.9	16.2
1.4	53.2	2.0	13.0
1.5	41.4	2.1	10.2
1.6	32.4	2.2	7.8
1.7	26.0		

2. **Acid phthalate buffer:** Place 50.0 mL of *0.2 M potassium hydrogen phthalate* in a 200 mL volumetric flask, add the specified volume of *0.2 M hydrochloric acid* **(Table 2.2)** and then add *water* to volume.

Table 2.2: Acid phthalate buffer (pH 2.2 to 4.0)

pH	0.2 M HCl, mL	pH	0.2 M HCl, mL
2.2	49.5	3.2	15.7
2.4	42.2	3.4	10.4
2.6	35.4	3.6	6.3
2.8	28.9	3.8	2.9
3.0	22.3	4.0	0.1

3. **Neutralised phthalate buffer; phthalate buffer:** Place 50.0 mL of *0.2 M potassium hydrogen phthalate* in a 200 mL volumetric flask, add the specified volume of *0.2 M sodium hydroxide* **(Table 2.3)** and then add *water* to volume.

Table 2.3: Neutralised phthalate buffer; phthalate buffer (pH 4.2 to 5.8)

pH	0.2 M NaOH, mL	pH	0.2 M NaOH, mL
4.2	3.0	5.2	28.8
4.4	6.6	5.4	34.1
4.6	11.1	5.6	38.8
4.8	16.5	5.8	42.3
5.0	22.6		

4. **Phosphate buffer:** Place 50.0 mL of *0.2 M potassium dihydrogen phosphate* in a 200 mL volumetric flask, add the specified volume of *0.2 M sodium hydroxide* **(Table 2.4)** and then add *water* to volume.

Table 2.4: Phosphate buffer (pH 5.8 to 8.0)

pH	0.2 M NaOH, mL	pH	0.2 M NaOH, mL
5.8	3.6	7.0	29.1
6.0	5.6	7.2	34.7
6.2	8.1	7.4	39.1
6.4	11.6	7.6	42.4
6.6	16.4	7.8	44.5
6.8	22.4	8.0	46.1

5. **Alkaline borate buffer:** Place 50.0 ml of *0.2 M boric acid* and *potassium chloride* in a 200 mL volumetric flask, add the specified volume of *0.2 M sodium hydroxide* **(Table 2.5)** and then add *water* to volume.

Table 2.5: Alkaline borate buffer (pH 8.0 to 10.0)

pH	0.2 M NaOH, mL	pH	0.2 M NaOH, mL
8.0	3.9	9.2	26.4
8.2	6.0	9.4	32.1
8.4	8.6	9.6	36.9
8.6	11.8	9.8	40.6
8.8	15.8	10.0	43.7
9.0	20.8		

6. **Acetate buffer:** Place the specified amount of sodium acetate ($NaC_2H_3O_2.3H_2O$) in a 1000 mL volumetric flask, add the specified volume of *acetic acid* solution **(Table 2.6)** and then add *water* to the volume and mix.

Table 2.6: Acetate buffer (pH 4.1 to 5.5)

pH	pH (measured)	$NaC_2H_3O_2 \cdot 3H_2O$, g	2 N CH_3COOH, mL
4.1	4.10	1.5	19.5
4.3	4.29	1.99	17.7
4.5	4.51	2.99	14.0
4.7	4.70	3.59	11.8
4.9	4.90	4.34	9.1
5.1	5.11	5.08	6.3
5.2	5.18	5.23	5.8
5.3	5.30	5.61	4.4
5.4	5.40	5.76	3.8
5.5	5.48	5.98	3.0

Note: In Pharmacopoeia, standard buffer solutions are referred to as "buffer solution pH" or "buffer pH".

2.2.14 Standardisation of Buffers

1. **For pH = 7.00**

   Add 29.1 mL of 0.1 M NaOH to 50 mL of 0.1 M potassium dihydrogen phosphate.

   Alternative method

   Dissolve 1.20 g of sodium dihydrogen phosphate and 0.885 g of disodium hydrogen phosphate in 1000 mL of distilled water.

2. **For pH = 4.00**

   Add 0.1 mL of 0.1 M NaOH to 50 mL of 0.1 M potassium hydrogen phthalate.

   Alternative method

   Dissolve 8.954 g of disodium hydrogen phosphate ($Na_2HPO_4.12H_2O$) and 3.4023 g of potassium dihydrogen phosphate in 1000 mL of distilled water.

2.2.15 General Procedure for Preparation of Pharmaceutical Buffer Solutions

Buffer for which formula and composition are not available in the literature includes the following steps for the development of new buffer:

(a) Select a weak acid having a pK_a approximately equal to the pH at which the buffer is to be used. This will ensure maximum buffer capacity.

(b) From the buffer equation, calculate the ratio of salt and weak acid required to obtain the desired pH. The buffer equation is satisfactory for approximate calculations within the pH range of 4 to 10.

(c) Consider the individual concentrations of the buffer salt and acid needed to obtain a suitable buffer capacity. A concentration of 0.05 to 0.5 M is usually sufficient and a buffer capacity of 0.01 to 0.1 is generally adequate.

(d) Other important factors in the choice of a pharmaceutical buffer include availability of chemicals, sterility of the final solution, stability of the drug and buffer on aging, cost of materials and freedom from toxicity. For example, a borate buffer, because of its toxic effects, certainly cannot be used to stabilise a solution to be administered orally or by parenteral route.

(e) Finally, one should determine the pH and buffer capacity of the completed buffered solution using a reliable pH meter. In some cases, sufficient accuracy is obtained by the use of pH papers. Particularly, when the electrolyte concentration is high, it may be found that the pH calculated by use of the buffer equation is somewhat different from the experimental value. This is to be expected when activity coefficients are taken into account and it emphasizes the necessity for carrying out the actual determination.

2.2.16 Commonly Used Buffer Solutions

A number of common buffer solutions are available and are enlisted in **Table 2.7**.

Table 2.7: Some common buffer solutions

Buffer	pH Range
KH phthalate/phthalic acid	2.1 - 4.1
CH_3COONa/CH_3COOH	3.8 - 5.8
KN_a phthalate/KH phthalate	4.4 - 6.4
Na_2HPO_4/KH_2PO_4	6.2 - 8.2
Tris (hydroxymethyl) aminomethane/HCl	7.1 - 9.1
Na borate/boric acid	8.1 - 10.1
$Na_2CO_3/NaHCO_3$	9.3 - 11.3
Na_3PO_4/Na_2HPO_4	11.3 - 13.3

2.2.17 Other Buffer Solutions Used in Pharmacy and Research

Other buffer solutions used in pharmacy and research are enlisted in **Appendix 2** along with their method of preparation.

2.2.18 Stability of Buffers

- It is required to make up and treat buffer solutions with care, since they being the measurement references.
- The typical shelf life for commercial technical buffers is 2 years, when unopened and 3-6 months when opened.
- However, this is not valid for alkaline buffers (pH buffer 10 or higher).
- Alkaline solutions will change their pH noticeably when they come into contact with carbon dioxide in air.
- The typical shelf life for alkaline buffers is 1 month when opened.
- So to maintain the stability of buffer solution, following points must be taken care of:
  (a) Check for expiry date on commercial buffer solution before using it (Note: The expiry date is for an unopened container.)
  (b) During the preparation of buffer solution, put a date on the label and also an expiry date, if possible, to remind that when to discontinue its use.
  (c) Keep the buffer solutions in closed plastic containers or within stoppered flasks/bottles.
  (d) Store the buffers at room temperature, i.e., 15 to 25°C.
  (e) For alkaline buffers, it is recommended to put the bottles in the refrigerator. When a pH buffer is stored in refrigerator, it is recommended to allow the buffer to come to room temperature prior to use.
  (f) Avoid storage close to a window or to a heat source. The temperature of a buffer is important because it is a function of its pH. At lower temperatures,

the evaporation of the water in the buffer is slower than at higher temperatures, which helps to keep the concentration of the buffer constant for a longer period of time.

2.2.19 Storage of Buffers

- At room temperature, buffers are stored at 15 to 30°C (60 to 90°F).
- When refrigerated, they should be stored at 2 to 8°C (35 to 45°F).
- Moreover, the prepared buffered solutions should be stored in chemically-resistant, tight containers, such as Type I glass bottles, with the label stating that these solutions should be used within 3 months.

2.3 BUFFERED ISOTONIC SOLUTIONS

2.3.1 Osmotic Pressure and Osmosis

- Osmotic pressure refers to the minimum pressure which needs to be applied to a solution to prevent the inward flow of water across a cell semipermeable membrane.
- Osmosis refers to the movement of water or other solvent through a plasma membrane (semipermeable membrane) from a region of low solute concentration to a region of high solute concentration **(Figure 2.1)**.

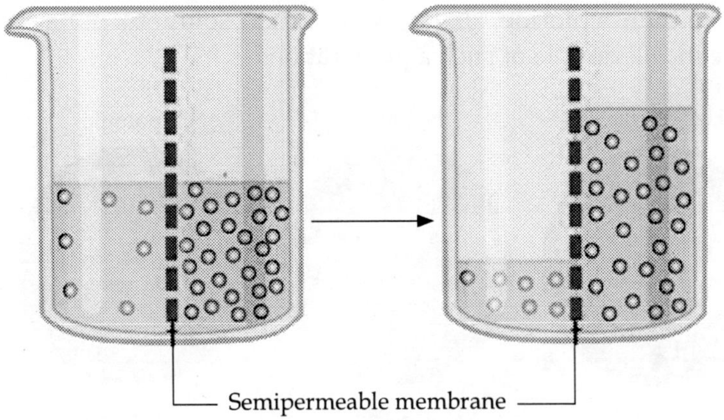

Figure 2.1: Osmosis

2.3.2 Tonicity

- The ability of an extracellular solution to make water move into or out of a cell by osmosis is known as its tonicity.
- A solution's tonicity is related to its osmolarity, which is the total concentration of all solutes in the solution.

Note: It is important to note that osmotic pressure and tonicity both often make confusion but actually osmotic pressure is the pressure of a solution against a semipermeable membrane to prevent water from flowing inward across the membrane and tonicity is the measure of this pressure. If the concentration of solutes on both sides of the membrane is equal, then there is no tendency for water to move across the membrane and hence, no osmotic pressure.

2.3.3 Isotonic Solutions

- It refers to two solutions having the same osmotic pressure across a semipermeable membrane.
- This state allows for the free movement of water across the membrane without changing the concentration for solutes on either side.
- Cell remains intact in isotonic solutions.

2.3.4 Importance of Isotonicity in Pharmaceutical Solutions

- Since pharmaceutical solutions are meant for application to delicate membranes of the human body, they should be adjusted to approximately the same osmotic pressure as that of the body fluids.
- Isotonic solutions cause no swelling or contraction of the tissues with which they come in contact and produce no discomfort when instilled in the eye, nasal tract, blood or other body tissues.
- Isotonic sodium chloride (0.9% w/v NaCl solution) is a well-known pharmaceutical example of such a preparation.

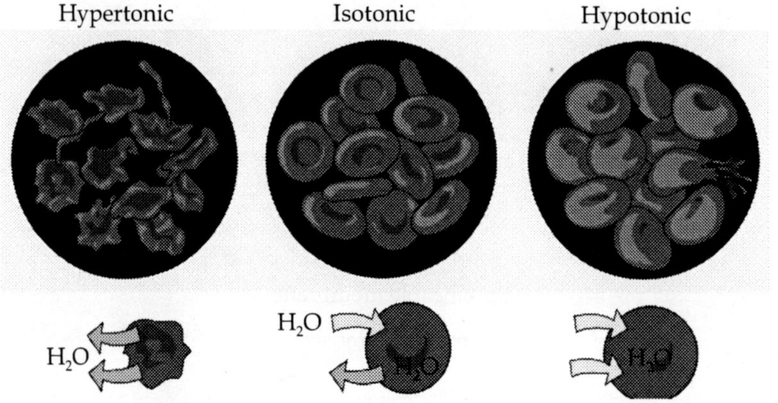

Figure 2.2: Tonicity

The need to achieve isotonic conditions with solutions to be applied to delicate membranes is dramatically illustrated by mixing a small quantity of blood with aqueous sodium chloride solutions of varying tonicity **(Figure 2.2)**. For example, a solution becomes:

(a) **Isotonic:** If a small quantity of blood is mixed with a solution containing 0.9 g of NaCl per 100 mL, the cells retain their normal size. The solution has essentially the same salt concentration and hence, the same osmotic pressure as the red blood cell contents.

(b) **Hypertonic:** If the red blood cells are suspended in a 2.0% NaCl solution, the water within the cells passes through the cell membrane in an attempt to dilute the surrounding salt solution. This outward passage of water causes the cells to shrink, become wrinkled or crenated.

(c) **Hypotonic:** If the blood is mixed with 0.2% NaCl solution or with distilled water, water enters the blood cells, causing them to swell and finally burst, with the liberation of haemoglobin. This phenomenon is called haemolysis.

2.3.5 Isosmotic Solution

- It refers to the solution having the same osmotic pressure as blood.
- The red blood cell membrane is not impermeable to all drugs, that is, it is not a perfect semipermeable membrane.
- Thus, it will permit the passage of not only water molecules but also solutes. such as urea, ammonium chloride, alcohol and boric acid.
- These solutes are regarded as solvent and they do not exert an osmotic pressure on the membrane (the solutions are isosmotic but not isotonic). A 2.0% solution of boric acid has the same osmotic pressure as the blood cell contents when determined by the freezing point method and is, therefore, said to be isosmotic with blood.
- The molecules of boric acid pass freely through the erythrocyte membrane, regardless of the concentration.
- As a result, this solution acts essentially as water when in contact with blood cells. Because it is extremely hypotonic with respect to the blood; boric acid solution brings about rapid haemolysis.
- Therefore, a solution containing a quantity of drug calculated to be isosmotic with blood is isotonic. Accordingly, a 2.0% boric acid solution serves as isotonic ophthalmic preparations.

2.3.6 Measurement of Tonicity

- Tonicity is a measure of the relative concentration of solute particles on either side of a semipermeable membrane (for example, inside a cell versus outside the cell).
- Only solutes that cannot cross the membrane contribute to tonicity.
- It determines the direction and extent to which water moves by osmosis.
- The higher the tonicity, greater the difference in the concentration of solutes (dissolved substances) and therefore, the concentration of water.

- Tonicity is generally classified in three ranges, viz., hypertonicity, hypotonicity and isotonicity.
- A solution containing a quantity of drug calculated to be isosmotic with blood is isotonic only when the blood cells are impermeable to the solute (drug) molecules and permeable to the solvent (water).
- The tonicity can be calculated by the following methods:
  (a) Haemolytic method
  (b) Measurement of the slight temperature differences
  (c) Calculating tonicity using L_{iso} values

(a) Haemolytic Method

- In this method, effect of various solutions of the drug is observed on the appearance of red blood cells suspended in the solutions.
- In the later work, a quantitative method developed by Hunter was used based on the fact that a hypotonic solution liberates oxyhaemoglobin in direct proportion to the number of cells haemolysed.
- The van't Hoff *(i)* factor can be determined and the value compared with that computed from cryoscopic data, osmotic coefficient and activity coefficient.
- Drug having the proper *i* value as measured by freezing point depression nevertheless may haemolyse human red blood cells. Based on this, scientists suggested restriction of the term 'isotonic' to the solutions having equal osmotic pressure with respect to a particular membrane.

(b) Measurement of the Slight Temperature Differences

- This method is based on rising measurement of the slight temperature differences from differences in the vapour pressure of thermally insulated samples contained in constant humidity chambers.
- One of the first references to the determination of the freezing point of blood and tears (as was necessary to make solutions isotonic with these fluids) is that -0.52°C and -80°C are the freezing points of both human blood and lachrymal fluid, respectively.
- This temperature corresponds to the freezing point of a 0.90% NaCl solution, which is therefore considered to be isotonic with both blood and lachrymal fluid.

(c) Calculating tonicity using L_{iso} values

- Because the freezing point depressions for solutions of electrolytes of both the weak and strong types are always greater than those calculated from the equation $\Delta T_f = K_f C$, a new factor, $L = iK_f$, is introduced to overcome this difficulty. Thus, the corrected new equation is as follows:

$$\Delta T_f = LC$$

- The value of L can be obtained from the freezing point lowering of solutions of representative compounds of a given ionic type at a concentration C that is isotonic with body fluids. This specific value of L is written as L_{iso}.
- The L_{iso} value for a 0.90% (0.154 M) NaCl solution which has a freezing point depression of 0.52°C and is thus, isotonic with body fluids, is 3.4, which can be obtained as follows:

$$L_{iso} = \frac{\Delta T_f}{C}$$

$$L_{iso} = \frac{0.52}{0.154} = 3.4$$

- The interionic attraction in solutions that are not too concentrated is roughly the same for all univalent electrolytes, regardless of the chemical nature of the various compounds of this class and all have about the same value for L_{iso}, i.e., 3.4.
- As a result of this similarity between compounds of a given ionic type, it will be observed that for dilute solutions of non-electrolytes, L_{iso} is approximately equal to K_f.
- **Table 2.8** represents the L_{iso} value for various types of electrolytes.

Table 2.8: Average L_{iso} value for various types of electrolytes

Type of electrolyte	L_{iso}	Examples
Non-electrolytes	1.9	Sucrose, camphor, propylene glycol, urea
Weak electrolytes	2.0	Boric acid, cocaine, phenobarbital
Di-divalent electrolytes	2.0	Magnesium sulphate, zinc sulphate
Uni-univalent electrolytes	3.4	Amphetamine hydrochloride, sodium chloride
Uni-divalent electrolytes	4.3	Atropine sulphate, sodium sulphate
Di-univalent electrolytes	4.8	Calcium bromide, zinc chloride
Uni-trivalent electrolytes	5.2	Sodium citrate, sodium phosphate
Tri-univalent electrolytes	6.0	Aluminium chloride, ferric chloride
Tetra borate electrolytes	7.6	Potassium borate, sodium borate

2.3.7. Methods of Adjusting Tonicity and pH

Any of the following methods can be used to calculate the quantity of sodium chloride, dextrose and other substances that may be added to solutions of drugs to render them isotonic.

These include:

(i) Class I methods

(ii) Class II methods

(i) Class I Methods

- According to these methods, sodium chloride or some other substance is added to the solution of the drug to lower the freezing point of the solution to –0.52°C and this makes it isotonic with body fluids.
- This class includes the following two methods:
  - (a) Cryoscopic method (freezing point depression method)
  - (b) Sodium chloride equivalent method

(a) Cryoscopic Method (Freezing Point Depression Method)

- The plasma and blood freezing point temperature = –0.52°C
- The dissolved substances in plasma or tear depress the solution freezing point to –0.52°C.
- Any solution that freezes at T = –0.52°C, is isotonic with blood and tear.
- Weight of the substance that needs to be adjusted to make it isotonic is given by the following formula:

$$W = \frac{0.52 - a}{b}$$

where, W = weight (in g) of the added substance in 100 mL of the final solution 'a'

a = the depression of the freezing point of water produced by the medicament already in the solution (calculated by multiplying the value of 'b' for the medicament by the strength of the solution expressed as % w/v)

b = the depression of freezing of water produced by 1% w/v of the added substance

- The isotonic values for various pharmaceutical substances are illustrated in **Table 2.9**.

Table 2.9: Isotonic values for various pharmaceutical substances

Substance	M	E	V	$\Delta T^{1\%}$	L_{iso}
Alcohol, dehydrated	46.07	0.70	23.3	0.41	1.9
Aminophylline	456.46	0.17	5.37	0.10	4.6
Ammonium chloride	53.50	1.08	36	0.64	3.4
Amphetamine sulfate (Benzedrine sulfate)	368.49	0.22	7.3	0.13	4.8
Antipyrine	188.22	0.17	5..7	0.10	1.9
Antistine hydrochloride (Antazoline hydrochloride)	301.81	0.18	6.0	0.11	3.2
Apomorphine hydrochloride	312.79	0.14	4.7	0.08	2.6
Ascorbic acid	176.12	0.18	6.0	0.11	1.9
Atropine sulphate	694.82	0.13	4.3	0.07	5.3

(Contd...)

Substance	M	E	V	$\Delta T^{1\%}$	L_{iso}
Aureomycin hydrochloride	544	0.11	3.7	0.06	3.5
Barbital sodium	206.18	0.29	10.0	0.29	3.5
Benadryl hydrochloride (Diphenhydramine hydrochloride)	291.81	0.20	6.6	0.34	3.4
Boric acid	61.84	0.50	16.7	0.29	1.8
Butacaine sulfate (Bulyn sulfate)	710.95	0.20	6.7	0.12	8.4
Bafileine	194.19	0.08	2.7	0.05	0.9
Calleine and sodium benzoate	-	0.25	8.7	0.79	-
Calcium chloride.$2H_2O$	147.03	0.51	17.0	0.30	4.4
Calcium gluconate	448.29	0.16	5.3	0.09	4.2
Calcium lactate	308.30	0.23	7.7	0.14	4.2
Camphor	152.23	0.20	6.7	0.12	1.8
Chloramphenicol (Chloromycetin)	323.14	0.10	3.3	0.06	1.9
Chlorobutanol (Chloretone)	177.47	0.24	8.0	0.14	2.5
Cocaine hydrochloride	339.81	0.16	5.3	0.09	3.2
Cupric sulfate.$5H_2O$	249.69	0.18	6.0	0.11	2.6
Dextrose.H_2O	198.17	0.16	5.3	0.09	1.9
Dibucaine hydrochloride (Nupercaine hydrochloride)	379.92	0.13	4.3	0.08	2.9
Emelina hydrochloride	553.56	0.10	3.3	0.06	3.3
Ephedrine hydrochloride	201.69	0.30	10.0	0.18	3.6
Ephedrine sulphate	428.53	0.23	7.7	0.14	5.8
Epinephrine bitartarate	333.29	0.18	6.0	0.11	3.5
Epinephrine hydrochloride	219.66	0.29	9.7	0.17	3.7
Ethylhydrocupreine hydrochloride (Optochin)	376.92	0.17	5.7	0.10	3.8
Ethylmorphine hydrochloride (Dionin)	385.88	0.16	5.3	0.09	3.6
Eucatropine hydrochloride (Euphthalmine hydrochloride)	327.84	0.18	6.0	0.11	3.5
Fluorescein sodium	376	0.31	10.3	0.18	6.9
Glycerin	92.09	0.34	11.3	0.20	1.8
Homotropine hydrobromide	356.26	0.17	5.7	0.10	3.6
Lactose	360.31	0.07	2.3	0.04	1.7
Magnesium sulfate.$7H_2O$	246.50	0.17	5.7	0.10	2.5
Menthol	156.26	0.20	6.7	0.12	1.8
Meperidine hydrochloride (Demerol hydrochloride)	283.79	0.22	7.3	0.12	3.7
Mercuric chloride (Mercuric bichloride)	271.52	0.13	4.3	0.08	2.1
Mercuric cyanide	252.65	0.15	5.0	0..09	2.2
Mercuric succinimide	396.77	0.14	4.8	0.08	3.3
Methacoline chloride (Mecholyl chloride)	195.69	0.32	10.7	0.19	3.7

(Contd...)

Substance	M	E	V	$\Delta T^{1\%}$	L_{iso}
Methamphetamine hydrochloride (Desoxyephedrine hydrochloride)	185.69	0.37	12.3	0.22	4.0
Melycaine hydrochloride	292.82	0.20	6.7	0.12	3.4
Mild silver protein	-	0.18	6.0	0.11	-
Morphine hydrochloride	375.84	0.15	5.0	0.09	3.3
Morphine sulphate	758.82	0.14	4.8	0.088	6.2
Neomycin sulphate	-	0.11	3.7	0.06	-
Neostigmine bromide (Prostigmine bromide)	303.20	0.22	6.0	0.11	3.2
Nicotinamide	122.13	0.26	8.7	0.15	1.9
Penicillin G potassium	372.47	0.18	6.0	0.11	3.9
Penicillin G procaine	588.71	0.10	3.3	0.06	3.5
Penicillin G sodium	356.38	0.18	6.0	0.11	3.8
Phenacaine hydrochloride (Holocaine hydrochloride)	352.85	0.20	5.3	0.11	3.3
Phenobarbital sodium	254.22	0.24	8.0	0.14	3.6
Phenol	94.11	0.35	11.7	0.20	1.9
Phenylephrine hydrochloride (Neosynephrine hydrochloride)	203.67	0.32	9.7	0.18	3.5
Physostigmine salicylate	413.46	0.16	5.3	0.09	3.9
Physostigmine sulphate	648.45	0.13	4.3	0.08	5.0
Pilocarpine nitrate	271.27	0.23	7.7	0.14	3.7
Potassium acid phosphate (KH_2PO_4)	136.13	0.43	14.2	0.25	3.4
Potassium chloride	74.55	0.76	25.3	0.45	3.3
Potassium iodide	166.02	0.34	11.3	0.20	3.3
Privine hydrochloride	246.73	0.27	7.7	0.16	3.3
Procaline hydrochloride	272.77	0.21	7.0	0.12	3.4
Quinine hydrochloride	396.91	0.14	4.7	0.08	3.3
Quinine and urea hydrochloride	547.48	0.23	7.7	0.14	7.4
Scopolamine hydrobromide (Hyoscine hydrobromide)	438.32	0.12	4.0	0.07	3.1
Silver nitrate	169.89	0.33	11.0	0.19	3.3
Sodium acid phosphate ($NaH_2PO_4.H_2O$)	138.00	0.40	13.3	0.24	3.2
Sodium benzoate	144.11	0.40	13.3	0.24	3.4
Sodium bicarbonate	84.00	0.65	21.7	0.38	3.2
Sodium bisulfite	104.07	0.61	20.3	0.36	3.7
Sodium borate.$10H_2O$	381.43	0.42	14.0	0.25	9.4
Sodium chloride	58.45	1.00	33.3	0.58	3.4
Sodium iodide	149.92	0.39	13.0	0.23	3.4
Sodium nitrate	85.01	0.68	22.7	0.39	3.4

(Contd...)

Substance	M	E	V	$\Delta T^{1\%}$	L_{iso}
Sodium phosphate, anhydrous	141.98	0.53	17.7	0.31	4.4
Sodium phosphate.$2H_2O$	178.05	0.42	14.0	0.25	4.4
Sodium phosphate.$7H_2O$	268.08	0.29	9.7	0.17	4.6
Sodium phosphate.$12H_2O$	358.21	0.22	7.3	0.13	4.6
Sodium propionate	96.07	0.61	20.3	0.36	3.4
Sodium sulfite, exsiccated	126.06	0.65	21.7	0.38	4.8
Streptomycin sulphate	1457.44	0.07	2.3	0.04	6.0
Strong silver protein	-	0.08	2.7	0.05	-
Sucrose	342.30	0.08	2.7	0.05	1.6
Sulfacetamide sodium	254.25	0.23	7.7	0.14	3.4
Sulfadiazine sodium	272.27	0.24	8.0	0.14	3.8
Sulfamerazine sodium	286.29	0.23	7.7	0.14	3.9
Sulfanilamide	172.21	0.22	7.3	0.13	2.2
Sulfathiazole sodium	304.33	0.22	7.3	0.13	3.9
Tannic acid	-	0.03	1.0	0.02	-
Tetracaine hydrochloride (Pontocaine hydrochloride)	300.82	0.18	6.0	0.11	3.2
Tetracycline hydrochloride	480.92	0.14	4.7	0.08	4.0
Pyribenzamine hydrochloride	291.83	0.30	7.3	0.17	3.8
Urea	60.06	0.59	19.7	0.35	2.1
Zinc chloride	139.29	0.62	20.3	0.37	5.1
Zinc phenolsulfonate	555.84	0.18	6.0	0.11	5.9
Zinc sulfate.$7H_2O$	287.56	0.15	5.0	0.09	2.5

Note: M is the molecular weight of the drug,
E is the sodium chloride equivalent of the drug,
V is the volume in mL isotonic solution that can be prepared by adding water to 0.3 of the drug (the weight of drug in 1 fluid ounce of a 1% solution),
$\Delta T_f^{1\%}$ is the freezing point of a 1% solution of the drug,
L_{iso} is the molar freezing point depression of the drug at a concentration approximately isotonic with blood and lacrimal fluid.

Numericals

Example 1: Prepare 500 mL of $NaHCO_3$ (ΔT_f, 1% = 0.38), so that when it is diluted with the same amount of water, it would be isotonic.

Solution: The solution is hypertonic even when diluted, so to find out the amount (W) of sodium bicarbonate needed to make 100 mL isotonic solution,

$$W = \frac{0.52 - a}{b} = \frac{0.52 - 0}{0.38} = 1.37 \text{ g}$$

$NaHCO_3$ required for making the solution isotonic upon dilution using the method of proportion,

$$\frac{1.37 \text{ g}}{100 \text{ mL}} = \frac{x}{500 \text{ mL}}$$

$$x = 6.85 \text{ g}$$

Hence, dissolve 6.85 g of $NaHCO_3$ in water and make its volume up to 500 mL to make the solution isotonic or 1.37% of its solution is isotonic in nature.

Example 2: Adjust isotonicity of procaine hydrochloride 3% using NaCl. Given that freezing point depression of 1% NaCl is 0.57°C and freezing point depression of 1% drug is 0.112°C.

Solution: a = 0.112°C (for 1%)

So, for 3%, a = 0.112 × 3 = 0.336

And b = 0.57

$$W = \frac{0.52 - a}{b} = \frac{0.52 - 0.336}{0.57} = \frac{0.184}{0.57} = 0.32$$

Thus, 0.32 g NaCl is dissolved to the given solution to make it isotonic.

Example 3: How much NaCl is required to render 100 mL of a 1% solution of apomorphine HCl isotonic with blood serum? Given that ΔT_f of 0.9% NaCl solution is 0.52°C (isotonic with blood), ΔT_f of 1% NaCl solution is 0.58°C and ΔT_f of 1% apomorphine HCl solution is 0.08°C.

Solution: Change in freezing point depression = 0.52 − 0.08 = 0.44°C

Now, ΔT_f of 1% NaCl solution is 0.58°C

So, the amount of NaCl required (x) for addition, by the method of proportion can be calculated as follows:

(NaCl) (Apomorphine)

$$\frac{1\%}{x} = \frac{0.58}{0.44}$$

or

$$x = 0.76 \text{ g}$$

Thus, 0.76 g sodium chloride will lower the freezing point to the required 0.44°C and will render the solution isotonic. So dissolve 1 g of apomorphine HCl + 0.76 g NaCl and add sufficient water to make 100 mL solution.

(b) Sodium Chloride Equivalent Method

- This method is developed by Mellen and Seltzer.
- It is based on the sodium chloride equivalents ($E_{1\%}$) of various drugs.
- $E_{1\%}$ is the amount of NaCl that is equivalent to (i.e., have the same osmotic effect or same freezing point depression) 1 g of drug.

- The sodium chloride equivalent can be calculated from the equation as follows:

$$E_{1\%} = \frac{\text{Sample or drug solution}}{\text{Freezing point depression by NaCl of same strength } (\Delta T_f)}$$

- Calculation of this method includes two basic steps:
  (1) Calculate or refer $E_{1\%}$
  (2) Add NaCl to reach 0.9% (i.e., isotonic concentration) by the formula given below:
- Amount of NaCl (w) to make the solution isotonic can be calculated by the following formula:

$$w\% = 0.9 - (\text{drug } \% \times E_{NaCl})$$

where, w% = weight of NaCl in g per 100 mL (to make the solution isotonic)
Drug% = weight of drug in g per 100 mL
E_{NaCl} = NaCl equivalent weight to 1 g of drug
0.9 = isotonic solution of NaCl

Numericals

Example 1: If $\Delta T_{f1\%}$ of ascorbic acid is 0.105°C and $\Delta T_{f1\%}$ of NaCl is 0.576°C, calculate the E for 1% ascorbic acid.

Solution: $E_{1\%} = \frac{\text{Sample or drug solution}}{\text{Freezing point depression by NaCl of same strength } (\Delta T_f)}$

$$= \frac{0.105}{0.576} = 0.18$$

Example 2: Calculate the amount of NaCl needed to adjust 1.5% atropine sulphate. Given that E for NaCl is 0.12 g.

Solution: $w\% = 0.9 - (\text{drug } \% \times E_{NaCl})$

$= 0.9 - (1.5 \times 0.12)$

$= 0.72$ g

Thus, 0.72 g of NaCl is needed to adjust 1.5% atropine sulphate to make it isotonic.

Example 3: Calculate the percentage of sodium chloride required to render a 0.5% solution of potassium chloride isosmotic with blood plasma.

Solution: Sodium chloride equivalent of 0.5% potassium chloride = 0.76

Therefore, the percentage of sodium chloride for adjustment = 0.9 − (0.5 × 0.76) = 0.9 − 0.38 = 0.52 g.

Hence, 0.52 g of NaCl is added to make the solution alkaline.

(ii) Class II Methods

- This class includes the following two methods:
  - (a) White-Vincent method
  - (b) The Sprowls method

(a) White-Vincent Method

- This method involves the addition of water to medicament to obtain an isotonic solution. This is followed by the addition of isotonic buffer solution or preservative isotonic solution to the required volume.
- White-Vincent developed a simplified equation for calculating the volume (V, mL) of osmotic solution prepared by mixing drug with water.

Principle

Isotonic solution A + Isotonic solution B = Isotonic solution C

- The 'V' value of the drug is defined as the volume of water in mL to be added to 0.3 g of the drug to make an isotonic solution. The addition of an isotonic vehicle (diluting vehicle) to make 30 mL yields a 1% solution (0.3 g drug in 30 mL). Solutions prepared by this method are isosmotic with 0.9% sodium chloride.
- Suppose that one wishes to make 30 mL of a 1% solution of procaine hydrochloride isotonic with body fluid. First, weight of the drug, w, is multiplied by the sodium chloride equivalent, E.

$$0.3 \text{ g} \times 21 = 0.063 \text{ g} \qquad \text{... (viii)}$$

- This is the quantity of sodium chloride osmotically equivalent to 0.3 g of procaine hydrochloride. Secondly, it is known that 0.9 g of sodium chloride when dissolved in enough water to make 100 mL, yields a solution that is isotonic with blood.
- The volume V of isotonic solution that can be prepared from 0.063 g of sodium chloride (equivalent to 0.3 g of procaine hydrochloride) is obtained by solving the proportion as follows:

$$\frac{0.9 \text{ g}}{100 \text{ mL}} = \frac{0.063}{V}$$

or

$$V = 0.063 \times \frac{100}{0.9} = 7.0 \text{ mL}$$

- The quantity 0.063 is equal to the weight of drug W multiplied by the sodium chloride equivalent E as seen in the above (viii). The value of the ratio 100/0.9 is 111.1.
- Thus, the formula obtained is

$$V = W \times E_{1\%} \times 111.1$$

where, V = volume of water to be added in the given amount of drug to make a solution isotonic

W = amount of drug in the formula

$E_{1\%}$ = NaCl equivalent of the drug

111.1 = a constant that could be found from volume for 1% isotonic NaCl

0.9% NaCl → 1% NaCl

0.9 g NaCl → 100 mL

1 g NaCl → 111.1 mL

Numericals

Example 1: Chloramphenicol (molecular weight = 323.13 g/mol) 1 g in sterile water for injection, q.s. and 100 mL is a total isotonic solution. Calculate the value of V, given that $E_{1\%}$ for chloramphenicol is 0.10.

Solution:

$$V = W \times E_{1\%} \times 111.1$$

or

$$V = 1.0 \times 0.10 \times 111.1 = 11.1 \text{ mL}$$

This means that 11.1 mL of water is added to 1 g chloramphenicol to make an isotonic solution and further, water for injection (q.s.) is added to make up the volume of isotonic solution up to 100 mL.

Example 2: Make the following solution isotonic with respect to an ideal membrane.

Phenacaine hydrochloride – 0.06 g

Boric acid – 0.30 g

Sterilized distilled water, enough to make 100.0 mL.

Given that $E_{1\%}$ for Phenacaine hydrochloride is 0.20 and that for boric acid is 0.50.

Solution: Based on the principle of White-Vincent method,

$$W = W_1 + W_2$$

where, W_1 = Phenacaine hydrochloride and W_2 = Boric acid

W_1 = % substance $\times E_{1\%} = 0.06 \times 0.20 = 0.012$

W_2 = % substance $\times E_{1\%} = 0.30 \times 0.50 = 0.15$

Total $W \times E_{1\%} = 0.012 + 0.15 = 0.162$

Now, $V = W \times E_{1\%} \times 111.1 = 0.162 \times 111.1 = 17.99$ mL (approximate 18 mL)

The drugs are mixed with water to make 18 mL of an isotonic solution. It means that 0.06 g phenacaine hydrochloride + 0.3 g boric acid + 18 mL of water makes an isotonic solution and the preparation is made up to volume of 100 mL by adding an isotonic diluting solution (like 0.9% NaCl).

Example 3: A solution contains ephedrine hydrochloride 1 g, chlorobutol 0.5 g in 200 mL solution. Calculate how much amount of NaCl is required to make the solution isotonic by Vincent Method. Given that $E_{1\%}$ for ephedrine hydrochloride and chlorobutol is respectively, 0.3 and 0.24.

Solution: Total volume = 200 mL

For ephedrine hydrochloride, $V = 1.0 \times 0.3 \times 111.1 = 33.33$ mL (final volume required to make isotonic)

For chlorobutol, $V = 0.5 \times 0.24 \times 111.1 = 13.33$ mL (final volume required to make isotonic)

Therefore, overall volume which is made to be isotonic = 20 − (33.33 + 13.33) = 153.34 mL

Hence, the amount of NaCl required (x) to adjust 153.34 mL volume to be isotonic is:

$$\frac{x}{153.34} = \frac{0.9\,g}{100\text{ mL}}$$

or

$$x = \frac{0.9}{100} \times 153.34 = 1.38\text{ g}$$

(b) Sprowls Method

- It is simplification of the method of White and Vincent.
- It was introduced by Sprowls.
- He used drug 'w' which was arbitrarily fixed.
- Sprowls chose the weight of drug as 0.3 g, the quantity for 1 fluid ounce (0.029 L) of a 1% solution.
- The volume of the isotonic solution that can be prepared by mixing 0.3 g of a drug with sufficient water may be computed for drugs commonly used in ophthalmic and parenteral solutions.

"0.3 g represents the amount of drug in a fluid ounce of a 1% solution".

$$V = 0.3 \times E_{1\%} \times 111.1 = 33.33 \times E_{1\%}$$

- Sprowls formula is as follows:

$$\frac{W \times E}{V} = \frac{0.9\text{ g}}{100\text{ mL}}$$

where, W = 0.3 g

E = sodium chloride equivalent of drug

V = amount of water needed to be added to the given amount of drug

Numericals

Example 1: If the Sprowls value of glycerine is 11.7, find out the E value of glycerine.

Solution:

$$V = 0.3 \times E_{1\%} \times 111.1$$

or

$$11.7 = 0.3 \times E_{1\%} \times 111.1$$

$$E_{1\%} = \frac{11.7}{0.3 \times 111.1} = 0.35$$

Example 2: How much silver nitrate is needed to prepare 100 mL of isotonic solution using Sprowls method? Given that $E_{1\%}$ for silver nitrate = 0.68.

Solution:

$$V = 0.3 \times E_{1\%} \times 111.1$$

or $$V = 0.3 \times 0.68 \times 111.1 = 22.66 \text{ mL} \qquad (\text{Since, } E_{1\%} \text{ for silver nitrate} = 0.68)$$

So, 22.66 mL water becomes isotonic with 0.3 g of silver nitrate.

Then, from the method or proportions, amount of silver nitrate needed to prepare 100 mL isotonic solution will be 'x' (say) and can be calculated as follows:

$$\frac{0.3}{22.66} = \frac{x}{100}$$

or $$x = 1.32 \text{ g}$$

2.3.8 Factors Affecting Buffers

For the selection of buffer, both chemical and pharmacological factors must be considered.

(i) Chemical Factors

- The buffer system should not react with other chemicals in the preparation.
- It should have reasonable chemical stability.
- That buffer acid should be selected which have the pK_a near the middle of the desired pH range of buffer.
- Buffer capacity has been found to depend on the absolute concentrations of each buffer compounds. The higher the actual concentration selected, the better the buffering capacity of the system.
- Temperature: Increase in temperature of buffer also causes an alteration in pH of buffer solution. For example, an increase in pH was found in the case of acetate buffers with increase in temperature whereas in case of boric acid-sodium borate buffer, pH was found to be decreased with increase in temperature.
- Addition of neutral salts to buffer causes changes in ionic strength and thereby, changes the pH.
- Dilution of buffer with water causes an alteration in the activity coefficient and causes a small negative or positive deviation in the buffer.

(ii) Pharmacological Factors

These include:

(a) Toxicity of buffers

(b) Effect of pharmacological action on the preparations

(c) Contamination by microorganisms

(a) Toxicity of Buffers

- Some of the buffers have limited use in pharmaceutical practice due to their toxicity.
- For example, use of borate buffers is restricted in pharmaceutical preparations intended for internal use but finds use in ophthalmic preparations and gargles.
- The phthalate buffer has toxic effect.
- Citrate buffers and phosphate buffers usually do not bring about complications until used in large excess.

(b) Effect of Pharmacological Action on the Preparations

- The buffer should neither contribute nor reduce the pharmacological action of the active ingredients from the preparation.

(c) Contamination by Microorganisms

- Many buffer solutions support microbial growth as they can serve as nutrient media for moulds and microorganisms particularly when pH is close to neutrality.
- Such buffers can be preserved by adding preservatives.

2.3.9 Importance of Buffer Solutions

(a) In Biological Processes

- The naturally occurring buffers in human body play a significant role in keeping the pH of blood constant (at about 7.4) despite various acids and bases producing reactions going in human body.
- The buffer action is due to the presence of carbonic acid (H_2CO_3), bicarbonate ion (HCO_3^-) and carbon dioxide in the blood.

(b) In Analytical Chemistry

- To calibrate the pH meters.
- In complexometric titration, for example, metal ion with EDTA (Ethylenediamine tetra acetic acid).
- In the removal of acid radicals such as phosphate, oxalate, and borate, which interfere in precipitation of radicals of group III (Al^{3+}, Fe^{3+} and Cr^{3+}) of salt analysis.

(c) In Bacteriological Research

- Culture media are generally buffered to maintain pH required for the growth of bacteria being studied.

(d) In Industrial Processes

- Buffers are used in a number of industrial processes like:
  - In electroplating
  - In the preservation of food articles
  - In the manufacture of leather, photographic material and dyes.

2.3.10 Role of Buffers in Pharmacy

- The buffers are important in pharmaceutical preparations to ensure stable pH for the medicinally active compounds.
- Solubility of many compounds is controlled by providing a suitable pH.
- pH imparts stability to different preparations.
- Colour of many compounds is pH-dependant.
- It provides patient comfort.
- Citric acid is used for stabilising milk of magnesia.
- Penicillin preparations are stabilised by addition of carbonates.
- Sulphonamide preparations are stabilised by the addition of sodium bicarbonate, sodium acetate or sodium citrate.

2.4 MAJOR INTRA- AND EXTRACELLULAR ELECTROLYTES

- The human body consists of fluids which contain various inorganic and organic compounds.
- The concentration of these inorganic and organic compounds in the various compartments has been balanced such that body cells and tissues have the same environment.
- In a healthy human, the electrolyte concentration is maintained constantly in body fluids.

2.4.1 Electrolytes

- **Electrolytes** are the inorganic ions carrying a positive or negative charge and their aqueous solutions are responsible for conducting electricity.
- For example, sodium chloride, magnesium, sulphate, potassium, calcium and sodium bicarbonates are the important human electrolytes.
- Types of electrolytes include:
  - Major intracellular ions; e.g., K^+, Mg^{2+}, HPO_4^{2-}, $H_2PO_4^-$.
  - Major extracellular ions; e.g., Na^+, Ca^{2+}, Cl^-, HCO_3^-.

2.4.2 Fluid Compartments

The electrolyte concentration of body fluids is different in various fluid compartments.

(a) Intracellular fluid (ICF)

(b) Interstitial fluid

(c) Plasma or vascular fluid

The various body fluid compartments have been classified as follows:

(a) Intracellular Fluid (ICF)

- It refers to the fluid which is present inside the cell, for example, cytoplasm.
- It constitutes 45 to 50% of body weight and its volume is 30 L.
- It contains small quantities of sodium and chloride ions, extremely small quantity of calcium ions, moderate quantities of sulphate and magnesium ions, whereas the quantities of potassium and phosphate ions are not very large.

(b) Interstitial Fluid

- It refers to the fluid which is present between the cells.
- It constitutes 12 to 15% of body weight and its volume is 10 L.

(c) Plasma or Vascular Fluid

- It refers to the fluid which is present within the blood vascular system.
- It constitutes 4 to 5% of body weight and its volume is 3 to 5 L.

Note: The fluids present in the interstitial and vascular compartments are collectively referred to as the extracellular fluid (ECF). It contains large quantities of sodium or chloride ions and reasonably large quantities of bicarbonate ion, while small quantities of potassium, calcium, magnesium, phosphate and sulphate ions.

2.4.3 Functions of Electrolytes

Electrolytes in our body perform various involuntary functions to maintain haemostasis. Some of these functions are as follows:

- Maintain electrolytic balance, including acid-base balance and osmotic equilibrium in various body fluids.
- To regulate the total amount of water in body fluids.
- To control the osmotic load between fluid compartments.
- To facilitate specific metabolic functions by supplying the specific ion to the body fluids associated with the concerning cell or organ.
- Human heart, muscle and nerve cells involve use of electrolytes to maintain voltages across their cell membranes and to carry electrical impulses to other cells.

- To generate action potentials and graded potentials and control secretion of some hormones and neurotransmitters.
- Muscle contraction needs the presence of calcium (Ca^{2+}), sodium (Na^{+}) and potassium (K^{+}). Wrong electrolyte levels can lead to either weak muscles or muscles that contract too severely.

2.4.4 Electrolytic Imbalance and its Causes

- Body is having a capacity to adjust slight variations in concentration of electrolytes in fluid compartments. Many electrolytes level is kept constant by our kidneys and several other hormones.
- In general, whenever there is change in the concentration of ions in any compartment, water will migrate across the cell membrane to re-establish osmotic equilibrium.
- In case of electrolytic imbalance, the body is not able to adjust the concentration of fluid electrolytes. Hence, externally "electrolyte replacement therapy" is used.
- As a result of this, the level of an electrolyte in blood can become too high or too low. Body electrolyte levels tend to alter when water levels in the body change.
- Several other causes are also reported, like:
  - Kidney disease
  - Vomiting for prolonged periods
  - Poor diet
  - Severe dehydration – water volume in every compartment becomes low
  - Diarrhoea
  - Edema – Fluids get accumulated in interstitial space between the cells due to low osmotic pressure
  - Heat waves – Cases of electrolyte imbalances increase significantly during heat waves
  - Acid/base, i.e., pH imbalance
  - Congestive heart failure
  - Cancer treatment
  - Bulimia – Disease related to self-induced vomiting in a strong desire to lose weight
  - Severe and persistent vomiting and nausea during pregnancy
  - Intake of some drugs, such as diuretics or ACE inhibitors. A study revealed that 20% of patients taking diuretics, commonly prescribed for high blood pressure or heart conditions, end up with reduced sodium and potassium levels.

2.4.5. Symptoms of Electrolytic Imbalance

- An electrolytic imbalance can be manifested in several ways.
- The symptoms depend upon which electrolyte is out of balance and whether that level is too high or too low.
- An altered level of magnesium, sodium, potassium or calcium may produce one or more of the following symptoms:
  - Irregular heartbeat
  - Bone disorders
  - Weakness
  - Twitching
  - Blood pressure changes
  - Confusion
  - Seizures
  - Numbness
  - Nervous system disorders
  - Fatigue, lethargy
  - Convulsions
  - Muscle spasm

2.4.6 Role of Major Physiological Cations and Anions

The body fluid consists of various inorganic ions which are either anionic or cationic in nature, a brief summary of which is given in **Table 2.10**.

- **Anionic electrolytes** include HCO_3^- (bicarbonate), Cl^- (chloride), SO_4^{2-} (sulphate) and HPO_4^{2-} (phosphate).
- **Cationic electrolytes** include sodium (Na^+), potassium (K^+), calcium (Ca^{2+}) and magnesium (Mg^{2+}), etc.

2.4.6.1 Extracellular Cations

(1) Sodium

- Sodium (Na^+) is considered the most abundant extracellular ion.
- It constitutes nearly 90% of extracellular ions.
- Normal plasma sodium concentration is 136 to 142 mEq/L.
- The normal intake of sodium chloride per day varies from 5 to 20 g and the daily requirement is between 3 and 5 g.
- The excess quantity of salt consumed gets excreted in the urine.
- The Na^+ level in the blood is controlled by aldosterone and antidiuretic hormones.

- The atria of the heart produce the hormone atrial natriuretic peptide, which opposes the actions of aldosterone and antidiuretic hormones.
- It increases Na^+ and water excretion by the kidneys.
- In the normal condition, the kidney excretes the excess of sodium and regulates the sodium content in the body.
- The sodium from the glomerular filtrate gets reabsorbed which is under the hormonal control. Prostaglandin is also considered responsible for the reabsorption of sodium.

Functions of sodium in human body

- The main component of ECF is sodium ions, which is associated with chloride and bicarbonate in regulating the acid-base equilibrium.
- It preserves the normal irritability of muscles.
- It is associated with permeability of the cells.
- It helps in maintaining osmotic pressure of various body fluids and thereby, protects the body against excessive fluid loss.
- It plays a vital role in the transmission of nerve impulses in the nerve fibres.

Conditions associated with sodium ion imbalance

- **Hyponatremia:** Condition associated with low sodium level in the blood.
- **Hypernatremia:** Condition associated with high sodium level in the blood.

Conditions causing hyponatremia

- Loss due to excessive urination as in case of diabetes insipidus.
- Diarrhoea and vomiting
- Due to excessive sodium excretion in 'metabolic acidosis.
- In Addison's disease, where decreased excretion of aldosterone occurs.

Symptoms associated with hyponatremia

- Muscle weakness
- Dizziness
- Headache
- Hypotension
- Tachycardia
- Shock

Conditions causing hypernatremia

- Severe dehydration
- Hyper adrenalism (as in Cushing syndrome)
- Certain types of brain damage
- Excessive treatment with sodium salts

Symptoms associated with hypernatremia

- Intense thirst
- Fatigue
- Restlessness
- Agitation
- Coma

Treatment

- Hyponatremia
  - Low sodium levels (hyponatremia) give rise to dehydration and acidosis.
  - Hence, to treat this, sodium salts have to be administered.
- Hypernatremia
  - High sodium levels (hypernatremia) give rise to oedema and hypertension.
  - Hence, to treat this, low salt diet and diuretics have to be administered.

(2) Calcium

- The total calcium (Ca^{2+}) content in the body is about 22 g per kg body weight.
- The daily requirement is about 0.8 g.
- Most of the calcium occurs in bones and the remaining is largely found in ECF compartment.
- Calcium can be absorbed by all parts of the small intestine through an active transport mechanism.
- Average daily intake for calcium in adults is about 800 to 1000 mg, whereas the minimum requirement is about 400 mg per day.
- However, greater amounts of calcium are needed in children and during pregnancy and lactation.
- The normal range for total plasma calcium is 2.2 to 2.6 mmol/L. About half of this is bound to plasma proteins while a small fraction gets complexed with citrate and phosphate and the balance amount circulates in the blood as ionised calcium.
- Calcium mainly gets excreted through sweat, urine and faeces.

Functions of calcium in human body

- It forms a major part of bones. Calcium is known to get associated with vitamin D and phosphorus in hardening of the bones.
- It plays a vital role in the functioning of nerves and muscles. It is involved in impulse muscle propagation and in muscle contraction.
- It is also needed for the release of acetyl choline from the preganglionic nerve terminals.
- It also gets involved in the coagulation of blood.

Conditions associated with calcium ion imbalance

- **Hypocalcaemia:** Condition associated with low calcium level in the blood.
- **Hypercalcaemia:** Condition associated with high calcium level in the blood.

Regulation of calcium ions

- The level of calcium ions in the plasma is regulated by the parathyroid hormone and calcitonin.

Conditions causing hypocalcaemia

- Low parathyroid hormone
- Vitamin D deficiency
- Renal failure
- Intestinal malabsorption

In these conditions, intestinal calcium absorption gets greatly reduced.

Symptoms associated with hypocalcaemia

- Tetanic spasms (due to low concentration of ionised calcium)
- Convulsions (due to low concentration of ionised calcium)
- Osteoporosis
- Mental problems like depression and irritability
- Dryness in skin
- Brittle nails

Conditions causing hypercalcaemia

- Excessive consumption of calcium-rich foods
- Certain bone diseases
- Extreme quadriplegic/paraplegic conditions where bones bear no weight

Symptoms associated with hypercalcaemia

- Disturbance of cardiac functions (due to high concentration of ionised calcium)
- Digestive problems
- Nausea
- Brain dysfunctioning
- Coma and even death in extreme instances

Treatment

- **Hypocalcaemia**
  - Calcium salts have to be administered. The main dietary sources of calcium include milk, cheese, green vegetables, eggs and some fish.
- **Hypercalcaemia**
  - Low calcium diet has to be administered.

2.4.6.2 Extracellular Anions

(1) Chloride

- It is a major anion of all the body fluids and constitutes about 66% of the anions present in plasma as chloride ion.
- The total chloride ion present in the body is nearly 50 mEq per kg body weight.
- The daily requirement of chloride is about 5 to 10 g as sodium chloride.
- It gets readily absorbed throughout the gastrointestinal tract (GIT).
- Chloride ions get excreted mainly through urine and through the skin during sweating. It occurs in all body secretions.

Functions of chloride (Cl^-) ions

- Chloride ions along with sodium ions are responsible for maintaining osmotic balance in different body fluids.
- Chloride ions are able to maintain the charge balance in the body fluids, i.e., extracellular and intracellular both, as they can pass through all membranes.
- Chloride ions participate in the formation of gastric hydrochloric acid.
- They are also involved in the maintenance of acid-base balance.

Conditions associated with chloride ion imbalance

- **Hypochloremia:** Condition associated with low chloride level in the blood.
- **Hyperchloremia:** Condition associated with high chloride level in the blood.

Condition causing hypochloremia

- Excessive fluid loss (e.g., diarrhoea)

Note: Hypochloremia occurs often along with hyponatremia and hypokalemia (low potassium cconcentration in blood).

Symptoms associated with hypochloremia

- Metabolic alkalosis (deficiency of chloride causes the blood to become less acidic and hence, the condition)
- Confusion
- Paralysis
- Difficulty in breathing

Conditions causing hyperchloremia

- Kidney failure
- Kidney dialysis
- Overproduction of parathyroid hormone

Symptoms associated with hyperchloremia

- Weakness
- Headache
- Nausea and vomiting

Treatment

- **Hypochloremia**
  - Chloride salts have to be administered. The dietary source of chloride ions is common table salt.
- **Hyperchloremia**
  - Low chloride diet has to be administered.

(2) Bicarbonate

- In the ECF compartment, it is the second largest anion.

Functions of bicarbonate (HCO_3^-) ion

- Along with carbonic acid, it acts as one of the important buffer systems.
- Plays an important role in the maintenance of the acid-base balance.
- Helps to maintain homeostasis.

Conditions associated with bicarbonate ion imbalance

- **Metabolic acidosis:** Condition associated with low bicarbonate level in the blood, resulting in the pH to go below 7.25.
- **Metabolic alkalosis:** Condition associated with high bicarbonate level in the blood.

2.4.6.3 Intracellular Cations

(1) Potassium

- It is the most abundant cation in the ICF.
- Its concentration in the ICFs is 23 times higher than ECFs. Active transport is able to maintain this concentration difference.
- Normal plasma K^+ concentration is 3.8 to 5.0 mEq/L.
- The normal intake of potassium chloride varies from 5 to 7 g per day.
- Human body usually has about 2.6 g per kg body weight of potassium (K^+).
- The daily requirement of potassium is about 1.5 to 4.5 g.
- It gets rapidly absorbed from diet through the GIT and is rapidly excreted through kidneys.
- The potassium also gets excreted in the digestive fluids but gets reabsorbed.
- The excretion of potassium through the kidney is influenced by changes in acid-base balance and activity of adrenal cortex.

Functions of potassium in human body

- It is involved in the transmission of nerve impulses.
- It is also involved in the contraction of muscles, especially, cardiac muscles.
- It plays a vital role in maintaining the electrolyte composition of the various body fluids.

- It plays an important role in many biochemical activities inside the cells.
- It helps to regulate pH by exchange against the hydrogen ions.

Conditions associated with potassium ion imbalance

- **Hypokalemia:** Condition associated with low potassium level in the blood.
- **Hyperkalemia:** Condition associated with high potassium level in the blood.

Conditions causing hypokalemia

- Loss of water due to severe vomiting or diarrhoea
- Malnutrition
- Metabolic alkalosis
- Use of diuretics like acetazolamide and chlorothiazide, which increases the excretion of potassium in urine. Hence in this case, potassium salts are given if these drugs are used for long.
- In case of heart disease, the potassium content of the myocardium gets depleted.
- During correction of dehydration or acidosis or alkalosis with sodium and water, there occurs depletion of potassium.

Symptoms associated with hypokalemia

- Muscle weakness and cramping
- Atrial fibrillation of the heart
- Anxiety
- Irritability

Conditions causing hyperkalemia

- Renal failure
- Shock
- In 'Addison's disease', there occurs an adrenal insufficiency, which elevates the serum potassium

Symptoms associated with hyperkalemia

- **High intracellular potassium symptoms**
  - Cardiac and CNS depressions
  - Bradycardia
  - Poor heart sound
  - Peripheral vascular collapse
  - Cardiac arrest
  - Electrocardiographic changes
- **High extracellular potassium symptoms**
  - Mental confusion
  - Weakness of respiratory muscles
  - Flaccid paralysis of extremities

Treatment

- **Hypokalemia**
  - Potassium salts have to be administered. The good sources of potassium include milk, certain vegetables, meat and whole grains.
  - However, its deficiency generally does not take place, except in certain pathological conditions.
- **Hyperkalemia**
  - Low potassium diet has to be administered.
  - It is fairly rare but can be fatal, if not treated quickly.

(2) Magnesium

- It is regarded as the second most common intracellular electrolyte.
- It is the body's fourth most abundant cation.
- In an adult human body, about 54% is present in the bones along with phosphorus, about 45% is present in the ICF and about 1% is present in the ECF.
- Nearly about 3.3 to 4.9 μmol of magnesium gets excreted through urine per day.
- The daily requirement of magnesium is about 350 mg.
- The magnesium ingested with food gets absorbed from the duodenum in the acidic media and this absorption is not related to magnesium stored in the body.

Functions of magnesium in body

- It plays an important role in activation of enzymes involved in carbohydrate and protein metabolism.
- It is of vital importance in neural transmission, myocardial function and neuromuscular activity.
- It is involved in Na^+ – K^+ – ATPase pump system.
- It promotes formation of bones and teeth.
- It stabilises blood sugar level.
- It boosts immune system.
- It plays an important role in the synthesis of both DNA and RNA, essential to every cell of every known living organism.

Conditions associated with magnesium ion imbalance

- **Hypomagnesemia:** Condition associated with low magnesium level in the blood (mostly found in alcoholics).
- **Hypermagnesemia:** Condition associated with high magnesium level in the blood.

Conditions causing hypomagnesemia

- Malabsorption
- Diarrhoea
- Chronic alcoholism
- Excessive loss of dietary magnesium

Symptoms associated with hypomagnesemia

- Weakness
- Irritability
- Tetany
- Delirium
- Convulsions
- Confusion
- Anorexia
- Nausea
- Cardiac arrhythmias

Conditions causing hypermagnesemia

- Addison's disease
- Acute diabetic acidosis
- Severe dehydration
- Hypothermia
- Renal failure

Symptoms associated with hypermagnesemia

- Slurred speech
- Drowsiness
- Impaired muscle coordination
- Hypotension
- Cardiac arrest

Treatment

- **Hypomagnesemia**
  - Magnesium salts have to be administered. The dietary sources of magnesium include various nuts, soybeans, whole grains and seafood.
- **Hypermagnesemia**
  - Low magnesium diet has to be administered.

2.4.6.4 Intracellular Anions

(1) Phosphate

- The phosphate ions such as $H_2PO_4^-$, HPO_4^{2-} and PO_4^{3-} are the main anions of the ICF compartment.
- Amongst these ions, HPO_4^{2-} has been found to be the most prevalent form at the physiological pH 7.4.
- Normal plasma phosphate concentration lies in the range 1.7 to 2.6 mEq/L.
- Its daily requirement is almost the same as that of calcium, especially in pregnant and lactating mothers and children.

Functions of phosphate in human body

- Almost 4/5th of the total body phosphate is present in teeth and bones in addition to calcium.
- It plays an important role in calcium metabolism and phosphorylation.
- Phosphate occurs in the cells as phospholipids, ATP or combined with nucleic acids (DNA and RNA).
- It is known to play a vital role in buffering systems of the body.
- Serum inorganic phosphate plays an important regulatory role in erythrocyte-glucose metabolism.

Conditions associated with phosphate ion imbalance

- **Hypophosphatemia:** Condition associated with low phosphate level in the blood (mostly found in alcoholics).
- **Hyperphosphatemia:** Condition associated with high phosphate level in the blood.

Conditions causing hypophosphatemia

- Crohn's disease
- Alcoholism

Symptoms associated with hypophosphatemia

- Joint pain
- Weak bones
- Fatigue
- Irregular breathing

Conditions causing hyperphosphatemia

- Kidney disease
- Calcium deficiency

Symptoms associated with hyperphosphatemia

- Increased risk of cardiovascular disease

Treatment

- **Hypophosphatemia**
  - Phosphate salts have to be administered. The main dietary sources of phosphorus are milk, milk products, whole grains, legumes, nuts, etc.
- **Hyperphosphatemia**
  - Low phosphate diet has to be administered.

(2) Sulphate

- This ion is present in very small quantities in plasma and interstitial fluids.
- Its main dietary sources include animal and plant proteins having sulphur, containing amino acids like cysteine and methionine.
- Sulphate ions are derived in the body by the metabolism of these two amino acids.
- The organic sulphur gets oxidised to sulphate.
- Drinking water source contains high levels of inorganic sulphate, which may cause osmotic diarrhoea resulting from unabsorbed sulphate. This is usually found in infants consuming fluids derived from water sources with high levels of sulphate.
- Some association between increased H_2S production and risk of ulcerative colitis has also been reported.
- Insufficient sulphur may lead to insulin resistance.
- Sulphur deficiency in the body may also contribute to obesity, heart disease, Alzheimer's disease, chronic fatigue, in addition to pain and inflammation-related muscle and skeletal disorders.
- Sulphur is also vital for regulating metabolism.

Functions of sulphate in human body

- Sulphates are also responsible for stabilisation of protein structures.
- It is also an element in the vitamin B, biotin and thiamine.
- It is also a component of hormone insulin.
- It is also involved in various enzymatic activities.
- Sulphur containing compounds play a vital role in detoxication mechanism.
- SH group containing organic compounds are important in tissue respiration.
- In addition to the above ions, the body needs smaller amounts of ions found in trace minerals.
- These include the ions like iron (II), chromium (III), copper (II), zinc, fluoride, iodide, including hydrogen ion.
- Additionally, trace elements like manganese, molybdenum and selenium also play an important role in maintaining homeostasis.

Table 2.10: Role of major physiological cations and anions

Electrolyte	Normal plasma range (mEq/L)	Functions in body	Deficiency leads to	Excess leads to
Extracellular ions				
Sodium	136-145	Maintains fluid balance, muscle contraction and nerve function	Hyponatremia	Hypernatremia
Calcium	4.5-5.5	Necessary for muscle contraction, blood clotting, nerve function, cell division, healthy bones and teeth	Hypocalcemia	Hypercalcemia
Chloride	97-107	Maintains fluid balance in the body	Hypochloremia	Hyperchloremia
Bicarbonate	25-31	Maintains homeostasis and regulates acid-base balance in the body fluids	Metabolic acidosis	Metabolic alkalosis
Intracellular ions				
Potassium	3.5-5.3	Regulates heart contraction, helps to maintain fluid balance	Hypokalemia	Hyperkalemia
Magnesium	1.5-2.5	Necessary for muscle contraction, nerve function, heart rhythm, bone strength, generating energy and building protein	Hypomagnesemia	Hypermagnesemia
Phosphate	1.2-3.0	Strengthening of bones and teeth, essential for production of energy within cells in the form of ATP/ADP	Hypophosphatemia	Hyperphosphatemia
Sulphate	0.3-1.5	Stabilise protein structure and regulation of various metabolic processes	Insulin resistance	Osmotic diarrhoea

2.4.7 Electrolyte Combination Therapy

- The purpose of this therapy is to restore the body volume and the composition of body fluids to their normal levels.
- This therapy is given when the body is unable to regulate an electrolyte imbalance.

Major causes of electrolyte imbalance

- Any accident, haemorrhage, surgery, etc.
- Diarrhoea, vomiting, dehydration due to GIT infection.
- Metabolic disorders.
- Deficiency or excessive presence of certain ions in body fluids.

Tonicity becomes an essential criterion for administration of electrolytes in the body. Hence, these are mainly given through IV (intra-venous) or oral route.

2.4.7.1 Types of Electrolyte Combination Therapy

It consists of two types:

(1) Fluid maintenance therapy

(2) Electrolyte replacement therapy

(1) Fluid Maintenance Therapy

- Maintenance therapy is needed when patients are unable to take food and fluids orally.
- Intravenous fluids are administered to such patients to supply water and electrolytes.
- Maintenance solutions contain small amounts of electrolytes and 5% dextrose.

(2) Electrolyte Replacement Therapy

- Electrolyte replacement therapy is given when there occurs heavy loss of water and electrolytes, which is usually associated with conditions like prolonged fever, severe vomiting or diarrhoea.
- In order to compensate this, administration of lost electrolyte in appropriate concentration of tonicity becomes essential.
- Electrolyte replacement contains infusions, which are used as replacement fluids.
- Two types of solutions of electrolytes are used in replacement therapy:
  (a) Solution for rapid initial replacement
  (b) Solution for subsequent replacement

(a) *Solution for Rapid Initial Replacement*

The formula consists of:

Ingredient	Amount (mEq/L)
Sodium	130-150
Chlorine	98-110
Bicarbonate	28-55
Potassium	4-12
Calcium	3-5
Magnesium	3

(b) *Solution for Subsequent Replacement*

The formula consists of:

Ingredient	Amount (mEq/L)
Sodium	40-120
Chlorine	30-105
Bicarbonate	16-53
Potassium	16-35
Calcium	10-15
Magnesium	3-6
Phosphorous	0-13

- Electrolyte replacement therapy includes:
  (i) Infusions
  (ii) Powders for oral solutions
- Other electrolyte infusions available are:
  (i) Sodium lactate injection (IP, BP)
  (ii) Compound sodium chloride injection IP (Ringer's solution)
  (iii) Compound sodium lactate injection IP (Ringer's lactate solution)

2.4.8 Sodium Chloride

Synonyms : Rock salt, common salt, table salt
Molecular formula : NaCl
Molecular weight : 58.45 g/mol
Category : Pharmaceutical aid, fluid and electrolyte replenisher
Natural sources : Rock salt, seawater
Dose : 1 to 2 g three times daily (oral)
1 to 2 L 0.45% sodium chloride injection daily
1 L 0.9% sodium chloride injection daily

Standards

It contains not less than 99.0% and not more than 100.5% of NaCl, calculated with reference to the substance dried at 130°C. It contains no added substances.

Methods of Preparation

- Industrially, it is prepared by (i) evaporating purified saline (seawater) deposits and further purification, and (ii) by purifying rock salt.
- In the laboratory, it is prepared from common salt (impure) in water by passing hydrochloric gas. The crystals precipitate.

Physical Properties

Colour : Colourless or white
Odour : Odourless
Taste : Saline
State : Crystalline powder
Solubility : (i) Freely soluble in water, readily soluble in boiling water
(ii) Insoluble in alcohol

Chemical Properties

- With silver nitrate solution, it gives a white water insoluble precipitate of silver chloride, which is soluble in ammonia.

$$NaCl + AgNO_3 \longrightarrow NaCO_3 + AgCl$$

- It reacts with sulphuric acid to give hydrochloric acid gas. This method is commonly used in laboratory for preparing HCl solution.

$$2NaCl + H_2SO_4 \longrightarrow 2HCl\uparrow + Na_2SO_4$$

Identification Test

- It gives reactions characteristic of sodium and chloride.

Tests for Purity

It is tested for acidity and alkalinity, As, Ba, Ca, Mg, Fe, heavy metals, bromide, iodide, sulphate and loss on drying.

- As should not be more than 1 ppm.
- Ca and Mg should not be more than 50 ppm.
- Heavy metals should not be more than 5 ppm.
- Fe should not be more than 20 ppm.
- Sulphate should not be more than 200 ppm.
- Loss on drying should not be more than 1% when dried in an oven at 130°C.

Assay

Method 1

Principle

- The assay is based on Argentometric titration.

Procedure

- 1 g of accurately weighed substance is dissolved in 50 mL water in a glass stoppered flask.

- To this, 50 mL of 0.1 N silver nitrate, 3 mL of nitric acid, 5 mL of nitrobenzene, and 2 mL of ferric ammonium sulphate solution are added.
- The solution is shaken well and titrated with 0.1 N ammonium thiocyanate solution until the water becomes reddish-yellow.

$$NaCl + AgNO_3 \longrightarrow 2AgCl\downarrow + NaNO_3$$

$$AgNO_3 + NH_4SCN \longrightarrow AgSCN + NH_4NO_3$$

$$3NH_4SCN + Fe^{3+} \longrightarrow Fe(SCN)_3 + 3NH_4^+$$

Equivalence Factor

- Each mL of 0.1 N $AgNO_3$ Ξ 0.005844 g of NaCl.

Method 2 (Volhard's Precipitation Method)

- Nowadays, it is analysed by Volhard's precipitation method with modification.
- In this method, the aqueous solution is acidified with nitric acid and excess of standard silver nitrate is added.
- Silver chloride gets precipitated.
- Then nitrobenzene is added and excess of silver nitrate is determined by titrating with standard ammonium thiocyanate solution using ferric ammonium sulphate as an indicator.
- Nitrobenzene prevents interaction of silver chloride with ferric thiocyanate.

Storage

- It is stored in tightly-closed containers in a dry place as it absorbs moisture.

Pharmaceutical Uses

- As a source of both sodium and chloride ions.
- 0.9% w/v solution of NaCl is isotonic and is used as wet dressing and irrigating body tissues and cavities.
- Used in treating dehydration and sodium depletion.
- As a first aid in poisoning.
- As emetic and topical anti-inflammatory.
- In the manufacture of dialysis fluids.
- As an ingredient of ORS with other salts and glucose.
- As a constituent of Ringer's solution.
- To improve caking and the flow properties.

Note

- Deficiency of sodium chloride is called "salt hunger".

- Sodium chloride is used for the preparation of parenteral formulation and dialysis fluids. Hence, it should comply with the tests for purity of potassium and aluminium in case of parenteral, and aluminium in case of dialysis fluids.

2.4.9 Official Preparations of Sodium Chloride

- Sodium chloride solution (IP, BP)
- Sodium chloride eye lotion (BP)
- Sodium chloride injection
- Sodium chloride hypertonic injection (IP, BP)
- Sodium chloride tablet (IP)
- Sodium chloride and dextrose injection
- Mannitol and sodium chloride injection (IP, BP)
- Ringer's solution (USP)
- Compound sodium chloride injection (IP, BP, USP)
- Normal saline solution (IP, BP)
- Dextrose and normal saline solution (IP, BP)
- Compound sodium chloride and dextrose solution (BP)
- Compound sodium chloride and dextrose powder (BP)
- Fructose and sodium chloride injection (NF)
- Lactated Ringer's injection

2.4.10 Some Marketed Preparations of Sodium Chloride

(a) Sodium Chloride Injection

- It is sodium chloride IV infusion, a 0.9% w/v NaCl sterile solution in water for injection, isotonic with blood.
- It contains no antimicrobial agent.
- Composition:

Ingredient	Quantity
Sodium chloride	9 g
Water for injection	Sufficient to produce 1000 mL

(b) Sodium Chloride Hypertonic Injection

- It contains 1.6% w/v NaCl.
- Composition:

Ingredient	Quantity
Sodium chloride	16 g
Water for injection	Sufficient to produce 1000 mL

Note: pH must be adjusted between 5 and 7.5.

(c) Compound Sodium Chloride Injection

- It is a sterile solution of NaCl (0.86% w/v), KCl (0.30% w/v) and $CaCl_2 \cdot 2H_2O$ (0.0335% w/v).
- Composition:

Ingredient	Quantity
Sodium chloride	9 g
Potassium chloride	3 g
Calcium chloride	0.3 g
Water for injection	Sufficient to produce 1000 mL

Note: This solution should be filtered aseptically and sterilized in an autoclave.

(d) Sodium Chloride and Dextrose Injection

- It is a sterile solution of NaCl and dextrose in water for injection. It contains not less than 95% and not more than 105% of the stated amount of NaCl and dextrose.
- Preparation: It is prepared by dissolving the calculated quantities of sodium chloride and dextrose in purified water. Finally, it is sterilized immediately by autoclaving or by filtration.
- The usual strengths of injections containing varying amounts of sodium chloride and dextrose ($C_6H_{12}O_6$) are presented in **Table 2.11**.

Table 2.11: Usual strengths of sodium chloride and dextrose injections

% of NaCl	% of Dextrose	% of NaCl	% of Dextrose
0.110	5.0	0.450	5.0
0.180	5.0	0.450	10.0
0.200	5.0	0.900	2.5
0.225	5.0	0.900	3.0
0.300	5.0	0.900	10.0
0.330	5.0	0.900	25.0
0.450	2.5		

Uses: It is used as a fluid, nutrient and electrolyte replenisher.

Note: pH 3.6 to 6.5.

(e) Sodium Chloride Tablet

- It can be prepared in different strengths of 0.3 g, 0.6 g, 0.9 g, 1.0 g and 2.25 g tablets by adding some lubricant and binding agent.

2.4.11 Potassium Chloride

Synonym : Kalii chlordium, chloropotassuril
Molecular formula : KCl
Molecular weight : 74.55 g/mol
Synonym : Kalii chlordium, chloropotassuril
Natural sources : Sylvine and carnallite (minerals)
Dose : 40 to 100 mEq per day orally in 2 to 5 divided doses

Standards

It contains not less than 99.5% and not more than 100.5% of KCl, calculated with reference to the substance dried at 105°C for two hours.

Methods of Preparation

- It can be obtained from natural minerals by fractional distillation and floatation process. In nature, it is available as sylvine and carnallite.
- Industrially, it is prepared from carnallite ($KCl \cdot MgCl_2 \cdot 6H_2O$). The raw salt deposit is first grounded and then treated with hot water when the less soluble KCl crystallises out on cooling. The process has to be repeated for achieving almost complete recovery of KCl from the mother liquor and wash water.
- In laboratory, it is prepared by the action of HCl on potassium carbonate or bicarbonate.

$$K_2CO_3 + 2HCl \longrightarrow 2KCl + H_2O + CO_2\uparrow$$

$$KHCO_3 + HCl \longrightarrow KCl + H_2O + CO_2\uparrow$$

Physical Properties

Colour : Colourless or white
Odour : Odourless
Taste : Saline
State : Crystalline powder; prismatic or cubical crystals
Solubility : (i) Freely soluble in water
(ii) Insoluble in alcohol and ether
Nature : 10% aqueous solution is neutral to litmus

Chemical Property

- KCl dissolves in water and gets fully ionised into solvated K^+ and Cl^- ions. Thus, aqueous solutions of KCl show electrical conductivity.

Identification Test

- It gives reactions characteristic of potassium and chloride.

Tests for Purity

It is tested for acidity and alkalinity, As, Ba, Ca, Mg, Fe, heavy metals, bromide, iodide, sulphate and loss on drying.

- As should not be more than 1 ppm.
- Ca and Mg should not be more than 50 ppm.
- Heavy metals should not be more than 10 ppm.
- Fe should not be more than 20 ppm.
- Bromide should not be more than 0.1%.
- Loss on drying should not be more than 1% when dried in an oven at 130°C.
- It should be free from barium and iodides.

Assay

Principle

- The assay is based on argentometric titration by Mohr's method.

Procedure

- 0.2 g of accurately weighed substance is dissolved in 50 mL water.
- The solution is then titrated with 0.1 N silver nitrate solution using potassium chromate as an indicator.

$$KCl + AgNO_3 \longrightarrow AgCl + KNO_3$$

Equivalence factor

- Each mL of 0.1 N $AgNO_3$ Ξ 0.007455 g of KCl.

Storage

- It is stored in air-tight containers, as it absorbs moisture.

Pharmaceutical Uses

- As electrolyte replenisher.
- As an adjunct in the treatment of 'Myasthenia gravis'.
- In the treatment of paralysis.
- As an antidote in digitalis poisoning.
- In the treatment of hypokalemia or hypochloric alkalosis.
- Used as diuretic.
- Used for oral replacement of potassium in the form of solution.

- It is a constituent of oral rehydration salt (ORS), sodium chloride, potassium chloride intravenous infusion, sodium and potassium chloride and glucose intravenous infusion, 'Ringer's solution'.

Note: Administered cautiously in cardiac and renal diseases.

2.4.12 Official Preparations of Potassium Chloride

- Potassium chloride oral solution (USP)
- Potassium chloride injection (IP, USP)
- Potassium chloride and sodium chloride intravenous infusion (BP)
- Potassium chloride tablet (USP)
- Potassium chloride and dextrose intravenous infusion (BP)
- Lactated Ringer's injection (USP)
- Ringer's solution (IP, BP, USP)
- Compound sodium chloride injection (IP, BP, USP)
- Lactated potassium saline injection (NF)
- Potassium chloride and glucose intravenous infusion (BP)
- Potassium chloride, sodium chloride and glucose intravenous infusion (BP)

2.4.13 Some Marketed Preparations of Potassium Chloride

(a) Potassium chloride and sodium chloride (IV) infusion

- It is a colourless, sterile solution of KCl (0.3%) and NaCl (0.9%) in water for injection.

(b) Potassium chloride and glucose (IV) infusion BP

- It is a colourless sterile solution of KCl and either anhydrous glucose or glucose in water for injection.

(c) Potassium chloride, sodium chloride and glucose (IV) infusion BP

- It is a sterile solution of KCl (0.3%), NaCl (0.18%) and glucose (4.0%) in water for injection.

(d) Effervescent KCl tablet

- Composition: KCl (600 mg) and $KHCO_3$ (400 mg).

(e) Sustained release KCl tablet

- It is also obtained as sustained release tablet containing 600 mg KCl.

(f) It is also formulated in the form of strong KCl solution, suspension, liquid, syrup or sorbitol base (10 to 15% KCl).

2.4.14 Calcium Gluconate

Synonym : Calcium D-gluconate, gluconic acid calcium salt

Molecular formula : $C_{12}H_{22}O_{14}Ca.H_2O$

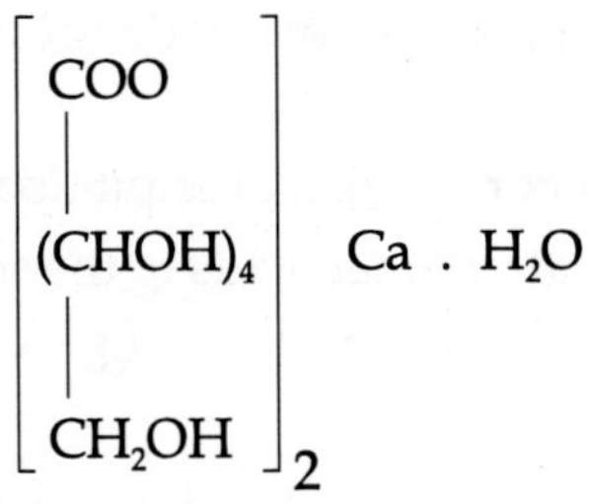

Molecular weight : 418.4 g/mol

Dose : 1 to 2 g per day when given intramuscularly or in IV injection. Tablets are given at a dose of 1 g per day.

Standards

It contains not less than 99.0% and not more than 103.0% of $C_{12}H_{22}O_{14}Ca \cdot H_2O$.

Method of Preparation

- It can be obtained by boiling the solution of gluconic acid with excess of calcium carbonate. The precipitate obtained is filtered and the product is concentrated to crystallisation.

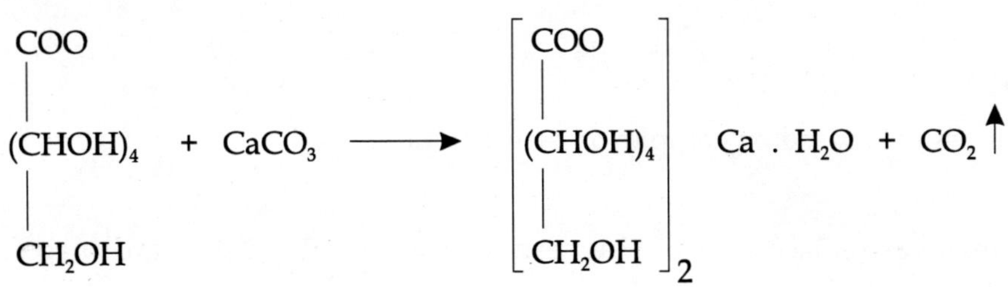

Physical Properties

Colour : White

Odour : Odourless

Taste : Tasteless

State : Crystalline granules or powder

Solubility : (i) Soluble in water, more soluble in boiling water
(ii) Insoluble in alcohol, chloroform and ether

Nature : 10% aqueous solution is neutral to litmus

Chemical Properties

- It is stable in air, but loses its water of crystallisation with decomposition at 100°C.
- Its aqueous solution has a pH in the range 6 to 7.

- Calcium salt can form complex with many drugs which leads to the formation of precipitates.
- The solution of calcium gluconate gets precipitated by oxalate, borate, etc.
- On adding hydrochloric acid or other acids to the solution, gluconic acid is said to be formed which gets converted easily to *d*-gluconolactone.

Identification Tests

- It gives reactions characteristic of calcium ions.
- Its aqueous solution gives yellow colour or precipitate with ferric chloride solution.
- It forms phenyl hydrazone on reaction with phenyl hydrazine in the presence of glacial acetic acid, melting point 200 to 202°C (decomposition).

Tests for Purity

It is tested for acidity and alkalinity, As, lead, heavy metals, chloride, sulphate, dextrose and sucrose.

- As should not be more than 2 ppm.
- Heavy metals should not be more than 20 ppm.

Assay

Principle

- The assay is based on complexometric titration.

Procedure

- It involves replacement of magnesium using 5 mL of standard magnesium sulphate solution.
- The pH can be adjusted with ammonia-ammonium chloride buffer.
- The volume of disodium edetate equivalent to magnesium sulphate solution is subtracted from total disodium edetate used and then results are calculated.

Equivalence factor

- Each mL of remainder of 0.05 M disodium edetate Ξ 0.02242 g of $C_{12}H_{22}O_{14}Ca \cdot H_2O$.

Incompatibility

- It is incompatible with oxidising agents and solution of calcium gluconate gives a precipitate with oxalates and borates.

Storage Condition

- It is stored in air-tight containers, as it absorbs moisture.

Pharmaceutical Uses

- As calcium replenisher.
- Acts as a source of calcium ion for treating hypocalcaemic tetany or in calcium deficiency.
- Its injection is found to be useful in the treatment of urticaria and black widow spider bite.
- Used in the treatment of burn from hydrofluoric acid as gel.
- Its tablet also finds use in supplementary diet of convalescent and expectant mothers.

2.4.15 Some Marketed Preparations of Calcium Gluconate

(a) Calcium Gluconate Injection

- It is a sterile solution of calcium gluconate in water for injection.
- The amount of calcium gluconate must be between 8.5 and 9.4% w/v.
- Calcium D-saccharate is added as a stabiliser, which also prevents the formation of precipitation of calcium gluconate.

(b) Calcium Gluconate Tablet

- Average weight of tablet should not be less than 95% but not more than 105% of the stated amount of calcium gluconate on label.
- Chewable tablets are available in the strength of 0.325 g, 0.5 g, 0.65 g and 1.0 g.

2.4.16 Physiological Acid-Base Balance

- Body fluids consist of balanced quantities of acids and bases, which are responsible for the maintenance of pH.
- These quantities are well-regulated by intricate mechanisms.
- The maintenance of the normal range within the body is essential because the biochemical reactions taking place in the living systems are very sensitive to even small changes in acidity and alkalinity.
- Hydrogen ion is highly reactive and has a prominent impact on the functioning of body enzymes, even at low concentrations.
- The pH of blood of a healthy person remains constant around 7.35.
- Decreased hydrogen ion concentration (or increased pH of blood) represents alkalosis, whereas increased hydrogen ion concentration (or increased pH of blood) represents acidosis.
- Generally, acidic metabolites are formed in higher quantity than basic metabolites. This is because CO_2, proteins and amino acids contribute to generation of acidic metabolites. These are then neutralised by bicarbonate ions.

Table 2.12: pH of certain body fluids

Body Fluids	pH Range
Gastric juice (stomach)	1.5-3.5
Saliva	5.4-7.5
Bile	6.0-8.5
Blood	7.4-7.5
Urine	4.5-8.0
Semen	7.2-7.6

2.4.17 Factors Responsible for Acid-Base Imbalance

These are categorized into the following two types:

(a) Factors causing acidosis

(b) Factors causing alkalosis

(a) Factors Causing Acidosis

(i) Increased production of CO_2

(ii) Increased production of organic acids

(iii) Greater intake of acid producing substances

(b) Factors Causing Alkalosis

(i) Reduced CO_2 concentration in body

(ii) Increased bicarbonate ion production

(iii) Decreased hydrogen ion concentration

Note: If the pH of the blood decreases to 6.8, the patient may die; whereas if the pH increases from 7.4 to 8.0, it is harmful and may lead to death.

2.4.18 Regulatory Mechanisms of Acid-Base Imbalance

- Even though strong acids and bases are continually taken into and formed by the body, the pH of the fluids inside and outside the cells remains almost constant due to the presence of buffer systems.
- The main function of the buffer system is to prevent the drastic changes in the pH values in the blood.
- The pH of the body fluid is maintained by the following mechanisms:
  1. Buffer Systems
  2. Elimination of some ions through urine by kidney (renal excretory mechanism)
  3. Through the respiratory centre (respiratory mechanism)

1. Buffer Systems

- Buffer system consists of a weak acid and the salt of that acid, which functions as a weak base.
- Buffer system of the body does not allow rapid and drastic changes in the pH of the body fluid by converting strong acids and bases into weak acids and bases.
- The major buffer systems existing in the body fluids are as follows:
  (a) Carbonic acid-bicarbonate buffer system
  (b) Phosphate buffer system
  (c) Protein (haemoglobin) buffer system

(a) Carbonic Acid-Bicarbonate Buffer System

- This kind of buffer system is mainly found in plasma and kidney.
- It is considered to be an important regulator of blood pH.
- If there occurs excess of H^+, the bicarbonate (HCO_3^-) ion acts as a weak base and accepts H^+ to form carbonic acid. The latter dissociates further to yield carbon dioxide and water.

$$\underset{\text{Strong acid}}{H^+} + \underset{\text{Weak base}}{HCO_3^-} \longrightarrow \underset{\text{Carbonic acid (Weak acid)}}{H_2CO_3} \longrightarrow CO_2 + H_2O$$

- If there is shortage of H^+ ions, the carbonic acid (another component of buffer system) ionises to release more H^+ ions and thus, maintains the pH.

$$H_2CO_3 \longrightarrow H^+ + HCO_3^-$$

- Similarly, in lungs, oxygen reacts with the protonated deoxyhaemoglobin, releasing protons. These protons combine with the bicarbonate, forming carbonic acid, which then dissociates to yield carbon dioxide and water. This carbon dioxide then gets exhaled out.

(b) Phosphate Buffer System

- This buffer system mainly works in cells and kidneys and helps to maintain the physiological pH of 7.4.
- Higher concentrations of phosphate ions are found in ICF, this system consists of monohydrogen phosphate/dihydrogen phosphate ($HPO_4^{2-}/H_2PO_4^-$) anions.
- If there occurs an excess of H^+ ions, the monohydrogen phosphate ion acts as a weak base by accepting the proton.

$$\underset{\text{Strong acid}}{HCl} + \underset{\text{Weak base}}{Na_2HPO_4} \longrightarrow \underset{\text{Salt}}{NaCl} + \underset{\text{Weak base}}{Na_2HPO_4}$$

- While the dihydrogen phosphate ion can act as a weak acid and is able to neutralize the alkaline condition.

$$\underset{\text{Strong acid}}{NaOH} + \underset{\text{Weak base}}{Na_2HPO_4} \longrightarrow H_2O + \underset{\text{Weak base}}{Na_2HPO_4}$$

(c) Protein (Haemoglobin) Buffer System

- It is considered to be the most abundant buffer in the body cells and plasma.
- Amino acids are the basic units of protein which contain at least one carboxyl (-COOH) group and at least one amino (-NH_2) group. Both these groups help in maintaining a constant pH.
- When there is excess of hydrogen ions, the amino group acts as a base and accepts the proton.

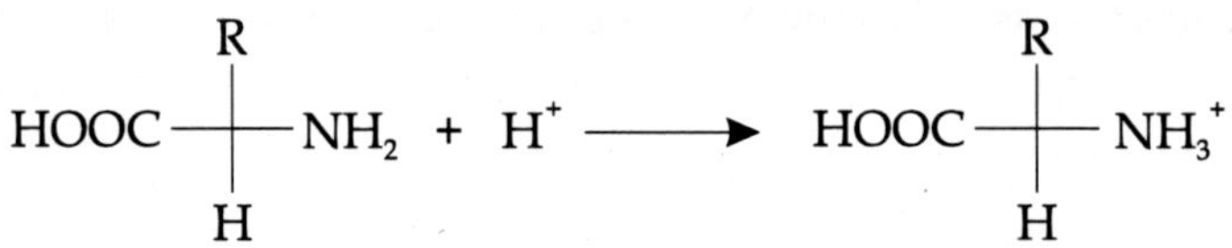

Amino acid   Accepted proton

- While the free carboxyl group can release protons so as to neutralise an alkaline condition.

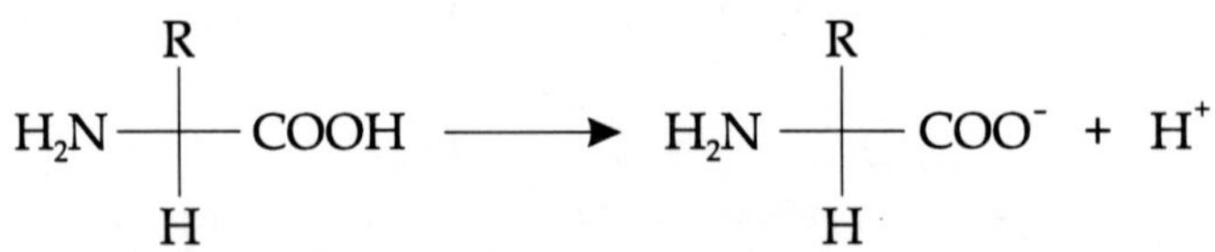

Amino acid   Liberated proton

2. Elimination of Some Ions Through Urine by Kidney (Renal Excretory Mechanism)

- Cells of proximal convoluted tubule and distal convoluted tubule of kidneys play a major role in secreting H^+ into the tubular fluid and that is why, pH of urine is usually found to be acidic.
- Renal excretory mechanism regulates the acid-base balance by the following three mechanisms:
  (a) Hydrogen ion elimination
  (b) Regeneration/reabsorption of bicarbonates
  (c) Regulating the flow of electrolytes
- Kidney is able to generate NH_3 (ammonia), which neutralizes the acidic products of protein metabolism. These products are then excreted from the body through urine.

- Fixed acids like sulphuric acid, phosphoric acid and hydrochloric acid are generally excreted by the kidneys while unstable carbonic acid (H_2CO_3) is removed mainly by the respiratory mechanism.

3. *Through the Respiratory Centre (Respiratory Mechanism)*

- The control of pH also occurs through the control of respiratory centre.
- If the respiratory centre is stimulated, it alters the rate of breathing.
- This change in rate of breathing is able to control the removal of CO_2 from the body fluids, which gives rise to the changes in pH of blood carbonic acid, leading to acidity or alkalinity.
- When respiration gets decreased, the accumulated CO_2 combines with water present in the blood, resulting in the formation of carbonic acid (H_2CO_3), which further dissociates to give H^+ ions, resulting in the condition called acidosis.

$$CO_2 + H_2O \longrightarrow H_2CO_3 \longrightarrow H^+ + HCO_3^-$$

- Similarly, in case of overbreathing, excess of CO_2 is excreted by lungs, giving rise to a condition called alkalosis.

If any one of these mechanisms does not function properly, the conditions of metabolic/respiratory acidosis or alkalosis may arise.

2.4.19 Some Important Terms

(a) Metabolic Acidosis

- It refers to the disturbed acid-base balance of the body and physiological fluids become acidic in nature.
- In this case, pH is decreased below 7.35.

Causes

- Failure to excrete metabolic acids by the kidney.
- Due to diarrhoea, vomiting or diabetes mellitus.
- Excess absorption of metabolic acids.
- Loss of alkali from the body.

Treatment

- Intake of sodium acetate, sodium citrate, potassium citrate, potassium acetate, etc.

(b) Metabolic Alkalosis

- It refers to the disturbed acid-base balance of the body and physiological fluids become more alkaline in nature.
- In this case, pH is more than 7.45.

Causes

- Excessive ingestion of alkaline drugs.
- Use of diuretics
- Treatment
- Intake of ammonium chloride and its injection, etc.

(c) Respiratory Acidosis

- It refers to the state in which carbon dioxide is retained in the body due to reduced ventilation.

Causes

- Due to mechanical/muscular impairment.
- Disease of lung due to CNS depression.

(d) Respiratory Alkalosis

- It refers to the state in which excess of carbon dioxide is lost from the body due to hyperventilation.

Causes

- Emotional factors
- Fever
- Salicylate poisoning

2.4.20 Electrolytes Used in Acid-Base Therapy

- Generally sodium/potassium compounds such as bicarbonates, lactate, acetate, etc., are used for treating metabolic acidosis.
- Whereas, the metabolic alkalosis can be treated with ammonium salt, important being ammonium chloride.

2.4.21 Sodium Acetate

It is sodium salt of acetic acid and is obtained as trihydrate.

Molecular formula : $CH_3COONa.3H_2O$

Molecular weight : 136.1 g/mol

Category : Pharmaceutical aid

Standards

It contains not less than 99.0% and not more than 101.0% w/w of $CH_3COONa \cdot 3H_2O$.

Method of Preparation

- It is prepared by neutralizing acetic acid with sodium carbonate. The solution is filtered, concentrated and allowed to crystallise.

$$2CH_3COOH + Na_2CO_3 \longrightarrow 2CH_3COONa + H_2O + CO_2\uparrow$$

Physical Properties

Colour : Colourless or white
Odour : Odourless
Taste : Slightly saline and bitter
State : Crystalline powder or crystals
Solubility : Freely soluble in water, soluble in alcohol
Nature : Alkaline (7.5 to 9)

Chemical Properties

- Sodium acetate forms ester on reaction with alkyl halide, such as bromoethane.

$$CH_3COONa + C_2H_5Br \longrightarrow CH_3COOC_2H_5 + NaBr$$

Identification Test

- It gives reactions characteristic of sodium and acetates.

Assay

Principle

- It may be assayed by non-aqueous titration method.

Procedure

- An accurately weighed sample is dissolved in glacial acetic acid and acetic anhydride (10:1 ratio) and titrated with perchloric acid using 1-naphthol benzene as an indicator.

Storage Condition

- It should be stored in tightly-closed containers in a cool place.

Pharmaceutical Uses

- Used as an ingredient of peritoneal dialysis fluid.
- Acts as alkalinizing agent.
- Used as a diuretic.
- Used as a pharmaceutical aid in haemodialysis.

2.4.22 Potassium Acetate

Molecular formula : CH_3COOK
Molecular weight : 98.14 g/mol
Category : Pharmaceutical aid and electrolyte replenisher

Standards

It contains not less than 99.0% of CH_3COOK, calculated with reference to the substance dried to constant weight at a temperature of 150°C.

Method of Preparation

- It is prepared by adding potassium carbonate or bicarbonate to acetic acid until the effervescence ceases. The neutralisation must be carried out carefully to avoid excess of the carbonate solution. The solution is filtered, evaporated to dryness; the residue is fused and allowed to solidify.

$$CH_3COOH + KNCO_3 \longrightarrow CH_3COOK + H_2O + CO_2\uparrow$$

Physical properties

Colour : White

Odour : Odourless

Taste : Saline and slightly alkaline

State : Powder, a fused mass or granules or monoclinic crystals

Solubility : Freely soluble in water and alcohol, insoluble in ether

Nature : Deliquescent

Dose : 1 to 3 g in divided doses in solution form

Chemical Properties

- It melts at 290°C and on strong heating, it leaves a residue of potassium carbonate.

$$2CH_3COOK + 4O_2 \xrightarrow{\Delta} K_2CO_3 + 3H_2O + 3CO_2\uparrow$$

- It gets hydrolysed in water and gives an alkaline reaction.

$$CH_3COO + H_2O \longrightarrow CH_3COOH + OH^-$$

- When warmed with ethyl alcohol and concentrated H_2SO_4, it evolves a pleasant smell of ethyl acetate.

Identification Test

- It gives reactions characteristic of potassium and acetates.

Test for Purity

- It has to be tested for Ca, Al, As, heavy metals, Na, chloride, sulphate, loss on drying and alkalinity.

Assay

Principle

- The assay is based on acid-base titration method.

Procedure

- An accurately weighed sample (2 g) is ignited in a crucible until the sample is completely carbonised.
- This residue contains potassium carbonate and carbon particles.
- This residue is treated with an excess of 50 mL of 0.5 N H_2SO_4.
- It is then boiled, filtered and washed with water.
- The combined filtrate and washings are back-titrated with 0.5 N NaOH using methyl orange as an indicator.

Equivalence Factor

- Each mL of 0.5 N $H_2SO_4 \equiv$ 0.04907 g of CH_3COOK.

Incompatibility

- It is incompatible with acids and silver, mercury and iron salt.

Storage

- It should be stored in tightly closed glass-stoppered bottles.

Pharmaceutical Uses

- Used as diuretic.
- Used as urinary alkaliser.
- Used for effects of potassium ion.
- Used as antacid in stomach.
- It stabilises purine alkaloids, if used in equimolar quantities.
- Used in the form of solutions.

Note: Indiscriminate use sometimes produces toxic manifestations of hyperkalemia.

2.4.23 Sodium Bicarbonate

Synonym : Baking soda, sodium hydrogen carbonate, meetha soda
Molecular formula : $NaHCO_3$
Molecular weight : 84.01 g/mol
Category : Antacid, electrolyte replenisher
Dose : 300 mg to 2 g

Standards

It contains not less than 99.0% and not more than 100.5% w/w of $NaHCO_3$, calculated with reference to the dried substance.

Methods of Preparation

- Industrially, it is obtained by the Solvay process. Brine solution (NaCl) is saturated with ammonia to remove traces of impurities like Mg and Fe. This solution is then filtered and passed through the carbonating tower, whereby the solution is allowed to come in contact with the current state of CO_2. The tower is then cooled to enhance precipitation, since sodium carbonate is less soluble in water below 15°C. The precipitate obtained is filtered and dried.

$$H_2O + CO_2 \longrightarrow H_2CO_3$$

$$NH_3 + H_2CO_3 \longrightarrow NH_4HCO_3$$

$$NaCl + NH_4HCO_3 \longrightarrow NaHCO_3 + NH_4Cl$$

- In laboratory, sodium bicarbonate is prepared from pure sodium carbonate. A solution of sodium carbonate is saturated with carbon dioxide and the reaction mixture is then cooled, which results in the precipitation of sodium bicarbonate.

$$Na_2CO_3 + H_2O + CO_2 \longrightarrow 2NaHCO_3$$

Physical Properties

Colour : White

Odour : Odourless

Taste : Saline

State : Crystalline powder or opaque monoclinic crystals

Solubility : Freely soluble in water but practically insoluble in alcohol

Nature : Effervescent and alkaline

Chemical Properties

- At 50°C, it loses CO_2 and when heated to 100°C, it gets converted into sesquicarbonate ($Na_2CO_3 \cdot NaHCO_3 \cdot 2H_2O$).
- Presence of moist air tends to decompose sodium bicarbonate. However, it is stable in dry air.
- On heating, it decomposes into sodium carbonate, carbon dioxide and water.

$$2NaHCO_3 \longrightarrow Na_2CO_3 + H_2O + CO_2\uparrow$$

- On reacting with acid, it forms salt.

$$2NaHCO_3 + H_2SO_4 \longrightarrow Na_2CO_3 + 2H_2O + 2CO_2\uparrow$$

Identification Tests

- It gives reactions characteristic of sodium and carbonate.
- Its 1% w/v solution has a pH not more than 8.6.
- An aqueous solution of sodium carbonate when boiled liberates carbon dioxide.

$$2NaHCO_3 \longrightarrow Na_2CO_3 + H_2O + CO_2\uparrow$$

- A solution of sodium bicarbonate when treated with solution of magnesium sulphate, no precipitate is formed. On heating, sodium carbonate produces hydroxide ions and CO_2 in solution. Magnesium sulphate reacts with the hydroxide ion to produce magnesium hydroxide which *in situ* reacts with CO_2 and forms white precipitates of magnesium carbonate.

$$2NaHCO_3 \longrightarrow Na_2CO_3 + H_2O + CO_2\uparrow$$

$$Na_2CO_3 + H_2O \longrightarrow 2Na^+ + 2OH^- + CO_2\uparrow$$

$$MgSO_4 + 2OH^- \longrightarrow Mg(OH)_2 + SO_4^{2-}$$

$$Mg(OH)_2 + CO_2 \longrightarrow MgCO_3 + H_2O$$

Tests for Purity

It is tested for alkalinity, Ca, Al, As, Fe, heavy metals, chloride, sulphate, ammonium compounds, insoluble matter and loss on drying.

- As should not be more than 2 ppm.
- Sulphate should not be more than 150 ppm.
- Chlorides should not be more than 200 ppm.
- Fe should not be more than 20 ppm.
- Heavy metals should not be more than 5 ppm.
- Loss on drying should not be more than 0.25%.

Assay

Principle

- It is based on acid-based titration technique.

Procedure

- 1.5 g of sample is accurately weighed and dissolved in 50 mL water.
- This solution is then titrated with 1 N HCl using methyl orange as an indicator.

$$2NaHCO_3 + 2HCl \longrightarrow 2NaCl + 2H_2O + 2CO_2$$

Equivalence factor

- Each mL of 1 N HCl Ξ 0.08401 g of $NaHCO_3$.

Incompatibility

- It is incompatible with mercury salts and acid.
- It inhibits the absorption of tetracycline from the GIT.

Storage

- It is stored in air-tight containers because of its hygroscopic nature in moist atmosphere. It releases carbon dioxide at 50°C and gets converted into sodium carbonate at 100°C.

Pharmaceutical Uses

- As antacid.
- As carminative.
- In the treatment of systemic acidosis.
- As electrolyte replenisher.
- To treat dyspepsia.
- For the preparation of buffer solutions.
- Its aqueous solutions are used as local applicants for burns, insect bites, etc.
- As a constituent of effervescent mixture.
- In the treatment of diarrhoea.
- In the treatment of acute poisoning from acidic drugs, like salicylates and phenobarbitone.
- Can be used in ear drops to remove ear wax, as eye lotions and as lubricating fluid for contact lens.

2.4.24 Sodium Bicarbonate Injection

Category : Fluid and electrolyte replenisher

Standards

It contains not less than 94.0% and not more than 106.0% w/v of $NaHCO_3$. The label should state the percentage of w/v sodium bicarbonate.

Method of Preparation

- It is a sterile solution of sodium bicarbonate in water for injection.

Identification Test

- Same as described under sodium bicarbonate.

Test for Purity

- Same as described under sodium bicarbonate.

Assay

- Same as described under sodium bicarbonate

Other Requirements

- It should comply with the requirements for injection.
- The injection is required to comply with the test for pyrogens, using a quantity containing not less than 0.25 g of sodium bicarbonate.

Pharmaceutical Uses

- Its 1.4% w/v solution is used for parenteral administration.

Note: The continuous use of sodium bicarbonate as an antacid has serious drawback. It can cause "rebound acidity".

2.4.25 Sodium Citrate

It is a dihydrate of trisodium 2-hydroxypropane-1,2,3-tricarboxylate.

Molecular formula : $C_6H_5O_7Na_3 \cdot 2H_2O$

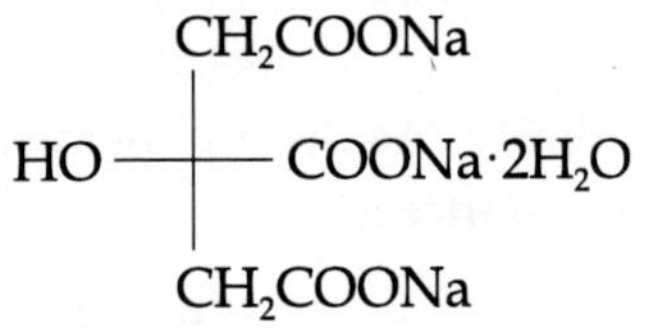

Molecular weight	: 294.1 g/mol
Category	: Systemic alkaliser
Dose	: 1 to 2 g with water as expectorant 1 to 4 g as systemic antacid

Standards

It contains not less than 99.0% and not more than 101.0% of $C_6H_5O_7Na_3$, calculated with reference to the anhydrous substance.

Method of Preparation

- It is prepared by neutralizing a solution of citric acid with sodium carbonate or sodium bicarbonate until the effervescence ceases. The solution is evaporated to crystallise the product.

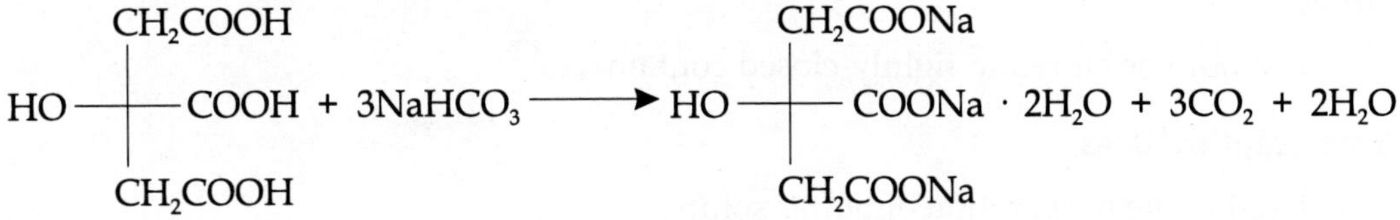

Physical Properties

Colour : White

Odour : Odourless

Taste : Cool and saline taste

State : Crystalline powder or granular crystals

Solubility : Insoluble in water and alcohol

Chemical Property

- When heated to 150°C, it becomes anhydrous. When it is further heated, it chars, leaving a residue of sodium carbonate.

$$2Na_3H_5O_7{\cdot}2H_2O + 9O_2 \longrightarrow 3Na_2CO_3 + 9H_2O + 9CO_2\uparrow$$

Identification Test

- It gives reactions characteristic of sodium and citrate.

Tests for Purity

- It is tested for acidity, alkalinity, As, heavy metals, chloride, sulphate, oxalate and readily carbonisable substances.

Assay

Principle

- It is assayed by potentiometric titration.

Procedure

- An accurately weighed 0.25 g sample is dissolved in 50 mL of glacial acetic acid by heating to about 5°C.
- The solution is cooled and titrated with 0.1 N perchloric acid determining the end-point potentiometrically.
- A blank determination is carried out and any correction, if necessary, is taken into account.

Equivalence factor

- Each mL of 0.1 N perchloric acid Ξ 0.008602 g of $C_6H_5Na_3O_7$.

Storage

- It should be stored in tightly-closed containers.

Pharmaceutical Uses

- Used in the preparation of buffer solutions.

- Acts as systemic antacid.
- Acts as anticoagulant.
- Used in the expectorant preparations.
- Acts as systemic alkaliser.

2.4.26 Potassium Citrate

Molecular formula : $C_6H_5O_7K_3 \cdot H_2O$

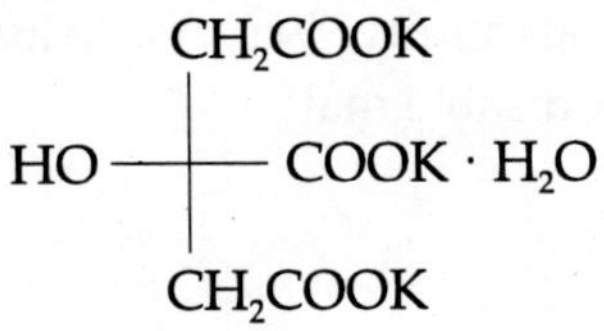

Molecular weight : 324.42 g/mol

Category : Pharmaceutical aid, acid-base regulator

Standards

It contains not less than 99.0% and not more than 101.0% of $C_6H_5O_7K_3$, calculated with reference to the anhydrous substance.

Method of Preparation

- It is prepared by neutralizing a solution of citric acid with potassium carbonate or sodium bicarbonate. The solution is filtered and evaporated to dryness with constant stirring. A fine powder is obtained by carrying out trituration in a warm mortar.

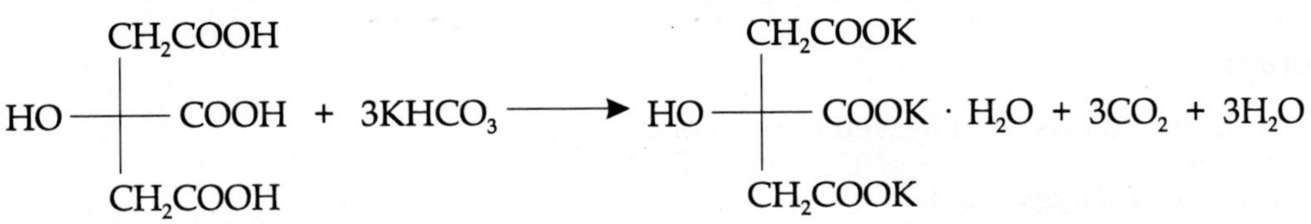

Physical Properties

Colour : Colourless or white

Odour : Odourless

Taste : Cool and saline

State : Crystalline powder or granular crystals

Solubility : Soluble in water and glycerine but insoluble in alcohol

Nature : Deliquescent in moist air

Chemical Property

- At higher temperature, it carbonizes and evolves inflammable gases, which have pungent acrid odour.

Identification

- It gives reactions characteristic of potassium and citrate.

Test for Purity

- It is tested for acidity or alkalinity, Na, As, heavy metals, chloride, oxalate, sulphate and readily carbonisable matter.

Assay

Principle

- The assay is based on acid-base titration method.

Procedure

- An accurately weighed sample (2 g) is ignited in a crucible until the sample gets completely carbonised.
- The residue is cooled.
- This residue is treated with 50 mL of water and of 50 mL of 0.5 N H_2SO_4.
- It is then boiled, filtered and washed with water.
- The combined filtrate containing excess of acid and washings are back-titrated with 0.5 N NaOH using methyl orange as an indicator.

Equivalence factor

Each mL of 0.5 N H_2SO_4 Ξ 0.05497 g of $C_6H_5O_7K_3.H_2O$.

Storage

- It should be stored in well-closed containers.

Pharmaceutical Uses

- Used as osmotic diuretic, expectorant and diaphoretic.
- Possesses slight laxative action.
- Acts as systemic alkaliser.
- Possesses anticoagulant action.

2.4.27 Sodium Lactate Injection

It is a sterile solution containing 1.85% w/v of sodium lactate in water for injection.

Molecular formula : $C_3H_5O_3Na$

Molecular weight : 112.06 g/mol

Category : Fluid and electrolyte replenisher

Standards

It contains not less than 1.75% and not more than 1.95% w/v of $C_3H_5O_3Na$.

Method of Preparation

- Specified quantity of lactic acid is accurately weighed and a small amount of sodium hydroxide is added. The mixture is subjected to autoclaving at 115°C for 60 minutes. Then excess alkali is neutralised with sufficient dilute HCl to attain pH 5.7. Then the volume of solution is made up to the desired volume using water for injection to yield 1.8% w/v solution of sodium lactate. The solution is finally filtered and sterilized using an autoclave.

Physical Properties

Colour : Colourless

Odour : Odourless

State : Clear solution

Pharmaceutical Uses

- Used as an alternative for sodium bicarbonate in treating electrolyte imbalance.
- Used as systemic alkaliser.
- Used to increase heart rate in conditions like hypokalemia.

2.4.28 Ammonium Chloride

Synonym	: Sal ammoniac, ammonium muriate, salmiac, amchlor
Molecular formula	: NH_4Cl
Molecular weight	: 53.49 g/mol
Category	: Expectorant, diuretic and electrolyte replenisher

Standards

It contains not less than 99.5% of NH_4Cl, calculated with reference to substance dried over silica gel for four hours.

Methods of Preparation

- Commercially, it is prepared by neutralizing ammonia with HCl. The solution is evaporated till crude, vitreous, crystalline mass of ammonium chloride is obtained. The crude salt is purified either by crystallisation or sublimation.

$$NH_3 + HCl \longrightarrow NH_4Cl$$

- It is also prepared by treating ammonium sulphate with sodium chloride.

$$2NaCl + (NH_4)_2SO_4 \longrightarrow 2NH_3 + 2HCl + Na_2SO_4$$

$$2NH_3 + 2HCl \longrightarrow 2Na_4Cl$$

- It is also obtained by treating ammoniacal gas liquors with lime and the liberated NH_3 is passed into hydrochloric acid solution. The crude ammonium chloride obtained is known as sal ammoniac and occurs as tough, crystalline masses.

Physical Properties

Colour : White

Odour : Odourless

Taste : Cool saline taste

State : Fine or coarse crystalline powder

Solubility : (i) Soluble in water and freely soluble in alcohol and glycerine
(ii) Sparingly soluble in boiling water

Nature : (i) Slightly hygroscopic
(ii) Its 0.8% w/v solution is isotonic with serum.

Chemical Properties

- Freshly prepared aqueous solutions are neutral to litmus but become quickly acidic on standing because of hydrolysis.

$$NH_4Cl + 2H_2O \longrightarrow NH_4OH + H_3O^+ + Cl^-$$

- In its vapour form, it dissociates in ammonia and hydrochloric acid.

$$NH_4Cl \rightleftharpoons NH_3 + HCl$$

Identification Tests

- It gives reactions characteristic of ammonium salts and chlorides.
- A few mg of substance is heated with sodium hydroxide solution, leading to the evolution of ammonia gas, which is recognisable by its odour and by its action on moist red litmus paper.

$$NH_4^+ + OH^- \longrightarrow NH_3 + H_2O$$

Tests for Purity

It is tested for As, sulphate, Ca, iodate, Fe, heavy metals, loss on drying and sulphated ash.

- As should not be more than 2 ppm.
- Sulphate should not be more than 150 ppm.
- Calcium should not be more than 200 ppm.

- Iron should not be more than 20 ppm.
- Heavy metals should not be more than 10 ppm.
- Loss on drying should not be more than 0.5% w/w.
- The sulphated ash should not be more than 0.1% w/w.
- The pH of a 5% w/v solution is between 4.5 and 6.0.

Assay

Principle

- Based on acid-base titration technique.

Procedure

- About 0.1 g of NH_4Cl sample accurately weighed is kept in a conical flask, about 50 mL water is added to dissolve it.
- 5 mL of neutral formaldehyde solution is then added so that ammonium chloride is converted to methanimine and hydrochloric acid.
- The liberated acid is titrated with 0.1 N NaOH using phenolphthalein as an indicator.

$$NH_4Cl + HCHO \longrightarrow CH_2NH + HCl + H_2O$$

$$HCl + NaOH \longrightarrow NaCl + H_2O$$

Equivalence factor

- Each mL of 0.1 N NaOH Ξ 0.05349 g of NH_4Cl.

Incompatibility

- It is incompatible with alkalis, carbonates of alkaline earths and lead and silver salts.

Storage

- It should be stored in tightly-closed containers in a dry place.

Dose

- 3 to 6 g daily in the divided dose.

Pharmaceutical Uses

- The ammonium ions (NH_4^+) are of vital importance in the maintenance of acid-base equilibrium of the body and are used in metabolic alkalosis.
- Ammonium chloride decreases the alkali reserve of the body and is administered as 2% solution intravenously with glucose.
- At large doses, it produces diuresis and makes the urine acidic.

- It is used as mild expectorant.
- It is used as a diaphoretic (increases sweating) and hence, reduces body temperature to a small extent.
- As an ingredient in cough preparations.

2.4.29 Ammonium Chloride Injection

Ammonium chloride injection contains concentration of 1% or 2% w/v administered by slow intravenous infusion.

Category : Diuretic and electrolyte replenisher

Pharmaceutical Uses

- Used in the treatment of hyperkalemia, hypernatremia, and systemic alkalosis.

Note: This preparation is not official in IP and is seldom used.

2.4.30 Combination of Oral Electrolyte Powders and Solutions

- These are also known as oral rehydration salts (ORS).
- These solutions are used to replace the lost electrolytes and fluids from the body, especially in case of diarrhoea, dysentery and severe vomiting.
- Various formulations of oral rehydration preparations are available in the market, which contain anhydrous glucose (or glucose), sodium chloride, potassium chloride, and either sodium bicarbonate or sodium citrate.
- These dry powder preparations are mixed in specified amount of water and used for oral rehydration therapy.
- These preparations may contain a flavouring agent and a suitable agent for free flow of the powder.
- Further, due to poor stability of sodium bicarbonate under tropical conditions, it may be packed separately such that the stability of ORS during storage is increased.
- Examples include electrol powder, paediatric powder, etc.
- Below mentioned are the formulas, the quantities of various ingredients for **preparation of one litre solution**:

Formula I

Ingredient	Amount (g)
Sodium chloride	1.0
Potassium chloride	1.5
Sodium bicarbonate	1.5
Anhydrous sodium citrate	-
Anhydrous glucose	36.4
OR Glucose	40.0

Formula II – WHO-UNICEF ORS

Ingredient	Amount (g)
Sodium chloride	3.5
Potassium chloride	1.5
Sodium bicarbonate	2.5
Sodium citrate	–
Anhydrous glucose	20.0
OR Glucose	22.0

Formula III – WHO-UNICEF ORS

Ingredient	Amount (g)
Sodium chloride	3.5
Potassium chloride	1.5
Sodium bicarbonate	–
Sodium citrate	2.9
Anhydrous glucose	20.0
OR Glucose	–

Formula IV – First aid ORS formula for emergency

Ingredient	Amount (g)
Sodium chloride	1 × 5 mL
Potassium chloride	–
Sodium bicarbonate	–
Sodium citrate	–
Anhydrous glucose	–
OR Glucose	–

The Formula II and III are recommended by WHO and UNICEF (United Nation International Children's Emergency Fund).

Pharmaceutical Use of ORS

- For the control of diarrhoeal diseases or diarrhoea related dehydration.

2.4.31 New Formulation of ORS With Reduced Osmolarity

- For more than 25 years, WHO and UNICEF have recommended a single formulation of glucose-based ORS to prevent or treat dehydration from diarrhoea, irrespective of the cause or age group affected.
- This product which provides a solution containing total osmolarity of 311 mOsm/L **(Table 2.13)** has proven to be effective without apparent adverse effects worldwide.

- It has contributed substantially to the dramatic global reduction in mortality from diarrhoeal disease during the period.
- The goal behind reduction in osmolarity to 245 mOsm/L **(Table 2.13.)** has been to make the product at least as safe and effective as standard ORS for preventing or treating dehydration from all types of diarrhoea, in addition to reducing stool output or other important clinical benefits.
- Apart from this, the other approach of reducing the osmolarity of ORS solution is to avoid possible adverse effects of hypertonicity on net fluid absorption. This was done by reducing the solution's glucose and salt (NaCl) concentrations.

Table 2.13: Composition of standard and reduced osmolarity of WHO-ORS

Ingredient	Amount	
	Standard WHO (1975)	**Reduced Osmolarity WHO (2002)**
Glucose, mmol/L	111	75
Sodium, mEq/L	90	75
Potassium, mEq/L	20	20
Chloride, mEq/L	80	65
Citrate, mmol/L	10	10
Osmolarity, mOsm/L	311	245

2.5 DENTAL PRODUCTS

- Maintenance of dental hygiene is crucial for human health.
- Numerous dental products are available for maintaining dental hygiene which help to keep the teeth clean and free from bacteria.
- A wide range of inorganic chemicals and their preparations are known to find applications in dental and oral diseases.
- Dental products may be defined as inorganic compounds and their preparations are meant for local application in the oral cavity for maintaining dental hygiene.

2.5.1 Ideal Characteristics of Dental Products

For any dental product to work properly and be considered effective, it must have certain properties as listed below:

- Easy to use and should be cheap.
- Aid in reducing dental plaque and gingivitis without harming the teeth.
- Should not alter dental tissues or teeth.
- Sustained release especially in case of sensitivity.
- Must not produce any stain on teeth.
- Must not produce nausea or vomiting sensation.
- Must contain specific amount of fluoride, especially in toothpaste.

2.5.2 Classification of Dental Products

Dental products are classified into the following:

(a) Anticaries agents
(b) Dentifrices
(c) Oral antiseptics and astringents
(d) Mouthwashes
(e) Cements and fillers
(f) Polishing agents

(a) Anticaries Agents

- These are used in the treatment of dental caries or tooth decay.

  Examples include:

  (i) **Fluorides:** Sodium fluoride, stannous fluoride, sodium monofluorophosphate, calcium fluoride, potassium fluoride, aluminium fluoride, ammonium fluoride, sodium silicofluoride, etc.

  (ii) **Phosphates:** Calcium monohydrogen phosphate, sodium dihydrogen phosphate, calcium sucrose phosphate, etc.

(b) Dentifrices

- These are also called cleaning agents or abrasives.
- These substances are used to clean the accessible surfaces of teeth and adjacent gums.
- They are mainly used to remove stains from the teeth.
- Examples include calcium carbonate, dibasic calcium phosphate, calcium phosphate, sodium metaphosphate, potassium nitrate, hydrated silica, zinc chloride, strontium chloride, etc.
- Dentifrices, when used in the treatment of dental hyperaesthesia caused by any dental irritant like physical effects (heat or cold contact), physiological effects (abrasion) and chemical agents (acid erosion) are known as **desensitising agents**.

(c) Oral Antiseptics and Astringents

- These are the inorganic substances which show antiseptic and astringent action in the oral cavity.
- Examples include hydrogen peroxide, magnesium peroxide, sodium perborate, etc.

(d) Mouthwashes

- These are non-sterile aqueous preparations usually used after brushing.

- These are mainly intended to provide fresh breath and to kill the bacteria that are responsible for plaque formation.
- They are also used to prevent gum diseases and to strengthen the enamel.
- Examples include zinc chloride (deodorant and desensitising action), zinc sulphate (mild antiseptic and astringent action), potassium permanganate (anti-infective and astringent action), sodium bicarbonate (antacid property), sodium chloride (irritant), ammoniacal silver nitrate solution (decreases hypersensitivity of teeth and gums), etc.

(e) Cements and Fillers

- These are the inorganic agents used temporarily to cover and protect areas that have undergone operation.
- The cementing material is applied as a paste, which gets hardened in a shortwhile forming a protective layer. After healing of the operated tissue, the hardened cement can be removed.
- The temporary cement is sometimes medicated, usually with eugenol, which is antiseptic and local anaesthetic.
- The consistency of the cement can be controlled by additives.
- A cement of suitable consistency finds use as temporary filler for cavities.
- Examples of temporary fillers include zinc oxide, arsenical paste, etc.
- More often noble metals and their alloys are used as permanent filling materials for cavities. For example, gold and silver are used as permanent filling materials.

(f) Polishing Agents

- These are the substances which provide whiteness to teeth by their abrasive action.
- Examples include stannous fluoride, calcium carbonate, etc.

2.5.3 Dental Caries

- Dental caries, also known as tooth decay, cavities or caries is a disease of tooth caused by the acids produced by micro-organisms on carbohydrates.
- It starts forming on the surface of the mouth.
- The cavities may be of different colours, from yellow to black.
- It is believed that food particles lodged between the teeth undergo decay because of bacterial action and produce acids (lactic acid which leads to increased acidity in mouth, which ultimately affects the teeth).
- This disease is characterised by decalcification of tooth with mouth odour.
- The acid so produced dissolves enamel and dentine.
- The bacteria break down the hard tissue of the teeth, viz., enamel, dentine and cementum, by making acid form food debris on the tooth surface.

- Symptoms may include pain and difficulty while eating.
- Complications may include inflammation of the tissue around the teeth, tooth loss and infection or abscess formation.

Causes of Dental Caries

There are four main criteria required for caries formation:

- A tooth surface (enamel or dentine)
- Caries causing bacteria
- Fermentable carbohydrates (such as sucrose)
- Time

Prevention and Prophylaxis

- Regular brushing with a toothpaste containing fluorides.
- Less sugar intake in regular diet.
- Use brine (NaCl) warm solution, it has antimicrobial action.
- Keep mouth clean after every food intake.

2.5.4 Fluorides

2.5.4.1 Role of Fluorides

Role of fluoride in preventing dental caries has been well accepted.

- It increases the resistance of teeth to demineralisation.
- It provides strength to the teeth attacked by caries or plaque and renders them more resistant to decay.
- However, the essential factor that governs the effectiveness of fluoride ion is its concentration (about 1 ppm).
- When the concentration of fluoride exceeds 2-3 ppm, the condition called **dental fluorosis** develops, which is characterized by mottled, chalky and soft teeth.

2.5.4.2 Sources of Fluorides

- Fluoride is present in the human body in trace amounts.
- It is adequately obtained from food and water.
- It can be administered through topical and oral routes by including fluoride ions in toothpastes and mouthwashes.

2.5.4.3 Mechanism of Action of Fluorides

The deposition of fluoride prevents formation of caries by the following mechanisms:

(i) Fluoride acts by rendering the enamel resistant towards acid attack by oral microbes.

(ii) Fluoride inhibits the action of several bacterial enzymes which are necessary for growth of bacteria.

2.5.5 Phosphates

2.5.5.1 Role of Phosphates

- Inorganic phosphate salts are useful in the reduction of dental caries.
- Phosphate ions are needed for stronger and healthy teeth.
- Role of phosphate as cleaning agent is also important.

2.5.5.2 Source of Phosphates

- Phosphate salts, both soluble and insoluble forms, are obtained from normal diets.

2.5.5.3 Mechanism of Action of Phosphates

- The hydroxyapatite of tooth enamel is primarily composed of phosphate ions and calcium ions.
- Under normal conditions, there is a stable equilibrium between the calcium and phosphate ions in saliva and the crystalline hydroxyapatite that comprises 96% of tooth enamel.
- When the pH on the tooth surface drops below a critical level (pH of 5.5), i.e., it becomes acidic, phosphate in oral fluids combines with hydrogen ions (H^+) to form hydrogen phosphate species.
- Under these conditions, phosphate is "pulled" from the tooth enamel to restore phosphate levels in the saliva and the hydroxyapatite dissolves.
- As pH returns to normal, the calcium and phosphate in saliva can crystallise into the hydroxyapatite, remineralising the enamel.

2.5.6 Sodium Fluoride

Synonym : Chemiflour, Natri fluoridum
Molecular formula : NaF
Molecular weight : 41.99 g/mol
Category : Prophylactic anticaries agent
Dose : 2.2 mg once a day or 1.5 to 3 ppm in drinking water
Topically as 2% solution applied to teeth

Standards

It contains not less than 98.0% of NaF, calculated with reference to substance dried.

Methods of Preparation

- It is prepared by neutralising hydrofluoric acid with sodium carbonate.

$$HF + Na_2CO_3 \longrightarrow 2NaF + H_2O + CO_2\uparrow$$

- It is also obtained by double decomposition of calcium fluoride with sodium carbonate, while insoluble calcium carbonate can be removed by filtration.

$$CaF_2 + Na_2CO_3 \longrightarrow 2NaF + CaCO_3$$

Physical Properties

Colour : Colourless or white
Odour : Odourless
Taste : Slightly bitter taste
State : Occurs as both powder and crystals
Solubility : Soluble in water but insoluble in alcohol.
Nature : Aqueous solutions are corrosive

Chemical Properties

- Aqueous solution of salt yields alkaline reaction.
- On acidification of the salt solution, hydrofluoric acid is produced, which is a weak acid and is poisonous.

Identification Tests

- 1 g of sodium fluoride is placed in a platinum crucible in a well-ventilated hood. To this, 15 mL of sulphuric acid is added and covered with a piece of clear polished glass. The crucible is heated on a water bath for 1 hour. After 1 hour, the glass cover is removed and rinsed with water and wiped dry. It is be observed that the surfaces of glass have been etched.
- A 4% w/v, solution responds to the test for sodium.

Tests for Purity

It is tested for the presence of chlorides, heavy metals, fluorosilicates, loss on drying and pH.

- Chlorides should not be more than 0.012%.
- Heavy metals should not be more than 0.003%.
- Fluorosilicates should be absent.
- Loss on drying should not be more than 1%.
- The pH of freshly prepared saturated solution is 7.4.

Assay

Principle

- The assay is based on complexometric titration using disodium edetate.

Procedure

- An accurately weighed quantity of sample is dissolved in water.
- To this, a small amount of sodium chloride and alcohol is added.
- Contents are heated to boiling and drop-wise excess lead nitrate is added with stirring.
- On cooling, coagulated precipitate is filtered, residue is washed with dilute alcohol and the combined filtrate and washings are made to titrate with disodium edetate using xylenol orange as an indicator.

Incompatibility

- It is incompatible with ordinary glass.

Storage Condition

- Its aqueous solutions corrode ordinary glass and hence, the solution should be prepared in distilled water and stored in dark, pyrex bottles.

Pharmaceutical Uses

- As dental products and anticaries agent.
- Its 2% aqueous solution is widely used topically and occasionally over the surface of teeth periodically to protect the enamel of the teeth.
- To treat abnormal development of teeth.
- Administered as tablets for treating osteoporosis.
- Also used as a household insecticide occasionally.

2.5.7 Stannous Fluoride

Synonym	: Tin fluoride
Molecular formula	: SnF_2
Molecular weight	: 156.7 g/mol
Category	: Anticaries agent

Standards

It contains not less than 71.2% of stannous (Sn^{2+}) ions and not less than 22.3% and not more than 25.5% of fluoride, calculated with reference to substance dried.

Method of Preparation

- It is obtained by reaction of stannous with hydrogen fluoride.

$$2HF + Sn \longrightarrow SnF_2 + H_2\uparrow$$

- It is also prepared by evaporating a solution of stannous oxide in hydrofluoric acid in the absence of oxygen.

$$SnO + 2HF \longrightarrow SnF_2 + H_2O$$

Physical Properties

Colour : White
Taste : Unpleasant astringent-salty taste
State : Crystalline powder
Solubility : Freely soluble in water and insoluble in alcohol and organic solvents
Nature : Acidic (freshly prepared solution shows a pH range of 2.8 to 3.5)

Chemical Properties

- An aqueous solution of stannous fluoride on standing causes formation of white precipitates of stannous hydroxide.

$$SnF_2 + 2H_2O \longrightarrow Sn(OH)_2 + 2HF$$

- Aqueous solution of stannous fluoride deteriorates rapidly on standing because of oxidation of stannous cation to stannic form causing turbidity.

Identification Tests

- To 5 mL of 10% w/v solution in a test tube, addition of 2 mL calcium chloride results in the formation of white precipitate of calcium fluoride.
- When 2 drops of 10% w/v solution of stannous fluoride and 2 drops of silver nitrate are mixed on a spot plate, a brown precipitate is formed.
- It gives reactions characteristic of stannous and fluoride ions.

Tests for Purity

- The pH of 0.4% solution lies in the range of 2.8 to 3.5.
- The other impurities tested in the sample of stannous fluoride are water insoluble substances and should not be more than 0.2%.
- Antimony should not be more than 0.2%.
- Loss on drying should not be more than 0.5%.

Assay

Method 1 (Complexometric Titration)

Principle

- The assay is based on complexometric titration method using disodium edetate.

Procedure

- An accurately weighed quantity of sample is dissolved in water.
- To this, a small amount of sodium chloride and alcohol is added.
- Contents are heated to boiling and drop-wise excess lead nitrate is added with stirring.
- On cooling, coagulated precipitate is filtered, residue washed with dilute alcohol and the combined filtrate and washings are made to titrate with disodium edetate, using xylenol orange as an indicator.

Method 2

The assay is carried out both for stannous ions as well as for fluoride ions.

Assay Procedure for Stannous Ions

Principle

- The assay is based on oxidation-reduction titration method.

Procedure

- An accurately weighed 250 mg of stannous fluoride is transferred to 500 mL of conical flask.
- 300 mL of hot boiled 3 N HCl is added and a stream of oxygen-free inert gas is passed to dissolve stannous fluoride.
- Then it is cooled at room temperature and 5 mL of potassium iodide is added.
- This mixture is then titrated with potassium iodide-iodate solution using starch solution as an indicator.
- At the end-point, a colour change is observed from colourless to violet colour.

$$IO_3^- + 2Sn^{2+} + 6H^+ + Cl^- \longrightarrow ICl + 2Sn^{4+} + 3H_2O$$

Equivalence factor

- Each mL of 0.1 N KIO_3 Ξ 0.005935 g of stannous ions.

Assay Procedure for Fluoride Ions

Principle

- The assay is based on potentiometric titration method.

Procedure

- Fluoride ions are estimated by measuring potentiometrically the pH of the standard and test solutions.
- A standard graph is plotted between log concentrations and potential in millivolts.
- From the graph, the concentration of the unknown is determined using the following formula:

$$C = W / 125$$

where, C is the concentration of fluoride in μg/mL

W is the weight of stannous fluoride taken in mg

Incompatibility

- It is incompatible with calcium pyrophosphate and other calcium compounds.

Storage Condition

- It should be stored in tightly-closed containers in a dark place.

Pharmaceutical Uses

- As anticaries agent.
- In fluoride treatment of teeth.
- A freshly prepared 8% aqueous solution of SnF_2 is applied to clean the dry teeth. A single application has been reported to be sufficient for 6 to 12 months.
- To clean dry teeth.
- As a source of fluoride in dentifrices, gels, mouthwashes and solutions.
- Decreases the resistance of amalgam to corrosion when mixed with silver-tin alloy.

Advantages over Sodium Fluoride

- Greater effectiveness
- Simple application

Note: Its taste is unpleasant and can cause decolouration of teeth.

2.5.8 Calcium Carbonate

Synonym : Precipitated chalk, limestone

Molecular formula : $CaCO_3$

Molecular weight : 100.09 g/mol

Category : Antacid, excipients (pharmaceutical aid), cleaning agents or dentifrices

Dose : 1-4 g repeated according to need; usually six times a day.

Standards

It contains not less than 98.0% and not more than 100.5% of $CaCO_3$, calculated with reference to the sample dried at 105°C.

Method of Preparation

- Commercially, calcium carbonate is obtained by mixing the boiling solutions of calcium chloride and sodium carbonate. The resulting precipitate is allowed to settle down and collect on *calico* filter, washed with boiling water until it is free from chloride ions and dried.

$$CaCl_2 + Na_2CO_3 \longrightarrow 2NaCl + CaCO_3\downarrow$$

- From quicklime: Carbon dioxide gas is passed through an aqueous suspension of slaked lime, calcium carbonate precipitates which is filtered and dried.

$$CaF_2 + CO_2 \longrightarrow CaCO_3$$

Physical Properties

Colour : White

Odour : Odourless

Taste : Tasteless

State : Fine microcrystalline powder

Solubility : (i) Soluble in water containing dissolved CO_2 and NH_3 salts

(ii) Soluble in dilute acids with effervescence due to the presence of CO_2

(iii) Insoluble in alcohol, water, mineral acids and other organic solvents

Nature : Stable in air

Chemical Property

- Calcium carbonate neutralises acids with effervescence.

$$CaCO_3 + 2HCl \longrightarrow CaCl_2 + H_2O + CO_2\uparrow$$

Identification Tests

About 5 g of $CaCO_3$ is dissolved in 1 M acetic acid; it results in the formation of effervescence. Once the effervescence ceases, the solution is boiled for two minutes, allowed to cool and diluted to 100 mL with 2 M acetic acid and filtered.

- The filtrate is tested for the presence of calcium and carbonate.
- The residue is tested for the presence of substance insoluble in acetic acid.

Tests for Purity

It is tested for the presence of As, heavy metals, Ba, Mg, chlorides, sulphates and loss on drying.

- As should not be more than 4 ppm.
- Heavy metals should not be more than 20 ppm.
- Barium should not be more than 100 ppm.
- Magnesium and alkali metals should not be more than 0.5%.
- Chlorides should not be more than 250 ppm.
- Sulphates should not be more than 0.5%.
- Loss on drying should not be more than 2%.
- Substances insoluble in acetic acid should not be more than 0.2%.

Assay

Principle

- The assay is based on the complexometric titration method.

Procedure

- Accurately weighed 0.1 g of sample is dissolved in 3 mL of dilute HCl and 10 mL of water.
- It is boiled for 10 minutes and the sample is cooled to room temperature.
- It is then diluted to 50 mL with water.
- The sample solution is then titrated with 0.05 M EDTA (ethylene diamine tetra acetic acid) solution.
- After a few mL of titrations, 8 mL of NaOH and 0.1 g of calcon mixture is added and titration is continued until the colour of the solution changes from pink to full blue colour.

Equivalence Factor

- Each mL of 0.05 M EDTA Ξ 0.00500 g of $CaCO_3$.

Storage

- It should be stored in tightly-closed containers.

Pharmaceutical Uses

- Externally as dentifrice.
- Internally as antacid.
- As absorbent in diarrhoea.
- As calcium supplement in deficiency diseases.
- As food additive in homeopathy.

- In various pharmaceutical formulations, like dusting powders and pastes.
- In cosmetics and antibiotics.

Note: The use of calcium carbonate may cause constipation because it tends to liberate CO_2 gas. To overcome this problem, Ca^{2+} supplements are given along with magnesium compounds.

Formulation

- Calcium carbonate is formulated in the form of chewable tablets, in the form of suspension and in combination with other antacids, such as aluminium hydroxide.

2.5.9 Strontium Chloride

It is not official in any pharmacopoeia.

Molecular formula : $SrCl_2 \cdot 6H_2O$

Molecular weight : 266.6 g/mol

Category : Dentifrice, pharmaceutical aid (excipient)

Method of Preparation

- It is obtained by treating strontium carbonate with hydrochloric acid.

$$SrCO_3 + 2HCl \longrightarrow SrCl_2 + H_2O + CO_2\uparrow$$

Physical Properties

Colour : Colourless to white

Odour : Odourless

Taste : Tasteless

State : Powder or crystals

Solubility : Soluble in water and alcohol

Nature : Efflorescent in dry air and deliquescent in moist air

Chemical Property

- It reacts with sodium chromate to form yellow coloured strontium chromate, which is used as a corrosion inhibitor for aluminium.

$$SrCl_2 + Na_2CrO_4 \longrightarrow SrCrO_4 + 2NaCl$$

Storage

- It should be stored in tightly-closed containers.

Pharmaceutical Uses

- As dentifrice.
- As desensitising agent.
- As abrasive agent in dental preparations, like tooth paste and tooth powder.
- As calcium supplement in deficiency diseases.
- As excipients in soaps and cleaning powders.

Formulation

- It is used as 10% w/w toothpaste to relieve dental hypersensitivity, occasionally in medicated dentifrices.

2.5.10 Zinc Chloride

Synonym : Buffer of zinc
Molecular formula : $ZnCl_2$
Molecular weight : 136.3 g/mol
Category : Astringent, deodorant and pharmaceutical aid

Standards

It contains not less than 95.0% and not more than 100.5% of $ZnCl_2$, calculated with reference to the dried sample.

Method of Preparation

- It is obtained by treating zinc metal with dilute hydrochloric acid.

$$Zn + 2HCl \longrightarrow ZnCl_2 + H_2$$

Physical Properties

Colour : White
Odour : Odourless
Taste : Tasteless
State : Powder or crystals
Solubility : Soluble in water, alcohol and glycerine.
Nature : Deliquescent

Chemical Properties

- When ammonia is bubbled through a solution of zinc chloride instead of hydroxides, compounds containing complexed ammonia (ammines) are produced, $Zn(NH_3)_4Cl_2 \cdot H_2O$ and on concentration $ZnCl_2(NH_3)_2$.

$$ZnCl_3 + 2NH_3 \longrightarrow ZnCl_2(NH_3)_2$$

- Aqueous solution is distinctly acidic (pH 4.0). This is ascribed to its hydrolysis to form hydrochloric acid and basic zinc chloride similar to aluminium salts.

$$ZnCl_2 + H_2O \rightleftharpoons Zn(OH)Cl + H^+ + Cl^-$$

Identification Test

- It gives reactions characteristic of zinc and chloride ions.

Assay

Principle

- The assay is based on the complexometric titration method using disodium edetate.

Procedure

- Accurately weighed sample is dissolved in water and a definite volume is made.
- To a known volume of the solution, ammonia-ammonium chloride solution is added as buffer and the solution is titrated with standard disodium edetate using Eriochrome black T as an indicator.

Storage

- It should be stored in tightly closed non-metallic containers.

Pharmaceutical Uses

- As desensitising agent.
- As astringent and deodorant in mouthwashes and gargles.
- As pharmaceutical aid in insulin preparations.
- As a topical agent for foul smelling wounds and ulcers in the form of 2 to 4% lotion.
- Strong zinc chloride solution in combination with zinc oxide as a cementing and filling agent.
- In talcum powders.

2.5.11 Zinc Oxide Eugenol Cement

Zinc Oxide Eugenol (ZOE) has been extensively used in dentistry since 1890s.

Methods of Preparation

- ZOE is a material formed by combination of zinc oxide and eugenol contained in the oil of cloves.
- An acid-base reaction takes place with the formation of zinc eugenolate chelate.

- The reaction is catalysed by water and is accelerated by metal salts.
- ZOE cements are noted for the sedative effect the eugenol has on the pulp of teeth.
- Eugenol is found in the oil of cloves.
- The two-component ZOE cements are available in paste, paste of powder, and liquid formulas.
- ZOE cements are commonly used as cavity liners under dental amalgams or as temporary filling material.

Classification of ZOE

ZOE is classified into four types on the basis of its purpose of use.

- Type-I ZOE: For temporary cementation
- Type-II ZOE: For permanent cementation
- Type-III ZOE: For temporary filling and thermal base
- Type-IV ZOE: Cavity liner

Composition of ZOE Cement

Zinc oxide – 69% (principle ingredient)

White rosin – 29.3% (to reduce the brittleness of set cement and to maintain homogeneity)

Zinc acetate – 1.0% (accelerator, improves strength)

Zinc stearate – 0.7% (accelerator, plasticiser)

Eugenol – 85% (react with zinc oxide, act as anaesthetic)

Olive oil – 15% (plasticiser)

Pharmaceutical Uses

- ZOE is used in temporary and permanent cementation.
- Also used as pulp capping agent.
- Prior to root canal treatment, ZOE is used to reduce pain sensation in teeth.
- It has anaesthetic and anti-bacterial activity.
- Used as an impression material during construction of complete dentures.
- Used as mucostatic in the technique of taking impressions of gums and teeth.
- Commonly used as cavity liners under dental amalgams or as temporary filling material.

MULTIPLE-CHOICE QUESTIONS

1. Which of the following are not the properties of an acid?
   (a) Sour taste (b) Turns blue litmus red
   (c) Reacts with base to form water (d) Feels slippery on the skin
2. Which of the following are not the properties of a base?
   (a) Bitter taste (b) Turns red litmus blue
   (c) Reacts with salts to form acid (d) Feels slippery on the skin
3. In general, when an acid and a base are mixed –
   (a) A new acid and salt are formed (b) A new base and salt are formed
   (c) No reaction occurs (d) Salt and water are formed
4. Which of the following is a conjugate acid-base pair?
   (a) CH_3COOH and OH^- (b) HCN and CN^-
   (c) HCN and OH^- (d) HCl and OH^-
5. Which buffer is used for maintaining acid-base balance in the blood?
   (a) Carbonic acid-bicarbonate ion b) Acetic acid and sodium acetate
   (c) NH_4OH-NH_4Cl d) Formic acid-sodium formate
6. Sodium hydroxide is commonly known as
   (a) Slaked lime (b) Spirit of salt
   (c) Caustic soda (d) Quicklime
7. The body fluids found within the cells are called
   (a) Plasma (b) Extracellular fluid
   (c) Interstitial fluid (d) Intracellular fluid
8. Blood plasma belongs to
   (a) Intracellular fluid (b) Extracellular fluid
   (c) Interstitial fluid (d) None of the above
9. Most solutes in body fluid are
   (a) Electrolytes (b) Proteins
   (c) Sugars (d) Amino acids
10. Water is lost from the body through the actions of the
    (a) Kidneys (b) Lungs
    (c) Skin (d) All of the above
11. Which of the following ions diffuse easily between extracellular and intracellular compartments?
    (a) Magnesium (b) Sodium
    (c) Potassium (d) Chlorine

12. The major route of excretion for sodium ions (under normal conditions) is the
    (a) Kidneys (b) Lungs
    (c) Skin (d) None of the above
13. Calcium is essential for
    (a) Blood clotting (b) Blood pontification to whaler bone
    (c) Myasthenia gravis (d) All of the above
14. Fluoride inhibits caries formation by
    (a) Decreasing acid solubility of enamel
    (b) Bacterial inhibition
    (c) Both (a) and (b)
    (d) None of the above
15. Hydroxyapatite is a mixture of Ca^{2+} salt of
    (a) CO_3^- (b) PO_4^-
    (c) OH (d) All of the above
16. Dental caries is a medical term of
    (a) Cleaning action (b) Polishing action
    (c) Tooth decay or cavities (d) None of the above
17. Fluoride can be administered either
    (a) Orally (b) Topically
    (c) Both (a) and (b) (d) None of the above
18. Desensitisers tend to
    (a) Decrease hypersensitivity of teeth
    b) Increase hypersensitivity of teeth
    (c) Bacterial inhibition
    (d) None of the above
19. Example of desensitiser is
    (a) Zinc chloride (b) Sodium fluoride
    (c) Stannous fluoride (d) Calcium carbonate
20. .... is known as 'butter of Zinc'.
    (a) Zinc chloride (b) Zinc carbonate
    (c) Zinc bicarbonate (d) None of the above
21. Which vitamin is necessary for tooth formation?
    (a) Vitamin A (b) Vitamin C
    9c) Vitamin D (d) All of the above
22. Phosphate is used as
    (a) Cleansing agent (b) Flossing agent
    (c) Removing stains (d) None of the above

FILL IN THE BLANKS

1. Buffer solutions are those which resist the change in ....
2. pH of blood in the human body is about ....
3. Acid turns .... litmus ....
4. Base has .... taste.
5. According to Bronsted Lowry concept, an acid is .... while base is ....
6. Sodium chloride is used as ....
7. .... and .... are found in plasma and interstitial fluid.
8. .... are found in intracellular fluid.
9. The basic objective of replacement therapy is ....
10. Replacement therapy is needed for ....
11. Electrolyte solution can be given by .... and ....
12. ORS stands for ....
13. The concentration of electrolytes is expressed in ....
14. Extracellular fluid includes ....
15. Dentifrices are the compounds that are used for ....
16. The cleaning action of dentifrices depends on their ....
17. To prevent dental caries, toothpaste containing .... should be used.
18. Soluble salts of phosphate are ....
19. .... is a medical term for tooth decay or cavities.
20. Concentration of fluoride in drinking water is ....
21. Stannous fluoride is prepared by heating .... with .... in the absence of oxygen.
22. Chemical formula of sodium fluoride is .... and stannous fluoride is ....
23. .... reduces the sensitivity of the teeth to heat and cold.
24. Precipitated chalk is ....

SHORT QUESTIONS

1. Define the following terms: (a) acid, (b) base, and (c) buffer solution.
2. What are conjugate acid-base pairs?
3. Mention the preparation and uses of boric acid.
4. Comment on the statement that "All Arrhenius acids are also Bronsted acids but all Arrhenius bases are not Bronsted bases".
5. Which concept deals with "Electron-Donor-Acceptor System"?

6. Name the major ions involved in the fluid and electrolyte balance.
7. Name the largest body fluid compartment.
8. Define electrolytes and classify them with examples.
9. Define intracellular and extracellular fluid.
10. What is ORS?
11. What are dentifrices? List the examples of inorganic compounds used as dentifrices.
12. Define anticaries agents.
13. Classify cements and fillers with examples.
14. Define desensitising agents with examples.
15. What are mouthwashes? Give examples.
16. Does the desensitizer increase or decrease the hypersensitivity of teeth?

LONG QUESTIONS

1. Discuss the various theories of acids and bases.
2. Mention the classification of Lewis acids and Lewis bases.
3. Write a note on relative strength of acids and bases.
4. Mention the pharmaceutical importance of acids and bases.
5. Write in brief about handling and storage of acids and bases.
6. Define buffer solution. What is buffer capacity?
7. Write a note on buffer action.
8. Discuss buffer equations.
9. Mention the various criteria for buffers.
10. Give a brief account of various types of buffers in pharmaceutical systems.
11. Enumerate the precautions needed to be taken while preparing actual pharmaceutical buffer solutions.
12. How can buffer solutions be standardised?
13. Write in brief about stability of buffers.
14. Write a short note on buffered isotonic solutions.
15. Discuss importance of isotonicity in pharmaceutical solutions.
16. How can tonicity be measured?
17. Discuss the methods of adjusting tonicity and pH.
18. Mention the importance of buffer solutions in pharmacy.
19. Enlist the properties of buffer solutions.
20. Enumerate the role of buffers in pharmacy.
21. Give examples of some commonly used buffer solutions with their pH range.

22. Mention the advantages, disadvantages and uses of (a) phosphate buffer system, and (b) borate buffer system.
23. What are the factors that affect the buffer system?
24. Enumerate the functions of electrolytes.
25. Write in brief about electrolytic imbalance.
26. Write a note on major physiological cations and anions.
27. Discuss various conditions associated with the imbalance of physiological cations and anions.
28. Write a note on electrolyte combination therapy.
29. Narrate the following in brief: (a) sodium chloride and its preparations, (b) potassium chloride and its preparations, and (c) calcium gluconate and its preparations.
30. Mention the official preparations of sodium chloride.
31. Mention the official preparations of potassium chloride.
32. Discuss physiological acid-base balance.
33. Mention factors responsible for acid-base imbalance.
34. Explain the regulatory mechanisms of acid-base imbalance.
35. Explain the following terms: (a) metabolic acidosis, (b) metabolic alkalosis, (c) respiratory acidosis, and (d) respiratory alkalosis.
36. Write a note on electrolytes used in acid-base therapy.
37. Write the method of preparation, physical and chemical properties, storage and pharmaceutical uses of (a) sodium acetate, (b) potassium acetate, (c) sodium bicarbonate, (d) sodium citrate, (e) potassium citrate, and (f) ammonium chloride.
38. Discuss the following: (a) sodium lactate injection, (b) ammonium chloride injection, and (c) sodium bicarbonate injection.
39. Write a note on the combination of oral electrolyte powders and solutions.
40. Discuss new formulation of ORS with reduced osmolarity.
41. What are dental products? Classify them with examples.
42. What is dental fluorosis? Explain the role of fluorides in the prevention of dental caries.
43. Explain the role of phosphates in the prevention of dental caries.
44. Mention the chemical formula, method of preparation, properties, storage and uses of (a) sodium fluoride, (b) zinc chloride, (c) stannous fluoride, (d) strontium chloride, and (e) calcium carbonate.
45. Write a note on zinc oxide eugenol cement.

ANSWERS

Multiple Choice Questions

1. (d) 2. (c) 3. (d) 4. (b) 5. (a) 6. (c) 7. (d) 8. (c)
9. (a) 10. (d) 11. (d) 12. (a) 13. (a) 14. (c) 15. (d) 16. (c)
17. (c) 18. (a) 19. (a) 20. (a) 21. (d) 22. (a)

Fill in the Blanks

1. pH
2. 7.3 to 7.4
3. Blue, red
4. Bitter
5. Proton acceptor, proton donor
6. Fluid and electrolyte replenisher
7. Na, Cl
8. K, Mg, phosphate
9. To restore the volume and composition of body fluids
10. Heavy loss of water, diarrhoea, prolonged fever
11. Oral, IV
12. Oral rehydration salt
13. Milliequivalents per litre
14. Intestinal and vascular fluids
15. Cleaning teeth and gums
16. Abrasives
17. Sodium fluoride
18. Sodium monohydrogen phosphate, sodium dihydrogen phosphate
19. Dental caries
20. 1.5 to 3.0 ppm
21. Stannous oxide, hydrofluoric acid
22. NaF and SnF_2
23. Dentifrices
24. Calcium fluoride

3

Gastrointestinal Agents

3.1 INTRODUCTION

- The gastrointestinal tract (GIT) consists of a group of organs for digesting food; right from ingestion of food to the expulsion of wastes or faeces.
- It extends from the oesophagus to the anus.
- The entrance of the GIT is called the buccal cavity.
- The main portions of the GIT include the stomach, small intestine (duodenum, jejunum and ileum), large intestine (caecum, ascending, transverse and descending colons) and the rectum, with exit as the anus.
- In the stomach, digestion of proteins takes place in acidic medium with pepsin enzyme. Both acid, i.e., HCl and enzyme, i.e., pepsin are secreted in the stomach by specialised cells.
- In the small intestines, digestion of proteins takes place in alkaline medium in the presence of various enzymes; digestion of carbohydrates and lipids take place in the presence of enzymes and bile salts; in addition to absorption of digested food, vitamins and minerals.
- Diseases or undesirable conditions occur whenever any of the above functions goes wrong.

3.2 UNDESIRABLE CONDITIONS OF THE GIT

- Inadequate secretion of acid in the stomach causes achlorhydria or hypochlorhydria.
- Excessive secretion of acid in the stomach results in hyperchlorhydria or acidity and ultimately ulcers, inflammation and even pain.
- Gastric and sometimes duodenal walls become sensitive and give rise to pain.
- Accumulation of toxic substances or gases may take place.
- Insufficient peristaltic movement of the large intestine results in constipation.

- Inadequate secretion of saliva causes difficulty in food swallowing.
- Inadequate absorption of fluids and minerals from large intestine result in diarrhoea.
- Ingestion of poisonous substances may occur accidently or intentionally by some persons.

Various agents are used to bring the above conditions to the normal state. These include:

- Products for altering gastric pH (acidifying agents and antacids)
- Cathartics or laxatives
- Protectives and adsorbents
- Emetics

3.3 ACIDIFYING AGENTS OR ACIDIFIERS

- These are inorganic chemicals or drugs that are used to increase the gastrointestinal acidity.
- These agents are used in a condition when there is absence of insufficient secretion of hydrochloric acid in the stomach, which results in achlorhydria or hypochlorhydria.
- Some of these drugs are used to increase metabolic acidosis, whereas some are used to increase the gastric hydrochloric acid.

3.3.1 Mechanism of Action of Acidifiers

- These substances increase the acidity in the stomach by one of the following mechanisms:
  (i) They increase the acidic concentration due to the acidic nature.
  (ii) They increase the acidity in the stomach by stimulating the secretory cells of the GIT.

3.3.2 Classification of Acidifiers

Acidifying agents or acidifiers are classified into the following four types:

(a) Gastric acidifiers
(b) Systemic acidifiers
(c) Urinary acidifiers
(d) Acids

(a) Gastric Acidifiers

- These are the inorganic compounds that enhance the gastric acidity or restore the acidity of the stomach for a certain period of time.

- These are useful for the management of achlorhydria (a condition wherein no acid is secreted by the stomach) or hypochlorhydria (a condition wherein adequate amount of acid is secreted by stomach).
- For example, dilute hydrochloric acid.

(b) Systemic Acidifiers

- These are the inorganic compounds that neutralise the alkaline body fluids, especially blood.
- These are used in the management of systemic alkalosis (excessive accumulation of alkali in the blood).

(c) Urinary Acidifiers

- These are the drugs that render the urine acidic.
- These are useful in the treatment of certain urinary tract disorders.

(d) Acids

- These are the acidifiers that serve as pharmaceutical aid in the preparation, laboratory quality control, etc.

Note

- Achlorhydria patients are sensitive to spicy food. They can be best treated using dilute hydrochloric acid.

3.3.3 Ammonium Chloride

Synonym	: Sal ammoniac, ammonium muriate, salmiac, amchlor
Molecular formula	: NH_4Cl
Molecular weight	: 53.49 g/mol
Category	: Acidifier, expectorant, diuretic and electrolyte replenisher

Standards

It contains not less than 99.5% of NH_4Cl, calculated with reference to substance dried over silica gel for four hours.

Methods of Preparation

- Commercially, it is prepared by neutralising ammonia with HCl. The solution is evaporated till crude, vitreous, crystalline mass of ammonium chloride is obtained. The crude salt is purified either by crystallisation or sublimation.

$$NH_3 + HCl \longrightarrow NH_4Cl$$

- It is also prepared by treating ammonium sulphate with sodium chloride.

$$2NaCl + (NH_4)_2SO_4 \longrightarrow 2NH_3 + 2HCl + Na_2SO_4$$

$$2NH_3 + 2HCl \longrightarrow 2NH_4Cl$$

- It is also obtained by treating ammoniacal gas liquors with lime and the liberated NH_3 is passed into hydrochloric acid solution. The crude ammonium chloride obtained is known as sal ammoniac and occurs as tough, crystalline masses.

Physical Properties

Colour : White

Odour : Odourless

Taste : Cool saline taste

State : Fine or coarse crystalline powder

Solubility : (i) Soluble in water and freely soluble in alcohol and glycerine
(ii) Sparingly soluble in boiling water

Nature : (i) Slightly hygroscopic
(ii) Its 0.8% w/v solution is isotonic with serum.

Chemical Properties

- Freshly prepared aqueous solutions are neutral to litmus but become quickly acidic on standing because of hydrolysis.

$$NH_4Cl + 2H_2O \longrightarrow NH_4OH + H_3O^+ + Cl^-$$

- In its vapour form, it dissociates in ammonia and hydrochloric acid.

$$NH_4Cl \rightleftharpoons NH_3 + HCl$$

Identification Tests

- It gives reactions characteristic of ammonium salts and chlorides.
- A few mg of substance is heated with sodium hydroxide solution, leading to the evolution of ammonia gas, which is recognisable by its odour and by its action on moist red litmus paper.

$$NH_4^+ + OH^- \longrightarrow NH_3 + H_2O$$

Tests for Purity

It is tested for As, sulphate, Ca, iodate, Fe, heavy metals, loss on drying and sulphated ash.

- As should not be more than 2 ppm.
- Sulphate should not be more than 150 ppm.
- Calcium should not be more than 200 ppm.
- Iron should not be more than 20 ppm.
- Heavy metals should not be more than 10 ppm.
- Loss on drying should not be more than 0.5% w/w.
- The sulphated ash should not be more than 0.1% w/w.
- The pH of a 5% w/v solution is between 4.5 and 6.0.

Assay

Principle

- Based on acid-base titration technique.

Procedure

- About 0.1 g of NH_4Cl sample accurately weighed is kept in a conical flask and about 50 mL water is added to dissolve it.
- 5 mL of neutral formaldehyde solution is then added, so that ammonium chloride will be converted to methanimine and hydrochloric acid.
- The liberated acid is titrated with 0.1 N NaOH using phenolphthalein as an indicator.

$$NH_4Cl + HCHO \longrightarrow CH_2NH + HCl + H_2O$$

$$HCl + NaOH \longrightarrow NaCl + H_2O$$

Equivalence Factor

- Each mL of 0.1 N NaOH Ξ 0.05349 g of NH_4Cl.

Incompatibility

- It is incompatible with alkalis, carbonates of alkaline earths, lead and silver salts.

Storage Condition

- It should be stored in tightly-closed containers away from moisture.

Dose

- 3 to 6 g daily in the divided dose.

Pharmaceutical Uses

- As systemic acidifier.
- As expectorant in cough mixtures in doses of 300 mg to 1 g.

- In the maintenance of acid-base balance of the body fluids.
- Maintains urine at acidic pH, which is beneficial in treating urinary tract infections.
- As diuretic especially to excrete over dosage of basic drugs like amphetamine.
- In the treatment of lead poisoning.
- As a diaphoretic (increases sweating) and hence, reduces body temperature to a small extent.

3.3.4 Hydrochloric Acid

Synonym : Muriatic acid, spirit of salt (since first obtained by distillation of sea salt with sulphuric acid)

Molecular formula : HCl

Molecular weight : 36.5 g/mol

Category : Acidifying agent or acidifier

Dose : 0.6 to 8.0 mL

Standards

It contains not less than 9.5% w/w and not more than 10.5% w/w of HCl.

Method of Preparation

- It is obtained by the action of sulphuric acid on sodium chloride.

$$NaCl + H_2SO_4 \longrightarrow NaHSO_4 + HCl$$

$$NaHSO_4 + NaCl \longrightarrow Na_2SO_4 + HCl$$

Sodium bisulphate formed in the process is further mixed with some more quantity of sodium chloride and heated strongly in furnace to get more hydrogen chloride. Thus, the overall reaction taking place is:

$$2NaCl + H_2SO_4 \longrightarrow NaHSO_4 + 2HCl$$

- During the formation of caustic soda by electrolysis, large quantity of hydrogen and chlorine gas is evolved, both of which are combined to obtain HCl.

$$2NaCl + 2H_2O \longrightarrow 2NaOH + H_2\uparrow + Cl_2\uparrow$$

Physical Properties

Colour : Colourless

Odour : Pungent

Taste : Tasteless
State : Clear fuming liquid
Density : 1.04 to 1.05 g/cc
Solubility : Soluble in water and organic solvents
Nature : Acidic

Chemical Properties

- Its fume and pungent odour disappear on dilution with twice the quantity of water.
- Even highly diluted form is very acidic to litmus paper (converts blue litmus red).
- It is a strong acid and attacks the metal forming their chlorides with the evolution of hydrogen gas.

$$Ca + 2HCl \longrightarrow CaCl_2 + H_2\uparrow$$

$$2Na + 2HCl \longrightarrow 2NaCl + H_2\uparrow$$

- It takes part in various neutralisation reactions.

$$NaHCO_3 + HCl \longrightarrow NaCl + H_2O + CO_2\uparrow$$

$$NaOH + HCl \longrightarrow NaCl + H_2O$$

$$NH_3 + HCl \longrightarrow NH_4Cl$$

$$Na_2CO_3 + 2HCl \longrightarrow 2NaCl + H_2O + CO_2\uparrow$$

$$Na_2SO_3 + 2HCl \longrightarrow 2NaCl + H_2O + SO_2\uparrow$$

- Quantitatively, it is recognised by the formation of white precipitates of silver chloride when reacted with silver nitrate.

$$AgNO_3 + HCl \longrightarrow AgCl\downarrow + HNO_3$$

Identification Tests

- It gives the reactions characteristic of chloride ion.
- $HCl + KMnO_4 \rightarrow$ Chlorine gas

Test for Purity

- It is tested for the presence of As, heavy metals, bromides, iodides, sulphates and free chlorides.

Assay

Principle

- Based on the acid-base titration technique.

Procedure

- An accurately weighed 4 g of HCl is transferred to a stoppered flask containing 40 mL of water.
- This solution is then titrated with 1 N NaOH using methyl orange as an indicator.

$$NaOH + HCl \longrightarrow NaCl + H_2O$$

Equivalence Factor

Each mL of 1 N NaOH Ξ 0.03646 g of HCl.

Incompatibility

- It is incompatible with base, alkali metals, metals, metal oxides, iron, oxidizing agents, etc.

Storage Condition

- It should be stored below 30°C in well-closed containers made up of glass or other inert material.

Pharmaceutical Uses

- As a gastric acidifier for the management of hypochlorhydria or achlorhydria.
- As a pharmaceutical aid.
- As a solvent.
- As a catalyst in basic pharmaceuticals.

3.3.5 Dilute Hydrochloric Acid

Molecular formula : HCl
Molecular weight : 36.5 g/mol
Category : Acidifying agent or acidifier
Dose : 0.6 to 8.0 mL

Standards

It contains not less than 9.5% w/w and not more than 10.5% w/w of HCl.

Method of Preparation

It is obtained by mixing 276 g of conc. HCl with 726 g of purified water.

$$H_2 + Cl_2 \longrightarrow 2HCl$$

Physical Properties

Colour : Colourless
Odour : Odourless
Taste : Tasteless
State : Clear liquid
Density : 1.04 to 1.05 g/cc
Solubility : Soluble in water and organic solvents
Nature : Acidic

Chemical Properties

- It reacts with iron to change its colour.
- Dil. HCl + $KMnO_4 \rightarrow$ Chlorine gas

Identification Test

- It gives the reactions characteristic or chloride ion.

Test for Purity

- It is tested for the presence of As, heavy metals, bromides, iodides, sulphates and free chlorides.

Assay

Principle

- Based on acid-base titration technique.

Procedure

- An accurately weighed 10 g of HCl is transferred to a stoppered flask containing 40 mL of water.
- This solution is then titrated using 1 N NaOH using methyl orange as an indicator.

$$NaOH + HCl \longrightarrow NaCl + H_2O$$

Equivalence Factor

Each mL of 1 N NaOH Ξ 0.03646 g of HCl.

Incompatibility

- It is incompatible with base, alkali metals, metals, metal oxides, iron, oxidising agents, etc.

Storage Condition

- It should be stored below 30°C in well-closed containers made up of glass or other inert material.

Pharmaceutical Uses

- As a gastric acidifier for the management of hypochlorhydria or achlorhydria.
- In the management of metabolic alkalosis in the form of IV infusion that has been previously diluted with water or suitable infusion fluid.
- In the treatment of hypochromic anaemia and pernicious anaemia.
- As a solvent.
- As a catalyst in basic pharmaceuticals.
- As acidifier in liquid oral preparations.

Caution

Drinking straw is recommended in case of dil. HCl to avoid direct exposure of HCl with dental enamel, as it can get scratched.

3.4 ANTACIDS

- **Antacids** may be defined as the inorganic substances or chemical agents which are used for neutralising excess acid in the stomach of patients suffering from hyperchlorhydria (hyperacidity).
- These are usually alkaline in nature.
- It is important to note that water soluble antacids may produce systemic alkalosis due to absorbable ions disturbing acid-base balance of body fluids.
- Except sodium bicarbonate, most antacids are usually water insoluble.
- Antacids act on the GIT after being converted into soluble salts by hydrochloric acid. The cations such as calcium and aluminium exhibit constipating effect while magnesium shows laxative effect. It is for this reason that calcium-magnesium or aluminium-magnesium salts are generally employed as antacids.
- These combinations help in overcoming constipative effect of aluminium and laxative effect of magnesium.

- Further, antacids give symptomatic relief from pain by neutralising excess of hydrochloric acid. Thus, antacids find use in the treatment of ulcers by reducing pain.

3.4.1 Evaluation of Antacid Activity

- The efficacy of an antacid is measured in terms of neutralising capacity.
- Acid-neutralising test is done, which is an in vitro test wherein a known quantity of an antacid is added to the given amount of hydrochloric acid and then pH of this acid is measured at different intervals for determining the amount of acid consumed by the sample.
- However, the in vivo tests for the same have been unsuccessful.
- Further, no method is available which could evaluate an antacid by measuring pain reduction.
- Besides having acid neutralising activity, antacids may cause inactivation of protease enzymes or denaturation of it by means of metal cations or by adsorption of enzyme by antacid itself. However, such tests have neither been conclusive nor official.

3.4.2 Symptoms of Gastric Acidity

- Uneasy feeling from overeating
- Heart burn
- Feeling hungry even after meals

3.4.3 Consequences of Gastric Acidity

- Gastritis, i.e., inflammation of gastric mucosa
- Gastric ulcers
- Duodenal ulcers

3.4.4 Classification of Antacids

Antacids are classified into the following two types:

(a) Systemic antacids
(b) Non-systemic (non-absorbable) antacids

(a) Systemic Antacids

- These are water-soluble.
- Examples include sodium bicarbonate.

(b) Non-Systemic (Non-Absorbable) Antacids

- These are water insoluble.
- Examples include aluminium hydroxide gel, calcium carbonate, magnesium trisilicate, magnesium carbonate, etc.

3.4.5 Requirements of an Ideal Antacid

- It should be water-insoluble.
- It should have fine particle size.
- It should be non-absorbable.
- It should not cause systemic alkalosis.
- It should be able to exert its effect gradually and for a longer period of time.
- It should neither show laxative effect nor should it result in constipation.
- It should be stable and readily available.
- It should be free from any side effects.
- It should buffer in the pH range of 4 to 6.
- It should not interfere with digestion.
- It should be non-toxic and non-irritant.
- The reaction between antacid and gastric hydrochloric acid should not evolve gas.

Although no preparation is considered to be ideal for the above criteria, yet some compounds of sodium, aluminium, calcium and magnesium are used.

3.4.6 Sodium Bicarbonate (Refer to Section 2.4.23, pp. 136-139)

3.4.7 Aluminium Hydroxide Gel

Aluminium hydroxide gel is an aqueous white viscous suspension of hydrated aluminium oxide having varied amounts of basic aluminium carbonate.

The preparation may sometimes have oil of menthol and peppermint as a flavouring agent; and glycerine, sucrose, saccharin, etc., as sweetening agents and up to 0.05% sodium benzoate as a preservative.

Molecular formula : $Al(OH)_3$
Molecular weight : 78 g/mol
Category : Antacid
Dose : 7.5 to 15 mL, 200 mg 2 to 4 tablets in a day

Standards

Aluminium hydroxide gel contains not less than 3.5% and not more than 4.4% w/w of aluminium oxide (Al_2O_3).

Dried aluminium hydroxide gel (aluminium hydroxide powder) contains not less than 47% of Al_2O_3 when ignited to constant weight.

Method of Preparation

It is prepared by addition of hot solution of potash alum slowly with constant stirring to a hot solution of sodium carbonate. After complete removal of carbon dioxide, the precipitated aluminium hydroxide is filtered and washed thoroughly with hot water, until it is free from sulphates.

$$3Na_2CO_3 + 2KAl(SO_4)_2 + 3H_2O \longrightarrow 2Al(OH)_3\downarrow + 3Na_2SO_4 + K_2SO_4 + 3CO_2\uparrow$$

Precautions to be taken while preparing the gel

- The alum solution is added to the solution of sodium carbonate and not vice versa because that would yield a precipitate having alkali sulphate, which would be difficult to wash.
- Hot water and not boiling water should be used for washing the precipitate of $Al(OH)_3$, since the use of the latter tends to decompose aluminium hydroxide.

Physical Properties

Colour : White

Odour : Odourless

Taste : Tasteless

State : Viscous suspension

Nature : Translucent

Chemical Properties

- Aluminium hydroxide is an ideal buffer in the range 3 to 5, due to its amphoteric nature.
- It slightly affects both red and blue litmus papers.
- Aluminium hydroxide gel gives astringent aluminium chloride when it reacts with gastric hydrochloric acid. This results in nausea, vomiting and constipation.

$$Al(OH)_3 + 3HCl \longrightarrow AlCl_3 + 3H_2O$$

- When heated to red hot, it decomposes into water and aluminium oxide.

$$2Al(OH)_3 \longrightarrow Al_2O_3 + 3H_2O$$

Identification Tests

- A solution of hydrochloric acid gives reactions characteristic of aluminium (Al^{3+}).
- When equal volume of gel is diluted with distilled water, the pH of the solution should not be more than 7.5.

Tests for Purity

It has to be tested for alkalinity, ammonium salts, arsenic, calcium, iron, heavy metals, sulphate and acid consuming capacity.

- As should not be more than 1 ppm.
- Sulphate should not be more than 0.3%.
- Calcium should not be more than 0.25%.
- Fe should not be more than 20 ppm.
- Heavy metals should not be more than 10 ppm.
- 1 mL of formulation must be free from microbes, such as *Escherichia coli*.

Assay

Principle

- It is based on complexometric titration technique.

Procedure

- 5 g of accurately weighed sample is taken in a flask.
- To this, 3 mL of hydrochloric acid is added.
- This solution is now warmed on the water bath.
- After cooling, the solution is transferred to a 100 mL volumetric flask and the volume is made up to 100 mL.
- Now 20 mL of this solution is taken from the volumetric flask into a conical flask and exactly 40 mL of 0.05 M disodium edetate is added to it, followed by about 80 mL of water and a few drops of methyl red solution.
- To this, 1 N sodium hydroxide solution is added to neutralise this solution.
- This can be recognised by the change of colour from red to yellow.
- The solution in flask is then warmed on a water bath for about half an hour.
- To this, 3 g hexamine is added and then 0.5 mL of xylenol orange solution is added to it as an indicator.
- This solution is then titrated with 0.05 M lead nitrate.

$$2NaHCO_3 + 2HCl \longrightarrow 2NaCl + 2H_2O + 2CO_2$$

Equivalence Factor

- Each mL of 0.05 M disodium edetate Ξ 0.002549 g of Al_2O_3.

Storage Conditions

- It should be stored in well-closed containers at room temperature. It should not be allowed to freeze. For attractiveness, it is usually dispensed in blue or amber colour bottles.

Pharmaceutical Uses

- It is a non-systemic gastric antacid used in the management of gastric hyperacidity and peptic ulcers. It does not get absorbed in the alimentary canal and does not produce carbon dioxide.

- Used widely in the treatment of intestinal toxaemia and hyperchlorhydria.
- As astringent and skin protectant.
- Exerts soothening effect due to its demulcent properties.

Formulation

- It is formulated as a chewable tablet and as suspension.

3.4.8 Magnesium Hydroxide Mixture

It is 8% w/w oral suspension of hydrated magnesium oxide. It may be prepared from a suitable grade of light magnesium oxide.

Ingredients of Mixture

Magnesium sulphate	47.5 g
Sodium hydroxide	15 g
Light magnesium oxide	52.5 g
Chloroform	2.5 mL

Purified water (freshly boiled and cooled)
Sufficient to produce 1000 mL

Method of Preparation

Dissolve sodium hydroxide in 150 mL purified water, add light magnesium oxide, mix to form a smooth cream and then add sufficient purified water to produce 2500 mL.

Pour this suspension in a thin stream into a solution of magnesium sulphate with continuous stirring.

Allow the precipitate to subside, decant the clear liquid, transfer the residue to a calico strainer and allow draining and washing the precipitate with purified water, until all the sulphates are washed away.

Mix the washed precipitate with purified water, dissolve the chloroform in the mixture and add sufficient purified water to produce 1000 mL.

Physical Properties

Colour : White
State : Viscous suspension
Nature : Does not separate easily on standing

Identification Tests

- Its sample is alkaline to moist litmus paper.
- Its solution in dilute nitric acid gives all reactions characteristic of magnesium (Mg^{2+}).

Test for Purity

It has to be tested for As, Ca, heavy metals, soluble alkalis, soluble salts, carbonates and acid insoluble matter. Total microbial count does not exceed 1000 per mL and 1 mL and is free from *Escherichia coli*.

Assay

Principle

- It is based on the acid-base titration technique.

Procedure

- An accurately weighed amount of sample (5 mL) is taken in a flask.
- To it, 25 mL of 1 N sulphuric acid is added.
- The excess of acid is back-titrated with 1 N sodium hydroxide using methyl red as an indicator.

Equivalence Factor

- Each mL of 1 N sulphuric acid Ξ 0.02917 g of hydrated magnesium oxide calculated as $Mg(OH)_2$.

Storage Condition

- It should be stored in tightly-closed containers. It should not be kept in a cold place.

Pharmaceutical Uses

- Suspension of magnesium hydroxide is mainly used as an antacid to neutralise the stomach acid as well as a laxative in occasional constipation.
- Oral suspension gives relief in heart burn and indigestion problem.
- Also prescribed in the stomach ulcer or the stomach cancer.

Dose

- 5 to 10 mL as an antacid and 15 to 30 mL as a laxative.

Labelling

- The label on the containers states, "Shake well before use".

3.5 PREPARATIONS CONTAINING COMBINATION OF ANTACIDS

It is well known that no antacid is available in the market which satisfies the requirements of an ideal antacid.

3.5.1 Complications Associated with Singly-Used Antacids

- Sodium carbonate is quick acting but it results in side effect termed 'systemic alkalosis'.

- Sodium containing antacids may produce hypertension.
- Magnesium containing compounds are contraindicated in patients with renal disorders.
- Calcium containing compounds are contraindicated in patients suffering from renal and cardiac disorders.
- Aluminium containing compounds are contraindicated in patients with hypophosphatemia.
- Aluminium and calcium containing compounds produce constipation.
- Magnesium containing compounds may show laxative action.

3.5.2 Advantages of Using Combination of Antacids

- Combinations of antacids are used to counteract the constipative action of calcium and aluminium containing antacids with laxative effect of magnesium containing antacid.
- Combination of antacid preparation results in the product showing rapid onset of action and longer duration of action.
- Combining antacids with simethicone which acts as an antiflatulent and antifoaming agent, results in dispersion of gases.
- Combination of drugs results in synergistic effect.
- Combination also reduces the dose of the drug required to produce action.

3.5.3 Examples of Combination Preparations

(a) Compound Magnesium Trisilicate Oral Powder

- It contains magnesium trisilicate, chalk powder, sodium bicarbonate and heavy magnesium carbonate, each 250 g.

(b) Magnesium Trisilicate Mixture

- It is a suspension containing 5% w/w each of magnesium trisilicate, light magnesium carbonate and sodium carbonate in a suitable vehicle with a peppermint flavour.

(c) Compound Magnesium Trisilicate Tablets

- It contains in each 250 mg magnesium trisilicate and 120 mg dried aluminium hydroxide gel. Peppermint is added for flavour.
- It is one of the most common combinations.
- It has laxative, constipative and protective effects.

(d) Magaldrate

- It is a crystalline, white colour powder containing 28 to 39% w/w magnesium oxide and 17 to 25% w/w aluminium oxide.

(e) Algicon Tablet

- It is a chewable tablet which is prepared by aluminium hydroxide and magnesium carbonate co-dried gel (360 mg), magnesium alginate (500 mg), magnesium carbonate (320 mg) and potassium bicarbonate (100 mg).

(f) Simeco Tablets

- It contains aluminium hydroxide-magnesium carbonate co-dried gel (282 mg), magnesium hydroxide (85 mg) and activated dimethicone (25 mg).

3.6 CATHARTICS

- Cathartics may be defined as the drugs which activate peristalsis and motility of the gut, thus enabling bowel evacuation.
- They either hasten the passage of stools or cause reduction in the consistency.
- They are administered either by oral route in the form of suspensions, powders or via rectal route, such as enemas or suppositories.
- Thus, cathartics are beneficial in constipation and for expulsion of intestinal parasites.

Purgatives

- These are also cathartics which act similarly but are generally less effective compared to cathartics in their nature of action.

Laxatives

- Laxatives are the mild purgatives.

All these bring about same effect but vary in nature and mechanism of action.

Cathartics (most powerful), purgatives (less powerful) and laxatives (least powerful) act by retaining fluid in the bowel.

3.6.1 Classification and Mechanism of Action of Cathartics

Cathartics are classified into the following four types:

(a) Bulk forming cathartics
(b) Osmotic/saline cathartics
(c) Stimulant cathartics
(d) Stool softening cathartics

(a) Bulk Forming Cathartics

- These are fibrous in nature and undergo partial digestion.
- The undigested portion of the cathartic is hygroscopic in nature; it absorbs water from the lumen and forms soft, bulky faeces.

- The bulky stool so formed eventually activates the muscle of the intestine and hasten the movement of bowel through the colon.
- Examples include methyl cellulose, bran, isabgol, etc.

(b) *Osmotic/Saline Cathartics*

- These are the inorganic chemicals which are partially absorbed by the intestine.
- They are hypertonic solutions and act by stimulating the movement of water from the tissues into the colon, thereby increasing peristalsis, bowel movement and excretion of well-formed stools.
- Examples include lactulose and salts of magnesium, sodium and phosphate.

(c) *Stimulant Cathartics*

- These are the inorganic chemicals which stimulate fluid secretion in the intestine and thus, alter the GI motility.
- They exert direct action on the intestinal tract; bring about its irritation, thereby subsequently increasing the peristaltic activity facilitating bowel evacuation.
- Examples include bisacodyl, cascara, castor oil, rhubarb, senna, etc.

(d) *Stool Softening Cathartics (emollients)*

- These promote penetration of water and lipids, which liquefy the stool and promote its easy evacuation.
- Examples include docusate sodium.

3.6.2 Applications of Cathartics

- In the treatment of constipation.
- For cleansing the bowel prior to surgery or diagnosis.
- To treat poisoning or overdose of drugs.
- To promote bowel evacuation in bedridden patients.
- To prevent unnecessary strain and pressure in patients suffering from cardiovascular diseases, hernia and haemorrhoids.

3.6.3 Magnesium Sulphate

Synonym : Epsom salt
Molecular formula : $MgSO_4.7H_2O$
Molecular weight : 246.5 g/mol
Category : Osmotic laxative

Standards

It contains not less than 99.0% and not more than 100.0% w/w $MgSO_4$, calculated with reference to the ignited substance.

Methods of Preparation

- It is obtained by the action of dilute sulphuric acid on magnesium carbonate or magnesium oxide.

$$MgCO_3 + H_2SO_4 \longrightarrow MgSO_4 + H_2O + CO_2\uparrow$$

$$MgO + H_2SO_4 \longrightarrow MgSO_4 + H_2O$$

- It is also prepared by passing sulphur dioxide and air over precipitated magnesium hydroxide.

$$2Mg(OH)_2 + 2SO_2 + O_2 \longrightarrow 2MgSO_4 + 2H_2O$$

Physical Properties

Colour : Colourless or white
Odour : Odourless
State : Crystalline powder or crystals
Taste : Cool, saline bitter
Solubility : Soluble in water and sparingly soluble in alcohol

Chemical Property

- On gentle heating, it loses some of its water of hydration and gets converted into its monohydrate (white powder), which on further heating at 200°C becomes anhydrous.

$$MgSO_4{\cdot}7H_2O \longrightarrow MgSO_4{\cdot}H_2O$$

Identification Tests

- It gives reactions characteristic of magnesium and sulphate.
- To 0.5 mL neutral or slightly acidic solution of $MgSO_4$, addition of 0.2 mL of 0.1% w/v solution of titan yellow and 0.5 mL of 0.1 N NaOH give bright red precipitate.
- To 15 mg of $MgSO_4$ in 2 mL of water, 1 mL of dilute ammonia solution is added, resulting in the formation of white precipitate, which gets redissolved on adding 1 mL of 2 M ammonium chloride solution. Thereafter, addition of 1 mL of 0.25 M disodium hydrogen phosphate to this solution results in reappearance of white crystalline mass.

Tests for Purity

It has to be tested for As, Fe, Zn, heavy metals and loss on drying.

- As should not be more than 2 ppm.
- Chloride should not be more than 300 ppm.
- Fe should not be more than 200 ppm.
- Heavy metals should not be more than 10 ppm.
- Loss on drying should be in the range of 48 to 52%.
- 1 g dissolved in 10 mL water is neutral to litmus.
- 5 g of magnesium sulphate in 50 mL water gives a clear and colourless solution.

Assay

Principle

- The assay is based on complexometric titration.

Procedure

- An accurately weighed 0.3 g of sample is dissolved in 50 mL of water.
- To this, 10 mL of strong ammonium chloride solution is added.
- This solution is then titrated with 0.05 M disodium ethylene diamine tetra acetate using 0.1 g of Mordant Black 11 mixture as an indicator, until the pink colour gets discharged from blue colour.

Equivalence Factor

- Each mL of 0.05 M disodium ethylene diamine tetra acetate Ξ 0.00602 g of $MgSO_4$.

Incompatibility

- It is incompatible with alkali carbonates and alkali bicarbonates.
- Strong solutions are incompatible with sodium, potassium and ammonium bromide.

Storage Condition

- It should be stored in tightly-closed containers in a cool place because it is effervescent in nature.

Pharmaceutical Uses

- Used as saline purgative.
- Used in the form of enemas.
- Used as electrolyte replenisher.
- Helpful to promote evacuation of the gall bladder contents in the treatment of cholecystitis.

- As an antidote for barium, barbiturates and other types of poisoning.
- Also used in hypertension and convulsions due to CNS depressant property of magnesium.
- Also used in ventricular tachycardia.
- Twenty-five per cent solution of $MgSO_4$ is used in wet dressing for treatment of boils.

Note

- It should not be given to renal impaired patients.

3.6.4 Sodium Orthophosphate

Synonym	: Disodium hydrogen phosphate
Molecular formula	: $Na_2HPO_4 \cdot 12H_2O$
Molecular weight	: 358.14 g/mol
Category	: Laxative
Dose	: 2 to 16 g in divided dose daily

Standards

It is dodecahydrate of disodium hydrogen phosphate. It contains not less than 98.5% and not more than 101.0% w/w Na_2HPO_4 calculated with reference to the substance dried at 130°C.

Methods of Preparation

- It is obtained by adding sodium carbonate to a hot solution of phosphoric acid. Sodium carbonate fails to affect the third hydrogen of phosphoric acid and causes the formation of disodium hydrogen phosphate.

$$MgCO_3 + H_2SO_4 \longrightarrow MgSO_4 + H_2O + CO_2\uparrow$$

$$MgO + H_2SO_4 \longrightarrow MgSO_4 + H_2O$$

- It is also prepared by treating orthophosphoric acid with sodium hydroxide.

$$H_3PO_4 + 2NaOH \longrightarrow Na_2HPO_4 + 2H_2O$$

- Industrially, it is prepared in a two-step process by treating calcium bisphosphate ($CaHPO_4$) with sodium bisulphate ($NaHSO_4$), which results in precipitation of calcium sulphate while monosodium phosphate (NaH_2PO_4) remains in the solution.

$$CaHPO_4 + NaHSO_4 \longrightarrow NaH_2PO_4 + CaSO_4$$

In the second step, the resulting solution of monosodium phosphate is partially neutralised resulting in the formation of sodium orthophosphate.

$$NaH_2PO_4 + NaOH \longrightarrow Na_2HPO_4 + H_2O$$

- It is also obtained from calcium phosphate which on being treated with sulphuric acid yields calcium sulphate, which gets precipitated while the monobasic calcium phosphate formed along with remains in the solution.

$$Ca_3(PO_4) + 2H_2SO_4 \longrightarrow Ca(H_2PO_4)_2 + 2CaSO_4\downarrow$$

The above mixture after the addition of boiling water is filtered. The filtrate is then treated with sodium carbonate when dibasic calcium phosphate gets deposited, leaving sodium phosphate (disodium hydrogen phosphate or sodium orthophosphate) in solution.

$$Ca(H_2PO_4)_2 + Na_2CO_3 \longrightarrow Na_2HPO_4 + CaHPO_4 + H_2O + CO_2\uparrow$$

The solution is filtered off and the crystals of sodium orthophosphate are obtained by concentrating the solution and crystallising it.

Physical Properties

Colour : Colourless or white

Odour : Odourless

State : Crystalline powder or crystals

Taste : Saline

Solubility : Soluble in water but insoluble in alcohol

Nature : Its aqueous solution has a pH between 8 and 11 (moderately basic)

Chemical Properties

- On heating over 300°C, it is converted into sodium pyrophosphate.

$$2Na_2HPO_4 \longrightarrow Na_4P_2O_7 + H_2O$$

- On hydrolysis, sodium orthophosphate yields sodium hydroxide and phosphoric acid back from which it is formed.

$$Na_2HPO_4 + 2H_2O \longrightarrow H_3PO_4 + 2NaOH$$

- On heating with ammonium chloride, table salt is formed.

$$Na_2HPO_4 + NH_4Cl \longrightarrow NaCl + Na{\cdot}NH_4HPO_4$$

Identification Tests

- Its 10% solution gives reactions characteristic of sodium and phosphate.
- To 5 mL neutral solution of sample, addition of 5 mL of silver nitrate solution causes the formation of light yellow precipitate; this colour retains even on boiling the solution. However, the precipitate dissolves in 10 M ammonia solution and in dilute nitric acid.

$$Na_2HPO_4 + 3AgNO_3 \longrightarrow Ag_3PO_4 + H_2PO_4^-$$

$$Ag_3PO_4 \rightleftharpoons 3Ag^+ + PO_4^{3-}$$

$$Ag^+ + 2NH_3 \rightleftharpoons Ag(NH_3)_2]^+$$

Test for Purity

It has to be tested for alkalinity, As, Ca, Mg, heavy metals, chloride, sulphate and loss on drying.

Assay

Principle

- The assay is based on the acid-base titration.

Procedure

- An accurately weighed 6 g of sample is dissolved in 100 mL of water.
- This solution is then titrated with 0.5 N sulphuric acid using bromocresol green as an indicator at pH of 4.5.
- The result may be expressed on the basis of the salt dried at 130°C, so it is neutralised to sodium acid phosphate.

$$2Na_2HPO_4 + 2H_2SO_4 \longrightarrow 2NaH_2PO_4 + Na_2SO_4$$

Equivalence Factor

- Each mL of 0.5 N H_2SO_4 Ξ 0.07098 g of Na_2HPO_4.

Storage

- It should be stored in tightly-closed containers.

Pharmaceutical Uses

- Used as saline laxative.
- Used as cathartics.
- Used as buffering agent (pharmaceutical aid).

- Used as anti-hypercalcemic in the form of oral solution.
- Used in conjunction with trisodium phosphate in water softening treatment.
- Used to treat constipation or to clean the bowel before colonoscopy.
- Its presence prevents coagulation, hence used in the preparation of condensed milk.
- Used as anti-caking additive in powdered products.

3.6.5 Kaolin

Synonym : The china clay, hydrated aluminium silicate
Molecular formula : $Al_2O_3 \cdot 2SiO_2 \cdot 2H_2O$
Molecular weight : 258 g/mol
Category : Pharmaceutical aid
Dose : 15 to 75 g in three divided doses daily

Methods of Preparation

- It is hydrated aluminium silicate, widely distributed in nature. It is prepared when rocks are mined, executed and the impurities are washed with the flow of water and then powdered.
- It exists in two forms, viz., heavy kaolin and light kaolin.
- The rock is elutriated with water and large-sized particles are separated. The turbid liquid is allowed to settle; **heavy kaolin** containing large particles and colloidal kaolin (light kaolin) containing particles of small size are separated and dried.

Physical Properties

Colour : Normally white in colour; sometimes tinged grey, yellow brown, blue or red due to impurities
Odour : When moistened with water, develops marked clay-like odour
State : Slightly plastic light, soapy to touch and its surface takes high polish on rubbing
Taste : Earthy or clay-like
Solubility : Insoluble in water

Chemical Properties

- Its fusion point ranges between 1700 and 1800°C.
- When moistened with water, it produces darker colour.
- On heating, it loses water molecules.
- It gets decomposed by prolonged boiling or on treatment with conc. sulphuric acid.
- It is treated to white heat and then it becomes more resistant to heat.

Identification Test

- It gives reactions characteristic of aluminium.

Tests for Purity

- Development of pink colour due to addition of phenolphthalein to an aqueous suspension indicates the presence of alkaline nature.
- For the determination of lead, the substance is digested with nitric acid. The reaction mixture is then centrifuged and in the supernatant liquid, limit test for lead is carried out.
- Iron is detected by triturating kaolin with water, sodium salicylate is added; the mixture does not acquire more than a slight reddish tint.

Pharmaceutical Uses

- Used as adsorbent, antidiarrhoeal and increases the bulk of faeces.
- Adsorbs toxins from the GIT and thus, beneficial in diarrhoea.
- Used in the treatment of chronic ulcerative colitis.
- Externally, heavy kaolin has some uses as poultice, dusting powder, foot powder and as an ingredient of toilet preparation.
- Used as filtering medium and clarifying and decolourising medium.
- Sometimes, used as tablet diluent.

3.6.6 Bentonite

Synonym : Clay

Molecular formula : $Al_2O_3.4SiO_2.H_2O$

Molecular weight : 422.286 g/mol

Category : Pharmaceutical aid, emulsifying and suspending agent

It is a colloidal hydrated aluminium silicate which occurs naturally.

It is obtained from the naturally occurring sources.

Bentonite was previously called Taylorite, which was named after William Taylor, who first began to draw attention to the clay deposits. This clay consists mostly of montmorillonite, a name of the particular clay that was discovered in Montmorillon, France, named by Mauduyt in 1847.

When bentonite is subjected to analysis, it is found that it is an aluminosilicate having SiO_2, Al_2O_3, Fe_2O_3, CaO, MgO and some sodium and potassium. In acid solution, the metallic ions have been readily exchangeable for hydrogen ions and hence, bentonite could not be readily maintained in an acidic medium.

Physical Properties

Colour : Pale buff or cream coloured

Odour : Odourless

State : Fine powder, free from grit

Taste : Slightly earthy taste

Solubility : Almost insoluble in water but swells to about twelve times its volume when added to water. It neither dissolves nor swells in organic solvents.

Nature : Possess swelling, absorptive and binding property, excellent plasticity, lubricity, high shear and compressive strength, low permeability and compressibility, good dry sealing property, etc.

Identification Tests

- When a sample of bentonite is fused with anhydrous sodium carbonate and extracted with water, followed by repeated extractions with dilute HCl, it yields a residue of silica.
- This acid solution so obtained, after neutralisation gives reactions characteristic of aluminium.

Tests for Purity

It has to be tested for pH, gel formation, swelling factor and loss on drying.

- pH of 2% suspension in water should lie in the range of 9 to 10.5.
- When bentonite is dried to constant weight at 105°C, it should not lose less than 5% and not more than 12% of its weight.

Incompatibility

- Its suspensions have been affected by electrolytes.
- It should be readily used in acidic media because metallic ions have been exchangeable for hydrogen ions.

Pharmaceutical Uses

- As a pharmaceutical aid.
- As a protective colloid to stabilise emulsions.
- Used to suspend other insoluble powders.
- Also used as a base for many pharmaceutical preparations, including plasters and ointments.
- Used as an emulsifier for oil in water emulsions.
- As an ingredient of calamine lotion IP.
- As cathartics. Bentonite has negatively charged molecules, which give adsorptive properties to it.

- Used as an antidote. It has the ability to pass through the intestinal tract and attract the toxins which are positively charged. When they (i.e., bentonite and toxin) are in contact with each other, they swap ions and are bound together and the toxic molecule is absorbed by the clay molecule.
- As an antidote in mercury poisoning.
- Used to remove toxic metals and chemicals following radiation treatments.
- Promotes healthy bacteria balance and detoxify the digestive system.
- Also supports liver detoxification.
- Helps to remove the internal parasites from the digestive system.
- Used as antioxidant, as it is found to be active against free radicals.
- Helps in colon cleansing.
- Supports to boost immune system.
- Used as a binder if chemically compatible with other ingredients.

3.7 ANTIMICROBIAL AGENTS

- These are the chemicals and their preparations which help in reducing or preventing infection due to pathogenic microbes.

3.7.1 Classification of Antimicrobial Agents

Antimicrobial agents are classified into the following types:

(a) Antiseptics
(b) Disinfectants
(c) Germicides
  (i) Bactericide
  (ii) Fungicide
  (iii) Virucide
  (iv) Amoebicide
(d) Bacteriostatics
(e) Sanitizers
(f) Sterilizers

(a) Antiseptics

- These substances kill or prevent the growth of micro-organisms.
- These preparations are meant to be applied to the living tissues only.
- The antiseptics are protein denaturants and act on the enzymes in the bacteria.
- Examples include hydrogen peroxide.

(b) Disinfectants

- These substances prevent infection by the destruction of pathogenic micro-organisms.
- These are meant to be applied to inanimate objects only.
- These are widely used for home and hospital sanitation.
- They are bactericidal and rapidly produce irreversible lethal effects.
- Examples include cresol with soap solution.

(c) Germicides

- These are the substances which kill micro-organisms.
  - (i) ***Bactericides*** kill bacteria.
  - (ii) ***Fungicides*** kill fungi.
  - (iii) ***Virucides*** kill viruses.
  - (iv) ***Amoebicides*** kill amoebas.

(d) Bacteriostatic

- These substances inhibit or arrest the growth of bacteria.

(e) Sanitizers

- These disinfectants are used to maintain general public health standards.
- Sanitation is mainly concerned with cleansing or washing away the organic matter like saliva, mucous membrane, etc.

(f) Sterilizers

- Sterilization is the process of complete destruction of all living micro-organisms, including bacterial spores.
- It can be done by physical methods (like application of heat or radiation) or by chemical means (such as use of chemical disinfectants).

3.7.2 Properties of Ideal Antimicrobial Agents

They should:

- possess antiseptic or germicide activity but not bacteriostatic activity,
- have rapid onset of action,
- have sustained activity,
- possess good therapeutic index,
- not cause local cellular damage,
- not interfere with 'body defences',
- not show systemic toxicity,
- possess broad spectrum of activity against bacteria, virus, protozoa, etc,

- possess adequate 'lipid-water distribution coefficient',
- be economical,
- be effective at low concentration, and
- be compatible with other ingredients.

3.7.3 Mechanism of Action

The mechanism of action of antimicrobial agents may range from mild astringent to powerful oxidative processes.

Inorganic compounds generally exhibit antimicrobial action by involving either of the following three mechanisms:

(a) Oxidation
(b) Halogenation
(c) Protein precipitation or binding

(a) Oxidation

- These are the anti-infective agents who bring about oxidation of active functional groups present in proteins or enzymes vital to the growth or survival of micro-organisms.
- It causes the change in conformation of the protein by converting the sulfhydryl group to disulphide form.
- Examples include hydrogen peroxide, potassium permanganate, halogens, non-metal anions, etc.

(b) Halogenation

- These substances act on the peptide linkage of micro-organisms and add halogens; thereby altering the normal functioning of the microbial cell.
- Examples include iodine, povidone iodine, chlorinated lime, hypohalites, hypochlorites, etc.

(c) Protein Precipitation

- The antimicrobial agents containing metallic ions react with the polar groups of proteins and form a complex, thereby causing precipitation of proteins and hence, their inactivation.
- Examples include boric acid, borax, silver nitrate, mercurial compounds, etc.

3.7.4 Potassium Permanganate

Synonym : Permanganic acid
Molecular formula : $KMnO_4$
Molecular weight : 158.03 g/mol
Category : Antiseptic, powerful oxidising agent

Standards

It contains not less than 99.0% and not more than 100.5% $KMnO_4$.

Methods of Preparation

- It is obtained by electrolytic oxidation of potassium manganate with boiling water.

$$2K_2MnO_4 + 2H_2O \longrightarrow 2KMnO_4 + 2KOH + H_2\uparrow$$

- It is prepared by mixing a solution of potassium hydroxide with powdered manganese dioxide and potassium chlorate. The mixture is boiled and evaporated to get the residue, which is heated in iron pans until it has acquired a paste-like consistency.

$$KOH + 3MnO_2 + KClO_3 \longrightarrow \underset{\text{Potassium manganate}}{K_2MnO_4} + KCl + 3H_2O$$

- Potassium manganate (green colour) so obtained is then extracted with boiling water and a current of chlorine, CO_2 or ozonised air is passed into the liquid until it gets converted into permanganate. The MnO_2 formed is removed continuously so as to prevent its breaking down to the permanganate.

$$6K_2MnO_4 + 3Cl_2 \longrightarrow 6KMnO_4 + 6KCl$$

When carbon dioxide is passed through the solution in place of chlorine, only two-thirds of manganate gets converted into $KMnO_4$. One third is converted into MnO_2.

$$3K_2MnO_4 + 2CO_2 \longrightarrow 2KMnO_4 + MnO_2 + 3K_2CO_3$$

The solution of $KMnO_4$ is drawn off from any precipitate of MnO_2, which is then concentrated and crystallised. The crystals are then centrifuged and dried.

Physical Properties

Colour : Dark purple
Odour : Odourless
Taste : Sweetish and astringent
State : Granular powder or monoclinic prismatic crystals with metallic lustre
Solubility : Soluble in cold water and freely soluble in boiling water
Nature : Almost opaque with a blue metallic lustre

Chemical Properties

- When heated, potassium permanganate decrepitates and decomposes at a high temperature (240°C).

$$2KMnO_4 \xrightarrow{\Delta} K_2MnO_4 + MnO_2 + O_2\uparrow$$

- When hydrochloric acid is added to a solution of potassium permanganate, chlorine gas is evolved.

$$2KMnO_4 + 16HCl \longrightarrow 2KCl + 2MnCl_2 + 8H_2O + 5Cl_2\uparrow$$

- When H_2S is passed through potassium permanganate solution, which is acidified with HCl, the violet colour disappears and sulphur gets precipitated.

$$2KMnO_4 + 6HCl + 5H_2S \longrightarrow 2KCl + 2MnCl_2 + 8H_2O + 5S\downarrow$$

- It is a powerful oxidising agent. Alkaline or neutral solution of potassium permanganate is able to oxidise iodide to iodate.

$$2KMnO_4 + H_2O + KI \longrightarrow 2MnO_2 + 2KOH + KIO_3$$

- While in acidic medium, iodine gets liberated from iodides.

$$2KMnO_4 + 10KI + 8H_2SO_4 \longrightarrow 6K_2SO_4 + 2MnSO_4 + 5I_2 + 8H_2O$$

- In acidic solutions, ferrous salts get oxidised to ferric salts.

$$2KMnO_4 + 10FeSO_4 + 8H_2SO_4 \longrightarrow K_2SO_4 + 2MnSO_4 + 5Fe_2(SO_4)_2 + 8H_2O$$

- When a solution of hydrogen peroxide is added to an acidified potassium permanganate solution, the colour of permanganate solution gets discharged.

$$2KMnO_4 + 3H_2SO_4 + 5H_2O_4 \longrightarrow K_2SO_4 + 2MnSO_4 + 8H_2O + 5Cl_2\uparrow$$

Identification Tests

- When $KMnO_4$ solution is acidified with sulphuric acid and heated to 70°C, it gets decolourised by a solution of hydrogen peroxide.
- When heated to redness, it decrepitates evolving oxygen and black residue remains. The residue gives potassium hydroxide when water is added. The resulting solution gives reactions characteristic of potassium.

Tests for Purity

It has to be tested for chloride and sulphate.

- $KMnO_4$ is boiled with 95% aqueous alcohol to destroy the purple colour, so that the colour does not interfere with the limit test. The precipitated manganese dioxide is removed by filtration.

$$2KMnO_4 + 3CH_3CH_2OH \longrightarrow 2KOH + 2MnO_2 + 3CH_3CHO + 2H_2O$$

The solution so obtained is then tested for chloride and sulphate.

Assay

Principle

- The assay is based on iodometric type of redox titration.

Procedure

- An accurately weighed 0.3 g of $KMnO_4$ is dissolved in 100 mL of water.
- 20 mL of this solution is taken in conical flask, 1 g of KI and 10 mL of 2 N HCl is added and the liberated iodine is titrated with 0.1 M $Na_2S_2O_3$ using starch solution as an indicator.

$$2KMnO_4 + 10KI + 8H_2SO_4 \longrightarrow 6K_2SO_4 + 2MnSO_4 + 5I_2 + 8H_2O$$

Equivalence Factor

- Each mL of 0.1 M $Na_2S_2O_3 \equiv$ 0.003160 g of $KMnO_4$.

Mechanism of Action

- Potassium permanganate releases the nascent oxygen, i.e. [O], which by oxidative mechanism inhibits the actions of micro-organisms and their growth.

Incompatibility

- It is incompatible with iodides, reducing agents, most organic substances, and H_2O_2.

Storage

- It is stored in tightly-closed containers.
- It must be handled with care because of chances of explosion when brought in contact with readily oxidisable substances.

Pharmaceutical Uses

- As antiseptic in mouthwash.
- As cleaning agent for wounds, ulcers, etc.

- As topical anti-infective agent.
- As antidote in barbiturate, chloral hydrate, alkaloid poisonings, etc.
- As deodorant.
- For gastric lavage treatment.
- It stains the skin or tissues.
- Its solution is used in bath for eczema and acute dermatoses patients.
- Commonly used as an antiseptic in veterinary practices.

Caution

- Great care should be taken in handling $KMnO_4$ because dangerous explosion may occur if it is brought in contact with organic matter or any rapidly oxidisable substance.

3.7.5 Boric Acid

Synonym : Boracic acid, orthoboric acid
Molecular formula : H_3BO_3
Molecular weight : 61.83 g/mol
Category : Local anti-infective

Free boric acid occurs in seawater, many plants and nearly in all fruits. Although, its largest natural source occurs in combined form.

$Na_2B_4O_7 \cdot 4H_2O$ (Resonite)
$Na_2B_4O_7 \cdot 10H_2O$ (Borax)
$CaB_4O_7 \cdot 4H_2O$ (Borocalcite)
$Ca_2B_6O_{11} \cdot 5H_2O$ (Colemanite)

Standards

It contains not less than 99.5% and not more than 100.5% of H_3BO_3 with reference to dried substance.

Methods of Preparation

- Boric acid is prepared from native borax and from borates by reacting them with hydrochloric acid or sulphuric acid.

$$Na_2B_4O_7 + H_2SO_4 + 5H_2O \longrightarrow Na_2SO_4 + 4H_3BO_3$$

- Commercially, boric acid is prepared by decomposing certain naturally occurring borates.

$$Ca_2B_6O_{11} \cdot 5H_2O + 2SO_2 + 2H_2O \longrightarrow 2CaSO_3 + 6H_3BO_3$$

$$Na_2B_4O_7 \cdot 10H_2O + 2HCl \longrightarrow 4H_3BO_3 + 2NaCl + 5H_2O$$

Physical Properties

Colour : Colourless or white

Odour : Odourless

Taste : Bitter and acidic

State : Crystalline powder, pearly scales or six-sided triclinic crystals

Solubility : (i) Soluble in water and alcohol

(ii) Freely soluble in boiling water and alcohol

Nature : Acidic in nature, unctuous, greasy or soapy to touch and stable in air

Chemical Properties

- Boric acid on heating to 100°C loses one molecule of water to give metaboric acid HBO_2, which on heating to 160°C further causes loss of one molecule of water to give tetraboric acid $H_2B_4O_7$. Heating to still higher temperature results in the formation of anhydride of boric acid, called boron trioxide, B_2O_3.
- With alkali substance, it forms salt due to its acidic nature.

$$H_3BO_3 + NaOH \longrightarrow NaBO_2 + 2H_2O$$

- On reaction with sodium carbonate, it liberates carbon dioxide and borax ($Na_2B_4O_7$) is formed.

$$4H_3BO_3 + Na_2CO_3 \longrightarrow Na_2B_4O_7 + CO_2 + 6H_2O$$

- It reacts with alkali acids and fluorides to form sodium fluoroborate ($NaBF_4$).

$$2NaHF_2 + H_3BO_3 \longrightarrow NaBF_4 + NaOH + 2H_2O$$

- On reaction with calcium fluoride and conc. sulphuric acid, it forms boron trifluoride.

$$2CaF_2 + 3H_2SO_4 + 2H_3BO_3 \longrightarrow 3CaSO_4 + 2BF_3 \quad 6H_2O$$

- Ethanolic solution of boric acid when heated, gives ethyl borate. This ethyl borate burns with green edge flame.

$$H_3BO_3 + 3CH_3CH_2OH \longrightarrow B(CH_3CH_2O)_3 + 3H_2O$$

Identification Tests

- Solution of boric acid in alcohol in the presence of few drops of conc. H_2SO_4 burns with a green border flame due to formation of ethyl borate.

$$H_3BO_3 + 3CH_3CH_2OH \longrightarrow B(CH_3CH_2O)_3 + 3H_2O$$

- Aqueous solution of boric acid is faintly acidic.
- An aqueous solution of boric acid on addition of HCl turns the turmeric paper to pink or brownish red, which upon being moistened with NH_3 solution changes to blue or greenish black.

Tests for Purity

It is tested for As, heavy metals, sulphate and loss on drying.

- Arsenic should not be more than 10 ppm.
- Sulphate should not be more than 450 ppm.
- Heavy metals should not be more than 20 ppm.
- Loss on drying should not be more than 0.5%.

Assay

Principle

- The assay is based on acid-base titration.

Procedure

- An accurately weighed 2 g of sample is dissolved in 50 mL of water and 100 mL glycerol previously neutralised with phenolphthalein.
- This solution is then titrated with 1 N NaOH using phenolphthalein as an indicator. At the endpoint, colour changes to red.

Equivalence Factor

- Each mL of 1 N NaOH Ξ 0.06183 g of H_3BO_3.

Incompatibility

- It is incompatible with alkali carbonates and hydroxides.

Storage

- It is stored in air-tight containers in a cool place.

Pharmaceutical Uses

- As a weak germicide.
- As local anti-infective.
- Its aqueous solutions are used as eyewash and mouthwash.
- Employed in dusting powder, ointments, lotions, local antiseptic creams, etc., meant for local application to mucous membrane, skin or eyes.
- As a buffer in epinephrine bitartrate ophthalmic solutions.
- As an ingredient of boroglycerine, which is used as suppository base.
- As an emollient antiseptic in the treatment of diaper rash.

Caution

- It can be dangerous if ingested. Therefore, its container should bear the warning "Not for internal use".

3.7.6 Hydrogen Peroxide

Synonym : Oxygenated water
Molecular formula : H_2O_2
Molecular weight : 34.016 g/mol
Category : Antiseptic

Standards

It should contain not less than 6% w/w H_2O_2, which corresponds to about 20 times its volume of available oxygen.

Methods of Preparation

- It is obtained by adding a thick paste of barium peroxide in ice cold water to a calculated quantity of ice cold dilute sulphuric acid. The insoluble barium sulphate is filtered off.

$$BaSO_4 + H_2SO_4 \longrightarrow H_2O_2 + BaSO_4 \downarrow$$

- It can also be prepared by decomposing barium peroxide with phosphoric acid or by passing carbon dioxide through suspension of barium peroxide in water.

$$3BaO_2 + 2H_3PO_4 \longrightarrow Ba_3(PO_4)_2 + 3H_2O_2$$

- It is also obtained by treating sodium peroxide with dilute H_2SO_4 at low temperature. Sodium sulphate crystallises and H_2O_2 is distilled under 10 mm pressure.

$$Na_2O_2 + H_4SO_4 \longrightarrow Na_2SO_4 + H_2O_2$$

- It can also be manufactured by electrolysis of ice cold 50% sulphuric acid. Persulphuric acid is formed, which on distillation under reduced pressure, gives H_2O_2.

$$2H_2SO_4 \longrightarrow H_2S_2O_8 \downarrow + H_2$$

$$H_2S_2O_8 + 2H_2O \longrightarrow 2H_2SO_4 + H_2O_2$$

Physical Properties

Colour : Colourless
Odour : Odourless
Taste : Slightly acidic
State : Liquid
Solubility : Soluble in water and can be extracted with solvent ether

Chemical Properties

- Hydrogen peroxide gets decomposed when it comes in contact with oxidisable matter or when made alkaline.

$$2H_2O_2 \longrightarrow 2H_2O + O_2$$

  The decomposition of hydrogen peroxide is promoted by catalysts, such as Cu, Fe, Mn, etc., while small quantity of acids like H_2SO_4, H_3PO_4 and alcohol, if added, retards the composition.
- It is a strong oxidising agent.

Identification Tests

- When made alkaline and heated, it gets decomposed with effervescence, evolving oxygen.
- To 1 drop, 20 mL of water, 1 drop of potassium chromate and 2 mL of solvent ether are added and shaken. The ether layer becomes blue.

Test for Purity

- It is tested for acidity, preservative, loss on evaporation, barium and stability.

Assay

Hydrogen peroxide and acidified potassium permanganate both are oxidising agents. They reduce one another with the evolution of gaseous oxygen. Hydrogen peroxide reduces $KMnO_4$ solution and causes its decolouration. At the end-point, excess drops of $KMnO_4$ give pink colour. Potassium permanganate itself acts as self-indicator.

Principle

- The assay is carried out by permanganate method.

Procedure

- 10 mL of the sample is diluted to 25 mL in a volumetric flask with purified water.
- To 25 mL of this solution, 10 mL 5 N sulphuric acid is added.
- The contents are titrated with 0.1 N potassium permanganate solution until a faint pink colour is obtained.

$$2KMnO_4 + 3H_2SO_4 + 5H_2O_2 \longrightarrow K_2SO_4 + 2MnSO_4 + 8H_2O + 5O_2\uparrow$$

Equivalence Factor

- Each mL of 0.1 N $KMnO_4$ Ξ 0.001701 g of H_2O_2.

Mechanism of Action

- Hydrogen peroxide releases the nascent oxygen, i.e., [O], which by oxidative mechanism inhibits the actions of microorganisms and their growth.

Incompatibility

- It is incompatible with reducing agents, oxidising agents, organic matter, heavy metals, etc.

Storage Conditions

- It is preserved in light-resistant containers with stoppers made of glass or plastic-resistant to hydrogen peroxide.
- It should be stored in dark and in a cool place.

Label

- The label should state whether or not the solution contains a stabilising agent.

Pharmaceutical Uses

- As antiseptic and germicide.
- As disinfectant (6% solution).
- Its 1.6% solution is used as deodorant, gargles and mouthwash.
- As strong oxidising agent.
- As bleaching agent.
- As cleaning agent for cuts and wounds.
- As an antidote for phosphorus and cyanide poisoning.
- Used to clean ears and remove the surgical dressings.

3.7.7 Chlorinated Lime

Synonym : Bleaching powder, chloride of lime
Molecular formula : $CaOCl(Cl)H_2O$
Category : Germicidal and disinfectant

Standards

It should contain not less than 30.0% w/w of available chlorine.

Method of Preparation

It is obtained by passing chlorine gas over calcium hydroxide.

$$Ca(OH)_2 + Cl_2 \longrightarrow Ca(OCl)Cl + H_2O$$

Physical Properties

Colour : Dull white

Odour : Characteristic odour of chloride

State : Powder

Solubility : Partially soluble in water and alcohol

Chemical Properties

- When exposed to air, it absorbs moisture and gradually decomposes.
- It reacts with HCl, liberating Cl_2 gas in large quantities.

$$ClO^- + HCl \longrightarrow Cl_2(g)\uparrow + OH^-$$

- When bleaching powder is put in water, hypochlorite goes out in solution because of its bleaching and oxidising properties.

$$2Ca(OCl)Cl + CO_2 + H_2O \longrightarrow CaCO_3 + CaCl_2 + 2HOCl$$

Identification Tests

- When HCl is treated with the sample, chlorine gas is evolved in large amount.
- The resulting reactions have been characteristic of calcium and chloride.

Test for Purity

- It has to be tested for its stability by heating it at 100°C for 2 hours. It must not lose more than 3% w/w of available chlorine.

Assay

Principle

- It is based on the redox titration method.
- In the presence of acid, the available chlorine is liberated form chlorinated lime (available chlorine may be defined as the chlorine that is liberated from a substance by acids).
- The free chlorine reacts with potassium iodide to liberate iodine quantitatively and the quantity of iodine set free is determined by titration with 0.1 N $Na_2S_2O_3$.

$$Ca(OCl)Cl + 2CH_3COOH \longrightarrow Ca(CH_3COO)_2 + H_2O + Cl_2$$

$$Cl_2 + 2KI \longrightarrow 2KCl + I_2$$

$$2Na_2S_2O_3 + I_2 \longrightarrow 2NaI + Na_2S_4O_6$$

Procedure

- 4 g of bleaching powder is triturated with successive small quantities of water.
- This is then transferred to a litre flask and the volume made up to the mark.
- A measured volume (100 mL) of the suspension is taken in a flask.
- This is then titrated with an excess of KI solution (3 g), acidified with 5 mL of acetic acid and the liberated iodine is titrated with 0.1 N sodium thiosulphate, employing starch mucilage as an indicator.

Equivalence Factor

- Each mL of 0.1 N sodium thiosulphate Ξ 0.003545 g of available chlorine.

Mechanism of Action

- It works by chlorination of microorganism's protein, which ultimately leads to destruction of protein and cell death.

Incompatibility

- It is incompatible with oxidising agents, reducing agents, etc.

Storage

- It is stored in a well-closed containers and kept in a cool place. It gets affected by light, moisture and heat.

Pharmaceutical Uses

- As disinfectant in wounds.
- As germicidal.
- To clean water closets (toilets), drains and effluents.
- As a bleaching powder.
- Used in the preparation of chlorinated soda.
- Chlorinated lime has bactericidal action.
- As an ingredient in the preparation of detergents.
- Used to decolorise most dyes.

3.7.8 Iodine and its Preparation

3.7.8.1 Iodine

Iodine commonly occurs in nature. Minute amounts of iodine are found as iodides in sea weeds like *Laminaria digitata, Fucus vesiculosus,* etc. and as iodates in nitrate minerals like Chile saltpeter. It is also present as a trace element in thyroid hormones of the human body.

Molecular formula : I_2

Molecular weight : 253.81 g/mol

Category : Antiseptic and disinfectant

Standards

It should contain not less than 99.5% and not more than 100.5% of iodine.

Methods of Preparation

- **From seaweeds:** Iodine is manufactured by extracting Kelp (seaweed's ash) with water. The solution obtained is concentrated such that sulphates and chlorides of sodium and potassium crystallise, which are then removed from the solution.

  The solution now contains iodides of sodium and potassium, which is then treated with small amounts of sulphuric acid to allow decomposition of sulphides and thiosulphates, precipitating sulphur. Finally, the solution is filtered such that the filtrate mostly consists of freely soluble iodides along with small amounts of chlorides and bromides.

  This filtrate is treated with manganese dioxide, warmed and distilled over to obtain iodine.

$$2NaI + 2H_2SO_4 + MnO_2 \xrightarrow{\Delta} I_2 + MnSO_4 + Na_2SO_4 + 2H_2O$$

- Alternatively, the solutions having freely soluble iodides are treated with the required proportion of chlorine and the precipitated iodine is collected and purified by sublimation.

$$2NaI + Cl_2 \longrightarrow 2NaCl + I_2$$

- More recently, iodine has been reported to be found in brine of oil wells and this source is nowadays being used for getting iodine in USA and Russia.
- Impurities like ICl, IBr, and ICN present in iodine are removed by heating crude iodine with potassium iodide.

$$ICl + KI \longrightarrow KCl + I_2$$

$$IBr + KI \longrightarrow KBr + I_2$$

$$ICN + KI \longrightarrow KCN + I_2$$

- **From Chile saltpeter:** Crude Chile saltpetre, which is found in Chile (South America), contains dosium nitrate and sodium iodate. During its crystallisation, sodium sulphate separates out as crystals whereas sodium iodate remains in mother liquor. Iodine is obtained by treating mother liquor with sodium hydrogen sulphite.

$$2NaIO + 5NaHSO_3 \longrightarrow 2Na_2SO_4 + 3NaHSO_4 + I_2 + H_2O$$

Physical Properties

Colour : Greyish violet or bluish black

Odour : Irritant

Taste : Brittle crystalline flakes or rhombic prisms with metallic lustre

State : Granular crystals

Solubility : (i) Insoluble in water but soluble in alcohol
(ii) Freely soluble in chloroform and solvent ether
(iii) Soluble in aqueous solutions of iodine

Nature : It volatilises slowly at room temperature

Chemical Properties

- It reacts directly with some non-metals and with many metals.

$$2P + 3I_2 \longrightarrow 2PI_3$$

$$Fe + I_2 \longrightarrow FeI_3$$

- At higher temperature, the density of iodine decreases as it dissociates.

$$I_2 \rightleftharpoons 2I^-$$

- Reducing agents react with the aqueous solutions of iodine and are oxidised.

$$H_3AsO_3 + I_2 + H_2O \longrightarrow 2HI + H_3AsO_4$$

$$H_2S + I_2 \longrightarrow 2HI + S\downarrow$$

$$2Na_2SO_2 + I_2 \longrightarrow 2NaI + Na_2S_4O_6$$

- With an alkali, iodine reacts to form an iodide and iodate, especially with the aid of heat.

$$3I_2 + 6NaOH \xrightarrow{\Delta} 5NaI + NaIO_3 + 3H_2O$$

- Potassium iodide is able to dissolve large quantities of iodine due to formation of the I_3^- ion.

$$I_2 + KI \rightleftharpoons KI_3$$

- Iodine is able to add to the unsaturated acid, which is present in the oils.

$$R\text{-}CH{=}CH\text{-}COOH + I_2 \longrightarrow R\text{-}CHI\text{-}CHI\text{-}COOH$$

Identification Tests

- When heated, iodine yields vapours of violet colour.
- With starch, a clear solution of iodine in KI produces a blue colour in solution, which disappears on heating and reappears on cooling.

Tests for Purity

- It is tested for chloride, bromide, cyanogens and non-volatile matter.

Assay

Principle

- The assay is based on the oxidation-reduction titration method.

Procedure

- About 0.5 g of iodine is first of all dissolved in a solution of 1 g of potassium iodide in 5 mL of water in an iodine flask.
- It is then diluted with 50 mL of water and acidified with 1 mL of acetic acid.
- This solution is then titrated with standard 0.1 N sodium thiosulphate using starch solution as an indicator.

$$2Na_2S_2O_3 + I_2 \longrightarrow 2NaI + Na_2S_4O_6$$

Equivalence Factor

- Each mL of 0.1 N sodium thiosulphate Ξ 0.01269 g of iodine.

Mechanism of Action

- Iodine in aqueous solution acts as a mild oxidising agent which is mediated through the formation of hypoiodous acid (HIO), which further releases the nascent oxygen [O], responsible for causing oxidation of protein of microorganisms.

Incompatibility

- It is incompatible with hydrogen peroxide, alkalis and alkali carbonates.

Storage

- It is stored in glass stoppered, amber colour bottles or earthenware and kept in cool place.

Pharmaceutical Uses

- As counter irritant and disinfectant.
- As a germicide.
- As antiseptic.
- 10% solution is used for cleaning of wounds.
- As an ingredient of gargles and mouthwashes.
- Used to treat vaginal infections.
- Used in burns and cuts.
- Required for the proper functioning of thyroid gland.

3.7.8.2 Solutions of Iodine

Various iodine preparations include:

(a) Aqueous iodine solution

(b) Weak iodine solution

(c) Strong iodine solution

(a) Aqueous Iodine Solution

It was first made in 1829 by a French physician, Jean Lugol.

It is on the WHO's List of Essential Medicines, the most effective and safe medicines needed in a health system.

It is a liquid made of two parts of potassium iodide (KI) for every one part elemental iodine (I_2) in water.

It is available as a generic medication and over the counter.

Synonym : Lugol's solution

Category : Antiseptic and disinfectant

Standards

It contains 5.0% w/v of iodine (4.9 to 5.1%) and 10.0% w/v of potassium iodide (9.8 to 10.2%) in purified water.

Method of Preparation

50 g iodine and 100 g potassium iodide are accurately weighed and dissolved in 100 mL water with continuous shaking until complete dissolution occurs. The resultant solution is made up to 1000 mL by adding purified water.

Physical Properties

Colour : Brown

Odour : Characteristic odour of iodine

State : Liquid

Nature : Transparent liquid

Identification Tests

- With starch, aqueous iodine solution gives a blue colour.
- The residue left after evaporation of the solution and after ignition yields reactions which are characteristic of potassium and iodine.

Assay

- The assay of aqueous iodine solution is carried out for iodine and potassium iodide.
- 25 mL of the aqueous iodine solution is first of all diluted to 100 mL with water.
- This diluted solution is then used for the following assays.

Assay for Iodine

Procedure

- A measured volume (20 mL) of the above solution is diluted with10 mL of water.
- This solution is then titrated with standard 0.1 N sodium thiosulphate using starch solution as an indicator.

Equivalence Factor

- Each mL of 0.1 N sodium thiosulphate Ξ 0.01269 g of iodine.

Assay for Potassium Iodide

- To 10 mL of the diluted solution, 20 mL of water and 40 mL of HCl is added.
- This solution is then titrated with 0.05 M potassium iodate, shaking vigorously until the brown colour becomes light.
- Then chloroform is added and titration is continued until chloroform layer is colourless and the supernatant liquid is clear yellow.

$$2KIO_3 + 6HCl + KI \longrightarrow 3KCl + 3ICl + 3H_2O$$

In the IP method, 20 mL of the sample is employed for iodine determination and 10 mL potassium iodide and hence, one has to subtract one quarter of the number of 0.1 N $Na_2S_2O_3$ needed in the assay for iodine from the number of mL of 0.05 M potassium iodate used in the titration.

Each mL of 0.05 M potassium iodate Ξ 0.0166 g of KI.

The above method of assay is called Andrew's method.

In this method, iodides get quantitatively oxidised by iodate to iodine, which reacts with more iodate in the presence of HCl to yield ICl. The first portion of the iodate is reduced to iodine, which makes chloroform layer violet. But this iodine gets oxidised to a yellowish iodine monochloride, on further addition of KIO_3. One cannot use a starch indicator in this titration due to the high concentration of acid used. Hydrolysis of ICl could be prevented by a high concentration of HCl. The end-point may be observed with the disappearance of violet colour in chloroform, which is very sharp.

Incompatibility

- It is incompatible with hydrogen peroxide.

Storage

- It is stored in glass stoppered, amber colour bottles or earthenware and kept in a cool place. It is not stored in metal containers because iodine attacks metals.

Pharmaceutical Uses

- Acts as a good source of iodine and is taken internally and topically.
- As a germicide and disinfectant.
- As a fungicide.
- As counter-irritant.
- Used to treat thyrotoxicosis prior to surgery.
- Helps to protect the thyroid gland from harmful effects of radioactive iodine and to treat iodine deficiency.
- When applied to cervix, it is used in the screening for cervical cancer.
- A small amount may also be used for emergency disinfection of drinking water.

Note: It does not bring irritation in cuts or wounds like the tincture of iodine.

(b) Weak Iodine Solution

Synonym : Iodine tincture or tincture of iodine

Category : Antiseptic and disinfectant

Standards

It contains 2.0% w/v of iodine (limit - 1.9 to 2.1%) and 2.5% w/v of potassium iodide (limit - 2.4 to 2.6%) dissolved in required quantities of 50% alcohol.

Method of Preparation

25 g potassium iodide and 20 g iodine are first dissolved in sufficient alcohol (50%). Then, the volume is made up to 1000 mL by adding more 50% alcohol.

Alcohol content is 45 to 48% w/v.

Physical Properties

Colour : Brown

Odour : Characteristic odour of iodine

State : Liquid

Nature : Transparent liquid

Identification Tests

- With starch, aqueous iodine solution gives a blue colour.
- The residue left after evaporation of the solution and after ignition yields reactions which are characteristic of potassium and iodine.

Assay

- The assay of aqueous iodine solution is carried out for iodine and potassium iodide.
- 25 mL of the aqueous iodine solution is first of all diluted to 100 mL with water.
- This diluted solution is then used for the following assays.

Assay for Iodine

Procedure

- A measured volume (10 mL) of the above solution is diluted with 20 mL of water.
- This solution is then titrated with standard 0.1 N sodium thiosulphate using starch solution as an indicator.

Equivalence Factor

- Each mL of 0.1 N sodium thiosulphate Ξ 0.01169 g of iodine.

$$2Na_2S_2O_3 + I_2 \longrightarrow 2NaI + Na_2S_4O_6$$

Assay for Potassium Iodide

- To 10 mL of the diluted solution, 40 mL of water and 16 mL of HCl and 10 mL of potassium cyanide solution are added.
- This solution is then titrated with 0.05 M potassium iodate, shaking vigorously until the brown colour becomes light (pale yellow).
- A solution of starch (5 mL) is then added and the titration is continued until the liquids colourless.
- From the number of mL's of 0.05 M KIO_3 is subtracted half the number of mL's of 0.1 N $Na_2S_2O_3$, which is needed for the assay of iodine.

Each mL of the remaining 0.05 M KIO_3 Ξ 0.0166 g of KI

Incompatibility

- It is incompatible with hydrogen peroxide.

Storage Condition

- It is stored in glass stoppered, amber colour bottles or earthenware and kept in cool place.

Pharmaceutical Uses

- Acts as a good source of iodine and is taken internally and topically.
- As a germicide and disinfectant.
- As a fungicide.
- Used to treat thyrotoxicosis prior to surgery.
- Helps to protect the thyroid gland from harmful effects of radioactive iodine and to treat iodine deficiency.
- When applied to cervix, it is used in the screening for cervical cancer.
- A small amount may also be used for emergency disinfection of drinking water.

Note: Application of weak iodine solution on cuts and wounds causes irritation.

(c) Strong Iodine Solution

Category : Antiseptic and disinfectant

Standards

It contains 10.0% w/v of iodine (limit – 9.5 to 10.0%) and 6.0% w/v of potassium iodide (limit – 5.7 to 6.3%) dissolved in required quantities of 74 to 79% alcohol.

Method of Preparation

60 g potassium iodide and 100 g iodine are first dissolved in 100 mL of purified water. Then, the volume is made up to 1000 mL by adding 90% alcohol.

Physical Properties

Colour : Brown

Odour : Characteristic odour of iodine

State : Liquid

Nature : Transparent liquid

Identification Tests

- With starch, aqueous iodine solution gives a blue colour.
- The residue left after evaporation of the solution and after ignition yields reactions which are characteristic of potassium and iodine.

Assay

- The assay of aqueous iodine solution is carried out for iodine and potassium iodide.
- 25 mL of the aqueous iodine solution is first of all diluted to 100 mL with water.
- This diluted solution is then used for the following assays.

Assay for Iodine

- 25 mL sample is first of all diluted with 90% alcohol to 100 mL.
- Then it is assayed by the method described under weak iodine solution.

Each mL of the remaining 0.05 M KIO_3 Ξ 0.0166 g of KI

Incompatibility

- It is incompatible with hydrogen peroxide.

Storage Condition

- It is stored in glass stoppered, amber colour bottles or earthenware and kept in cool place.

Pharmaceutical Uses

- Acts as a good source of iodine and is taken internally and topically.
- As a germicide and disinfectant.
- As antiseptic.
- As a fungicide.
- It is used to make aqueous iodine solution and weak iodine solution, provided potassium iodide is replaced by sodium iodide.

3.7.8.3 Povidone-Iodine

Povidone-iodine solution is an aqueous solution of povidone-iodine.

It is a complex produced by the interaction between iodine and povidone (polyvinyl pyrrolidine).

It is an iodophoric complex that contains nearly 10% w/v of available iodine. The iodophoric complex releases iodine very slowly.

Category : Antiseptic, topical anti-infective

Standards

It contains nearly 10% w/v of available iodine.

Method of Preparation

It is prepared by interacting povidone (a polymer of vinyl pyrrolidine) with iodine.

Physical Properties

Colour : Yellowish brown
Odour : Slight and characteristic odour of iodine
Taste : Acidic taste
State : Amorphous powder
Solubility : (i) Soluble in water and alcohol
(ii) Practically insoluble in chloroform, acetone and ether
Nature : Acidic

Assay

- It could be analysed for the available iodine content.
- For the povidone-iodine complex, a known weight of sample is made to dissolve in water (using stirrer for complete solution) and it is titrated against standard sodium thiosulphate (0.02 N) using starch as an indicator.
- A blank is also carried out.

Incompatibility

- It is incompatible with hydrogen peroxide.

Storage

- It is stored in well-closed container and remains stable.

Pharmaceutical Uses

- As bactericidal agent – In 10% povidone-iodine, the free iodine content is only 0.001%. If this is diluted to 0.1%, the free iodine content increases and becomes more powerful bactericidal. Thus, povidone-iodine has to be diluted before use.
- As disinfectant.
- Effective in the management of burns and cuts.
- In the preparation of products to be applied to skin and mucous membrane.
- As antiseptic.
- To treat oral cavity infections in the form of gargles and mouthwashes.

Advantages of Povidone-iodine solution over other iodine preparations

- Water solubility
- Non-irritation
- Less toxicity
- Non-staining nature, can be easily removed from skin and clothes by washing.

MULTIPLE-CHOICE QUESTIONS

1. Which of the following compounds neutralises the alkaline body fluids?
   (a) Urinary acidifiers (b) Acids
   (c) Gastric acidifiers (d) Systemic acidifiers
2. What is the alternative name of ammonium chloride?
   (a) Ammonium muriate (b) Sal ammoniac
   (c) Both (a) and (b) (d) None of the above
3. What is the alternative name of HCl?
   (a) Spirit of salt (b) Salmiac
   (c) Baking soda (d) None of the above
4. Sodium bicarbonate is also called
   (a) Baking soda (b) Sodium hydrogen carbonate
   (c) Meetha soda (d) All of the above
5. Which process is used to prepare sodium bicarbonate?
   (a) Solvay process (b) Haber's process
   (c) Both (a) and (b) (d) None of the above
6. Which of the following compounds are fibrous in nature and undergo partial digestion?
   (a) Saline cathartics (b) Bulk forming cathartics
   (c) Stimulant cathartics (d) Stool softening cathartics
7. Docusate sodium is an example of
   (a) Saline cathartics (b) Bulk forming cathartics
   (c) Stimulant cathartics (d) Stool softening cathartics
8. Example(s) of bulk forming cathartics
   (a) Methyl cellulose (b) Bran
   (c) Isabgol (d) All of the above
9. Example(s) of stimulant cathartics
   (a) Bisacodyl (b) Castor oil
   (c) Cascara (d) All of the above
10. Alternative term for emollients
    (a) Saline cathartics (b) Bulk forming cathartics
    (c) Stimulant cathartics (d) Stool softening cathartics
11. The disinfectants used to maintain general public health are known as
    (a) Bacteriostatic (b) Sanitizers
    (c) Sterilisers (d) Antiseptics

12. Which of the following is not an ideal property of antimicrobial agent?
    (a) Rapid onset of action (b) Sustained activity
    (c) Poor therapeutic index (d) Does not cause local cellular damage
13. Which of the following compounds exhibit antimicrobial action by oxidation?
    (a) Hydrogen peroxide (b) Potassium permanganate
    (c) Halogens (d) All of the above
14. Which of the following antimicrobial compounds exhibit antimicrobial action by halogenation?
    (a) Povidone iodine (b) Chlorinated lime
    (c) Hypohalites (d) All of the above
15. Which of the following antimicrobial compounds exhibit antimicrobial action by protein precipitation?
    (a) Borax (b) Mercurial compounds
    (c) Silver nitrate (d) All of the above
16. Lugol's solution is
    (a) Weak iodine solution (b) Strong iodine solution
    (c) Aqueous iodine solution (d) None of the above

FILL IN THE BLANKS

1. Acidifying agents are the inorganic chemical compounds that either .... in the GIT tract.
2. Gastric acidifiers are the drugs which are used to .... the acidity of the stomach.
3. .... are the drugs which are used to remove acidic urine from the body or to maintain the pH of the urine.
4. .... are the drugs which are able to neutralise the alkaline body fluids.
5. Hydrochloric acid is also known as ....
6. Hydrochloric acid can be prepared by the action of .... on ....
7. Antacids are the drugs which are able to ....
8. Systemic antacid is .... in nature while non-systemic antacid is ....
9. Example of systemic antacid is ....
10. Neutralising capacity of an antacid is expressed in ....
11. .... is the aluminium containing salt as antacids.
12. .... are used to bring defecation.

13. Cathartics are used to ....
14. Laxatives are .... cathartics while purgatives are .... cathartics.
15. Alternative names of sodium potassium tartarate are ....
16. .... inorganic compounds are used as saline cathartics.
17. Excessive use of magnesium sulphate as saline cathartics causes ....
18. Epsom salt is ....
19. .... is the process of complete destruction of all living micro-organisms, including bacterial spores.
20. .... acts as germicidal and disinfectant.
21. Crude *Chile saltpeter* contains .... and ....

SHORT QUESTIONS

1. Define acidifying agents.
2. What is the difference between urinary acidifier and systemic acidifier?
3. What is achlorhydria?
4. By which other names hydrochloric acid is known?
5. What are antacids?
6. What is systemic antacid?
7. What is non-systemic antacid?
8. What do you understand by neutralising capacity?
9. How do you prepare sodium bicarbonate?
10. Define cathartics. Classify them with mechanism of action and examples.
11. What are purgatives and laxatives?
12. What are the side effects of magnesium sulphate when consumed in excessive amount?
13. Mention the alternative names of sodium potassium tartarate.
14. Mention the pharmaceutical uses of kaolin.
15. Define antimicrobial agents.
16. Define the following terms: a) bactericide, (b) fungicide, (c) virucide, and (d) amoebicide.

LONG QUESTIONS

1. What are acidifiers? How do they act?
2. Classify acidifying agents. Give an example of an acidifier.
3. Give a brief account of the preparation, properties, identification tests and uses of dilute HCl and ammonium chloride.

4. Mention the procedure to perform assay of ammonium chloride.
5. What are antacids? Classify them with examples.
6. How can the antacid activity be evaluated?
7. Mention the symptoms and consequences of gastric acidity.
8. Enlist the requirements of ideal antacid.
9. Mention the chemical formula, methods of preparation, properties, tests for purity, storage conditions and medicinal uses of (a) sodium bicarbonate, (b) aluminium hydroxide gel, and (c) magnesium hydroxide mixture.
10. Mention the procedure to perform assay of sodium bicarbonate.
11. Write a note on the preparations containing combination of antacids.
12. What are the limitations of singly-used antacids?
13. Mention the advantages of using combination of antacids.
14. Mention the applications of cathartics.
15. Mention the chemical formula, methods of preparation, identification tests, tests for purity, medicinal uses and storage conditions of (a) sodium orthophosphate, and (b) magnesium sulphate.
16. Write a short note on kaolin and bentonite.
17. How antimicrobial agents are classified?
18. Mention the ideal properties of antimicrobial agents.
19. Explain the mechanism of action of antimicrobial agents.
20. Mention the chemical formula, methods of preparation, properties, identification tests, tests for purity, applications and storage conditions of (a) hydrogen peroxide, (b) potassium permanganate, (c) chlorinated lime, and (d) boric acid.
21. Write a note on iodine and its preparations.

ANSWERS

Multiple-Choice Questions

1. (d)	2. (c)	3. (a)	4. (d)	5. (a)	6. (b)	7. (d)	8. (d)
9. (d)	10. (d)	11. (b)	12. (c)	13. (d)	14. (d)	15. (d)	16) c

Fill in the Blanks

1.	Produce or increase acid	2.	Increase
3.	Urinary acidifier	4.	Systemic acidifier
5.	Spirit of salt, muriatic acid	6.	Conc. sulphuric acid, sodium chloride
7.	Neutralise the gastric contents	8.	Absorbable, non-absorbable

9. Sodium bicarbonate
10. Milliequivalents of hydrochloric acid
11. Aluminium hydroxide gel
12. Cathartics
13. To relieve constipation
14. Mild, strong
15. Rochelle salt, Seignette's salt
16. Magnesium sulphate, sodium potassium tartarate
17. GIT irritation and waking diarrhoea
18. Magnesium sulphate
19. Sterilization
20. Chlorinated lime
21. Dosium nitrate, sodium iodate

4

Miscellaneous Compounds

4.1 EXPECTORANTS

- These are the chemical agents that assist in removing sputum from the respiratory tract, either by increasing the fluidity (or reducing the viscosity) of sputum or by increasing the volume of fluids that have to be expelled from the respiratory tract by coughing.
- As a result, expectorants act either by mucolytic action or by mucokinetic action.

4.1.1 Classification of Expectorants

Based on the mechanism of action, expectorants are classified into the following two types:

(a) Sedative expectorants

(b) Stimulant expectorants

(a) Sedative Expectorants

- These are also referred to as **stomach irritant expectorants**.
- These act by stimulating the gastric reflexes for producing the desired effect.
- Examples include ammonium chloride, antimony potassium tartarate, potassium iodide, sodium citrate, etc.
- These also include bitter drugs like ipecac, senega, Indian squill, etc.

(b) Stimulant Expectorants

- These expectorants cause direct or indirect stimulation of the secretory cells of respiratory tract.
- They enhance the respiratory secretions in the respiratory tract. As a result, more fluid is produced in the respiratory tract and sputum is diluted.
- Examples include eucalyptus oil, anise oil, lemon oil, etc.

4.1.2 Mechanism of Action of Expectorants

- They act on respiratory tract in two different ways:
    (a) By decreasing the viscosity of bronchial secretion, it facilitates their easy removal by coughing.
    (b) By increasing the amount of respiratory tract fluids, demulcent action is exerted by dry mucosal linings, thus relieving the unproductive cough.
- In case of dry cough, the expectorants act reflexly by irritating the gastric mucosa, which in turn, stimulates the gastric mucosa to produce the respiratory tract secretion.

4.1.3 Examples of Expectorants

- Volatile oils, such as eucalyptus oil, act as direct expectorants.
- Iodides, such as potassium iodide, liquefy the mucus and aid in its expulsion.
- Ammonium chloride and ammonium bicarbonate act as reflux saline expectorants which irritate gastric mucosa and stimulate respiratory tract secretions.
- Alkaloidal vasicine isolated from *Adhatoda vasicine* shows bronchodilatory action.

4.1.4 Contraindications of Expectorants

Expectorants should not be used in conditions like:

- Unconscious or semi-consciousness or coma situations.
- Significant CNS depression and shock.
- Patients with heart disease.
- In debilitated patients (i.e., weak patients and who cannot bear their body weight).
- In tuberculosis, hernia and advanced pregnancy cases.
- Poisoning caused by corrosive or petroleum products.

4.1.5 Potassium Iodide

Synonyms : Potide, Kalii iodidum
Molecular formula : KI
Molecular weight : 166.0 g/mol
Category : Expectorant, diuretic, antifungal and antithyroid

Standards

It contains not less than 99.0% of KI, calculated with reference to substance dried to a constant weight at 105°C.

Methods of Preparation

- **Industrial method:** It may be obtained by action of iodide on moist iron fillings to form ferro-ferric iodide (FeI_3 or FeI_2, $2FeI_2$), which then gets decomposed with potassium carbonate.

$$Fe + I_2 \longrightarrow FeI_2 ;\ 3FeI_2 .\ 2FeI_3$$

$$FeI_2 . 2FeI_3 + 4K_2CO_3 \longrightarrow 8KI + FeO . Fe_2O_2 + 4CO_2$$

  Ferroso-ferric oxide is filtered out. The filtrate is concentrated to get KI. The salt may be purified by recrystallisation.

- **Laboratory method:** It is also prepared by treating a hot aqueous solution of potassium hydroxide with iodine in slight excess to form a mixture of potassium iodide and potassium iodate.

$$6KOH + 3I_2 \longrightarrow KIO_3 + 5KI + 2H_2O$$

$$KIO_3 + 3C \longrightarrow KI + 3CO\uparrow$$

  The solution is concentrated and treated with excess of charcoal powder. Then the mixture is evaporated to dryness, followed by ignition. The charcoal (carbon) reduces the iodate to iodine, utilising the total iodine to get the potassium iodide. The product is lixiviated with water. Then it is filtered and potassium iodide is obtained by recrystallisation.

Physical Properties

Colour : Colourless or white
Odour : Odourless
Taste : Saline and bitter
State : Transparent or opaque crystals or granular powder
Solubility : Soluble in water, glycerine, alcohol and acetone
Nature : Deliquescent in moist air, solution is alkaline

Chemical Properties

- When KI is added to water to prepare solution, the temperature of the solution gets lowered.
- Iodine readily gets dissolved in aqueous solution of KI to form dark brown coloured solution of potassium tri-iodide.

$$KI + I_2 \rightleftharpoons KI_3$$

- With silver nitrate solution, it gives yellow precipitate of silver iodide.

$$KI + AgNO_3 \longrightarrow \underset{\text{Yellow}}{AgI\downarrow} + KNO_3$$

- Iodide ion gets easily oxidised to iodine when treated with oxidising agents like chlorine, copper, nitric acid, etc.

$$2I^- \longrightarrow I_2 + 2e^-$$

Identification Tests

- It gives reactions which are characteristic of potassium and iodide.
- Addition of mercuric chloride solution to 1 mL of sample solution of potassium iodide resulted in the formation of dark red precipitate of mercuric iodide, which is slightly soluble in excess of this reagent and completely soluble in excess of potassium iodide solution by forming potassium mercuri-iodine.

$$2KI + HgCl_2 \longrightarrow \underset{\text{Dark red ppt.}}{HgI_2\downarrow} + 2KCl$$

$$2KI + HgI_2 \longrightarrow \underset{\text{Potassium mercuri-ibdine}}{K_2HgI_4}$$

Tests for Purity

It is tested for As, sulphate, iodate, Fe, heavy metals and loss on drying.

- As should not be more than 2 ppm.
- Sulphate should not be more than 1 ppm.
- Iodate should be absent.
- Iron should not be more than 20 ppm.
- Heavy metals should not be more than 10 ppm.
- Loss on drying should not be more than 1%.

Assay

Principle

- Based on oxidation-reduction titration using iodometric method.

Procedure

- 0.5 g of KI is weighed and dissolved in a solution containing 10 mL of water.
- 3.5 mL of HCl and 5 mL of chloroform is added.
- This solution is then titrated with a standard solution of 0.05 M potassium iodate added from burette.

- In this reaction, potassium iodate liberates iodine from potassium iodide in the presence of acid.

$$KIO_3 + 5KI + 6HCl \longrightarrow 6KCl + 3I_2 + 3H_2O$$

- The iodine is further converted to iodine monochloride with more of iodate in presence of acid.

$$KIO_3 + 2I_2 + 6HCl \longrightarrow KCl + 5ICl + 3H_2O$$

- The chloroform which is heavier than water sinks to the bottom of the flask and appears bright.
- Free iodine being more soluble in chloroform, dissolves and colours the chloroform layer bright violet.
- If the yellow colour of the aqueous layer gets completely discharged but chloroform layer is still of violet colour, addition of potassium iodate from the burette is made drop wise and the flask is shaken vigorously to also allow iodine dissolved in chloroform to react with iodate.
- If the chloroform layer also becomes colourless, the end-point is reached.
- The total reaction can be summarised as follows:

$$KIO_3 + 2KI + 6HCl \longrightarrow 3KCl + 3ICl + 3H_2O$$

Equivalence Factor

- Each mL of 0.05 M KIO_3 Ξ 0.0166 mg of KI.

Incompatibility

- It is incompatible with salts of iron, bismuth, copper, lead and mercury.
- It is also incompatible with potassium chlorate and other oxidising agents, mineral acids, quinine sulphate and other alkaloid salts.
- Its use should be avoided in children.

Storage

- It should be stored in tightly-closed containers in a dark place.

Dose

- 250 to 300 mg daily.

Pharmaceutical Uses

- As expectorant in cough preparations.
- As a source of iodine.

- In thyroid deficiency.
- As saline diuretic.
- As antifungal agent.
- As reducing agent.
- Used in the synthesis of compounds like potassio-mercuric iodide and potassio-bismuth iodide.
- As electrolyte replenisher.
- As a stabiliser for iodine solution.

4.1.6 Ammonium Chloride

Synonym : Sal ammoniac, ammonium muriate, salmiac, amchlor
Molecular formula : NH_4Cl
Molecular weight : 53.49 g/mol
Category : Expectorant, diuretic and electrolyte replenisher

Standards

It contains not less than 99.5% of NH_4Cl, calculated with reference to substance dried over silica gel for four hours.

Methods of Preparation

- Commercially, it is prepared by neutralising ammonia with HCl. The solution is evaporated till crude, vitreous, crystalline mass of ammonium chloride is obtained. The crude salt is purified either by crystallisation or sublimation.

$$NH_3 + HCl \longrightarrow NH_4Cl$$

- It is also prepared by treating ammonium sulphate with sodium chloride.

$$2NaCl + (NH_4)_2SO_4 \longrightarrow 2NH_3 + 2HCl + Na_2SO_4$$

$$2NH_3 + 2HCl \longrightarrow 2NH_4Cl$$

- It is also obtained by treating ammoniacal gas liquors with lime and the liberated NH_3 is passed into hydrochloric acid solution. The crude ammonium chloride obtained is known in commerce as sal ammoniac and occurs as tough, crystalline masses.

Physical Properties

Colour : White
Odour : Odourless
Taste : Cool saline taste

State : Fine or coarse crystalline powder

Solubility : (i) Soluble in water and freely soluble in alcohol and glycerine
(ii) Sparingly soluble in boiling water

Nature : (i) Slightly hygroscopic
(ii) Its 0.8% w/v solution is isotonic with serum

Chemical Properties

- Freshly prepared aqueous solutions are neutral to litmus but become quickly acidic on standing because of hydrolysis.

$$NH_4Cl + 2H_2O \longrightarrow NH_4OH + H_3O^+ + Cl^-$$

- In its vapour form, it dissociates in ammonia and hydrochloric acid.

$$NH_4Cl \rightleftharpoons NH_3 + HCl$$

Identification Tests

- It gives reactions characteristic of ammonium salts and chlorides.
- A few mg of substance is heated with sodium hydroxide solution, leading to the evolution of ammonia gas, which is recognisable by its odour and by its action on moist red litmus paper.

$$NH_4^+ + OH^- \longrightarrow NH_3 + H_2O$$

Tests for Purity

It is tested for As, sulphate, Ca, iodate, Fe, heavy metals, loss on drying and sulphated ash.

- As should not be more than 2 ppm.
- Sulphate should not be more than 150 ppm.
- Calcium should not be more than 200 ppm.
- Iron should not be more than 20 ppm.
- Heavy metals should not be more than 10 ppm.
- Loss on drying should not be more than 0.5% w/w.
- The sulphated ash should not be more than 0.1% w/w.
- The pH of a 5% w/v solution is between 4.5 and 6.0.

Assay

Principle

- Based on acid-base titration technique.

Procedure

- About 0.1 g of NH_4Cl sample accurately weighed is kept in a conical flask, about 50 mL water is added to dissolve it.
- 5 mL of neutral formaldehyde solution is then added so that ammonium chloride is converted to methanimine and hydrochloric acid.
- The liberated acid is titrated with 0.1 N NaOH using phenolphthalein as an indicator.

$$NH_4Cl + HCHO \longrightarrow CH_2NH + HCl + H_2O$$

$$HCl + NaOH \longrightarrow NaCl + H_2O$$

Equivalence Factor

- Each mL of 0.1 N NaOH Ξ 0.05349 g of NH_4Cl.

Incompatibility

- It is incompatible with alkalis, carbonates of alkaline earth and lead and silver salts.

Storage

- It should be stored in tightly-closed containers away from moisture.

Dose

- 3 to 6 g daily in divided doses.

Pharmaceutical Uses

- As expectorant.
- As an acidifying agent.
- In the maintenance of acid-base balance of the body fluids.
- Maintains urine at acidic pH, which is beneficial in treating urinary tract infections.
- As diuretic.
- As a diaphoretic (increases sweating) and hence, reduces body temperature to a small extent.

4.2 EMETICS

- Emetics are defined as chemicals which give rise to forced regurgitation (emesis), thereby causing the contents of the stomach to be expelled through the oral cavity (mouth).
- These drugs act either by causing the GIT irritation or by stimulating chemoreceptor trigger zone (CTZ) in the floor of IV ventricle in medulla.
- Although vomiting is primarily considered to be a respiratory function, its result would be to evacuate the stomach.
- Emetics constitute a valuable part of the treatment during poisoning cases.

4.2.1 Classification of Emetics

Emetics are classified into two groups:

(a) Irritant emetics

(b) Stimulant emetics

(a) Irritant Emetics

- These agents are responsible for causing local irritation of cells of gastric mucosa and by reflex mechanism, vomiting is observed.
- Examples include antimony potassium tartarate, copper sulphate, sodium chloride, etc.

(b) Stimulant Emetics

- These agents cause stimulation of CTZ in the medulla oblongata and induce vomiting.
- These are also referred to as centrally acting emetics.
- Examples include morphine, ergot alkaloids, etc.

4.2.2 Mechanism of Action of Emetics

Emetics generally act in two ways:

- By stimulation of CTZ located in the areas of the postrema medulla oblongata in the brain.
- By refluxly producing irritation on the GIT. For example, copper sulphate, sodium chloride, zinc sulphate antimony potassium tartrate, etc.

Note: The common side effect of emetics is dehydration. Hence, patients must be kept hydrated.

4.2.3 Examples of Emetics

- Commonly used emetics include salt water and mustard.
- Inorganic salt includes copper sulphate, sodium chloride, zinc sulphate, antimony potassium tartrate, etc.

4.2.4 Uses of Emetics

- These are given in combination with expectorants in low doses to stimulate flow of respiratory tract secretions.
- These are used to treat certain types of poisoning to remove poison from the GIT.

4.2.5 Copper Sulphate

Synonym : Cupric sulphate, blue vitriol
Molecular formula : $CuSO_4 \cdot 5H_2O$
Molecular weight : 249.7 g/mol
Category : Expectorant, emetic

Standards

It contains not less than 98.5% and not more than 101.0% of $CuSO_4 \cdot 5H_2O$ calculated with reference to the dried substance at 250°C.

Method of Preparation

$$3Cu + S \xrightarrow{3O_2} CuSO_4 + 2CuO$$

$$2CuO \xrightarrow{\text{Dil. } H_2SO_4} 2CuSO_4 + H_2O$$

It is obtained by heating copper granules with sulphur, which results in the formation of solution containing mixture of copper sulphate and cupric oxide (CuO). This solution is then filtered to separate copper sulphate crystals.

Further, the above residue, i.e., CuO is then treated with dilute sulphuric acid to convert it completely into copper sulphate.

Physical Properties

Colour : Deep blue
Odour : Odourless
State : Triclinic crystals of the pentahydrate or as blue crystalline granules or powder.
Solubility : (i) Soluble in water and very soluble in boiling water.
(ii) Slowly soluble in glycerol and almost insoluble in alcohol.
Nature : (i) Acidic in nature, changes blue litmus red.
(ii) It effloresces slowly in dry air and the crystals get covered with a white anhydrous salt.

Chemical Properties

- The salt has been stable to heat up to 60°C. However, on heating at 100°C, it loses two molecules of water, at 140°C another molecule of water is lost and then at 200°C, a white anhydrous salt is formed.

$$CuSO_4{\cdot}5H_2O \xrightarrow{100°C} CuSO_4{\cdot}3H_2O + 2H_2O$$

$$CuSO_4{\cdot}3H_2O \xrightarrow{140°C} CuSO_4{\cdot}2H_2O + H_2O$$

$$CuSO_4{\cdot}2H_2O \xrightarrow{200°C} \underset{\text{(Anhydrous salt)}}{CuSO_4}$$

- At very high temperature, it decomposes to black cupric oxide, sulphur dioxide and oxygen.

$$2CuSO_4 \xrightarrow{400°C} 2CuO + 2SO_2 + O_2$$

Identification Test

- A 5% w/v sample solution of cupric sulphate gives reactions characteristic of copper and sulphate.

Tests for Purity

It is tested for Cl, Fe, Pb, As and loss on drying.

- Cl should not be more than 100 ppm.
- Fe should not be more than 10 ppm.
- Pb should not be more than 50 ppm.
- As should not be more than 8 ppm.
- Loss on drying should not be more than 33 to 36.5%.

Assay

Principle

- Based on the oxidation-reduction titration technique.
- It is based on the instability of cupric iodide formed in the reaction of copper sulphate and potassium iodide, which decomposes to give cuprous iodide with the liberation of free iodine.

Procedure

- Accurately weighed copper sulphate is dissolved in water.

- To this, a slight excess of potassium iodide is added, followed by acetic acid.
- The liberated iodine is titrated with standard sodium thiosulphate solution by using starch as an indicator.
- The titration is continued until faint blue colour persists.

$$2CuSO_4 + 4KI \longrightarrow 2CuI_2 + 2K_2SO_4$$

$$2CuI_2 \longrightarrow Cu_2I_2 + I_2$$

- 2 g of potassium thiocyanate is then added and titrated until the blue colour disappears.

$$I_2 + 2Na_2S_2O_3 \longrightarrow 2NaI + Na_2S_4O_6$$

$$Cu_2I_2 + KCNS \longrightarrow 2CuCNS + 2KI$$

Equivalence Factor

Each mL of 0.1 N sodium thiosulphate Ξ 0.02497 g of $CuSO_4 \cdot 5H_2O$.

Incompatibility

- It is incompatible with alkalies, phosphates, β-naphthol, propylene glycol and sulphathiazole.

Storage Condition

- It should be stored in air-tight containers protected from air, heat and moisture.

Dose

- 300 mg in 30 mL of water.

Pharmaceutical Uses

- As emetic but in large doses, it is corrosive in nature.
- As chemical antidote in phosphorus poisoning.
- Externally, as astringent and fungicidal (1.5% solution).
- As an ingredient of Benedict's and Fehling's reagents.
- In the detection of water.
- In the preparation of absolute alcohol.

4.2.6 Sodium Potassium Tartarate

Synonym : Rochelle salt, Seignette salt

Molecular formula : $C_4H_4KNaO_6 \cdot 4H_2O$

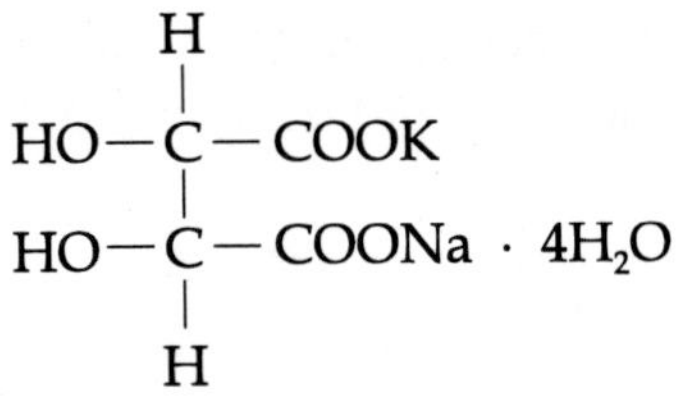

Molecular weight : 282.22 g/mol

Category : Emetic

Method of Preparation

It is obtained by the reaction of tartaric acid with sodium and potassium chloride with the evolution of HCl gas.

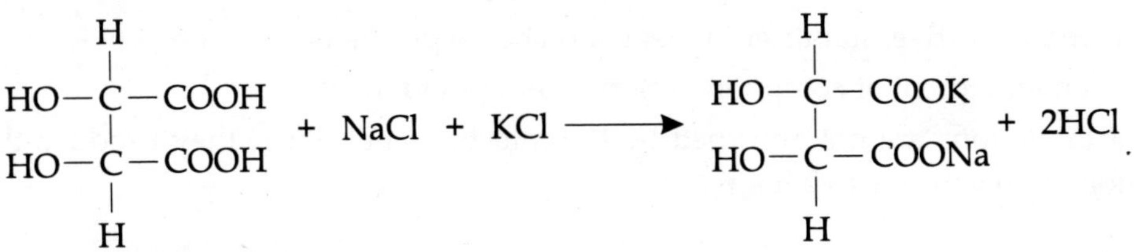

Physical Properties

Colour : White or colourless

Odour : Odourless

Taste : Cool saline taste

State : Fine or coarse crystalline powder or prismatic crystals

Solubility : Freely soluble in water but insoluble in alcohol

Nature : On exposure to air, crystals effloresces

Chemical Properties

- When heated to 74°C, it gives inflammable vapours of burnt sugar with residue of potassium and sodium carbonate.

$$C_4H_4KNaO_6 + 5O_2 \longrightarrow K_2CO_3 + Na_2CO_3 + 6CO_2 + 4H_2O$$

Identification Tests

- It gives reactions characteristic of sodium and potassium.
- When its salt is heated, it emits odour of burning sugar and leaves a residue behind. The residue produced is alkaline to litmus paper and gives effervescence with mineral acids.

$$C_4H_4O_6KNa.4H_2O + 5O_2 \longrightarrow K_2CO_3 + Na_2CO_3 + 6CO_2 + 4H_2O$$

- When equal volume of acetic acid is added to a 5% solution of salt, a white crystalline precipitate of potassium bi-tartarate is obtained after 15 minutes.

Storage Conditions

- It should be stored in air-tight containers.

Dose

- 10 g (range 8 to 16 g). Children may be given half the adult dose.

Pharmaceutical Uses

- As saline cathartic and mild laxative.
- As emetic.
- As diuretic and urinary alkaliser.
- As food additive, stabiliser in meat and cheese products.
- As an ingredient of compound effervescent powder.

Note: Tartarate ions are not absorbed by the intestine and hence, they produce the evacuation of bowels in 1 to 2 hours.

4.3 HAEMATINICS

- These are the agents which are required for the formation of blood cells and used in the treatment of anaemia.
- The main haematinics include iron, vitamin B_{12} and folate ions.
- Haematinic drugs are available in combination with folic acid + zinc + vitamin B_{12} in tablet, capsule, syrup and suspension forms.
- These agents increase the number of erythrocytes or haemoglobin content in the blood.

4.3.1 Iron

- Iron is considered to be one of the most essential constituents of the body. Its usual content is about 45 mg/kg body weight.
- The total body content of iron is estimated to be about 3 to 4 g.
- The main portion of body iron (70%) occurs in haemoglobin and myoglobin.
- The remaining portion of the body iron is in the form of storage iron, transport iron and enzyme iron.
- In normal adults, about 1 mg of iron is lost from the body daily.
- The amount of iron in the body is controlled by regulating the absorption but not by excretion because the body recycles the iron obtained from the breakdown of RBC and hence, the daily requirement of iron is quite low.

- Iron is essential to elementary metabolic processes. It is responsible for the transport of molecular oxygen from the respiratory chain.
- It is an essential constituent of blood system and tissues. It is generally associated with the various types of proteins, viz.:
  (i) **Haemoproteins** include cytochrome C, catalase, peroxidise, haemoglobin, myoglobin, etc.
  (ii) **Iron storage and/or transport proteins** include ferritin, haemosiderin, transferrin, etc.

4.3.2 Causes of Deficiency of Iron

Deficiency of iron may be because of the following reasons:

- Decreased absorption of iron because of the presence of intestinal parasites.
- Increased losses of iron under certain conditions (e.g., haemorrhage and menstrual flow).

4.3.3 Official Compounds of Iron

- Ferrous fumarate
- Ferrous gluconate
- Iron and ammonium citrate
- Ferrous sulphate
- Dried ferrous sulphate
- Iron and dextran injection (IP, BP)
- Iron sorbitol injection (BP)
- Ferrous succinate (BP)

4.3.4 Other Ferrous and Ferric Compounds

- Ferrous carbonate
- Ferrous iodide
- Iron phosphate
- Ferrous lactate
- Ferrous tartrate
- Ferrous glycine sulphate
- Ferric chloride

4.3.5 Other Less Commonly Used Iron Compounds

- Ferro cholinate
- Ferric cacodylate
- Ferric citrate

- Ferric glycerophosphate
- Ferric hypophosphite

4.3.6 Incompatibilities of Iron Compounds

- Iron compounds are incompatible with mineral acids, alkali, alkali-carbonates and tannates.
- Ferrous gluconate is unstable in alkaline and neutral solutions and undergoes rapid oxidation. The solutions have been incompatible with ascorbic acid, glycine and pyridoxine.
- Ferrous sulphate has been incompatible with alkali, arsenates and mercuric salts, in addition to phosphates, tannates and benzoates.
- Sugars, glycine and alkali citrates do not allow the precipitation of ferric salts.

4.3.7 Storage of Iron Compounds

- Most of the iron compounds and preparations get oxidised by air and hence, should be stored in air-tight containers in cool and dark place.

4.3.8 Action and Uses of Iron Compounds

- In the iron-deficiency anaemia.
- In haemorrhagic condition.
- As haematinics (substances which increase the haemoglobin content).
- Ferrous sulphate mixture is used for paediatric purposes.

4.3.9 Ferrous Sulphate

Synonyms : Green vitriol, iron vitriol

Ferrous sulphate is available in two forms: Ferrous sulphate heptahydrate and dried ferrous sulphate.

Molecular formula : $FeSO_4.7H_2O$

Molecular weight : 278.0 g/mol

Category : Haematinic

Standards

Ferrous sulphate contains not less than 98.0% and not more than 103.3% of $FeSO_4 \cdot 7H_2O$.

Dried ferrous sulphate contains not less than 80.0% and not more than 90.0% of $FeSO_4$.

Methods of Preparation

- It is obtained by adding iron to excess of dilute sulphuric acid. The liquid is filtered only after the effervescence has ceased. It is then concentrated and allowed to cool and crystallise. At room temperature, transparent pale green crystals are formed.

$$Fe + H_2SO_4 \longrightarrow FeSO_4 + H_2\uparrow$$

- Commercially, it is obtained by exploring moist iron pyrite (FeS_2) to air, it gets oxidised slowly and forms ferrous sulphate.

$$2FeS_2 + 2H_2O + 7O_2 \longrightarrow 2FeSO_4 + 2H_2SO_4$$

Physical Properties

Colour : Greenish or bluish-green

Odour : Odourless

Taste : Metallic and astringent taste

State : Crystalline powder

Solubility : Soluble in water but insoluble in alcohol

Nature : (i) Efflorescent

(ii) Undergoes oxidation and turns brownish yellow when exposed to air

Chemical Properties

- Ferrous sulphate when heated decomposes to yield ferric oxide, sulphur dioxide and sulphuric acid.

$$2(FeSO_4{\cdot}7H_2O) \longrightarrow Fe_2O_3 + SO_2 + H_2SO_4 + 13H_2O$$

- Ferrous sulphate reduces the salts of silver and gold to their corresponding metals.

$$Ag^{+} + Fe^{2+} \longrightarrow Ag + Fe^{3+}$$

$$Au^{3+} + 3Fe^{2+} \longrightarrow Au + 3Fe^{3+}$$

- With some alkali sulphates, it forms double salts.
- In the presence of light, ferrous sulphate reduces mercuric chloride to mercurous chloride.

$$2HgCl_2 + 2Fe^{2+} \longrightarrow Hg_2Cl_2 + 2Fe^{2+} + 2Cl^{-}$$

- It decolourises acidified potassium permanganate and turns acidified potassium dichromate green.
- When ferrous sulphate reacts with sodium carbonate solution, CO_2 is evolved.

$$FeSO_4 + Na_2CO_3 \longrightarrow FeCO_3 + Na_2SO_4$$

$$FeCO_3 + 2H_2O \longrightarrow Fe(OH)_2 + CO_2$$

- With ammonium sulphate, it forms Mohr's salt, i.e., $(NH_4)_2Fe(SO_4)_2 \cdot 6H_2O$.

Identification Test

- It gives reactions characteristic of ferrous and sulphate ions.

Tests for Purity

- It is tested for acidity, As, Cu, heavy metals and basic sulphates.

Assay

Method 1

Principle

- Based on the oxidation-reduction titration technique by using potassium permanganate solution. The same, i.e., potassium permanganate solution acts as self-indicator.

Procedure

- An accurately weighed, about 1 g of ferrous sulphate is dissolved in 20 mL of dilute H_2SO_4 and titrated with 0.1 N $KMnO_4$.

$$2FeSO_4 + 2KMnO_4 + 4H_2SO_4 \longrightarrow K_2SO_4 + 2MnSO_4 + Fe_2(SO_4)_3 + 4H_2O$$

Equivalence Factor

- Each mL of 0.1 N $KMnO_4$ Ξ 0.0291 g of $FeSO_4 \cdot 7H_2O$.

Method 2

Principle

- Based on the oxidation-reduction titration technique by using ceric ammonium sulphate. Solution of ferroin sulphate solution is used as an indicator.

Procedure

- An accurately weighed, about 1 g of ferrous sulphate is dissolved in about 30 mL of water and 20 mL of dilute H_2SO_4 in a conical flask and titrated with 0.1 M ceric ammonium sulphate solution in the burette, using ferroin sulphate solution as an indicator.
- At the end-point, the red colour changes to light blue.

$$2FeSO_4 + 2Ce(SO_4)_2{\cdot}2(NH_4)_2SO_4 \longrightarrow Fe_2(SO_4)_3 + Ce_2(SO_4)_3 + 2MnSO_4 + 4(NH_4)_2SO_4$$

Equivalence Factor

- Each mL of 0.1 M ceric ammonium sulphate Ξ 0.0278 g of $FeSO_4 \cdot 7H_2O$.

Incompatibility

- Ferrous sulphate is incompatible with alkali, arsenates, mercuric salts, phosphates, tannates and benzoates.

Storage

- It gets oxidised by air and hence, should be stored in air-tight containers in a cool and dark place.
- In order to stabilise the ferrous form, certain reducing agents like hypophosphorous acid and dextrose are included in formulations.

Dose

- 60 to 200 mg tablets.

Pharmaceutical Uses

- In the iron-deficiency anaemia.
- As haemopoietic.
- As haematinic, i.e., it promotes formation of haemoglobin.
- Ferrous sulphate mixture is used for paediatric purposes.
- Used to dye fabrics and in tanning clothes.
- Used in the manufacture of ink.
- In photography.
- As disinfectant.
- As insecticide in agriculture.

Cautions

- Ferrous sulphate solutions may bring about discolouration of teeth.
- Excessive consumption by children may cause the GIT irritation or shock.

4.3.10 Ferrous Gluconate

Synonyms : Iron gluconate, glucoferron

Molecular formula : $C_{12}H_{22}O_{14}Fe \cdot 2H_2O$

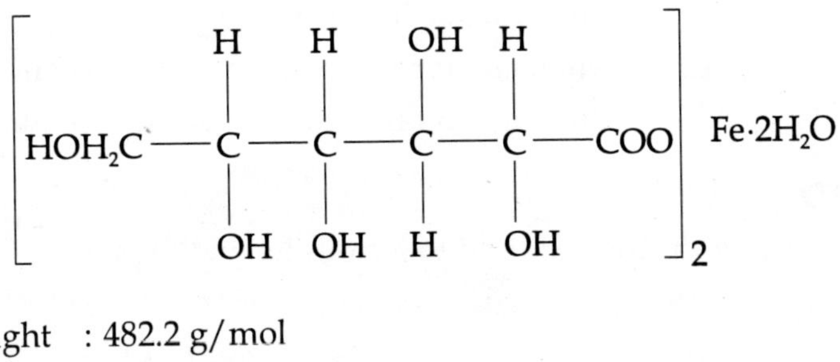

Molecular weight : 482.2 g/mol

Category : Haematinic

Standards

It contains not less than 95.0% of $C_{12}H_{22}O_{14}Fe$, which is calculated with reference to the substance dried at 105°C for 5 hours.

Methods of Preparation

- It is prepared by heating freshly prepared solution of ferrous carbonate with calculated amount of gluconic acid in aqueous media.

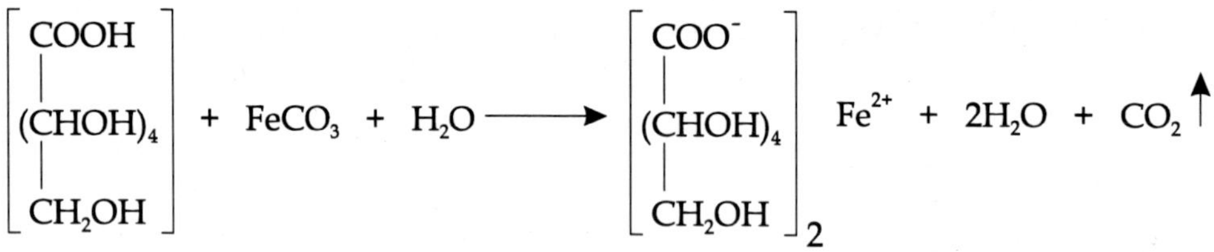

- It can also be obtained by double decomposition reaction between calcium gluconate and ferrous sulphate. The calcium sulphate is insoluble and filtered. The solution of ferrous gluconate is concentrated to get grey powder or granules of ferrous gluconate.

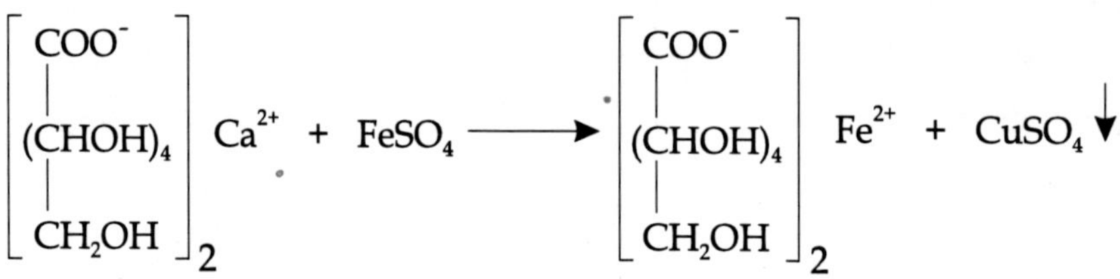

Physical Properties

Colour : Yellowish grey or pale greenish yellow

Odour : Slight odour resembling that of burnt sugar

State : Fine powder

Solubility : Soluble in water and almost insoluble in alcohol. Its solubility is increased by addition of citric acid.

Nature : (i) Its aqueous solution is acidic in nature.

(ii) Undergoes oxidation and turns brownish yellow when exposed to air.

(iii) Its aqueous solution is stabilised by the addition of glucose.

Chemical Property

- It is light sensitive, as it is oxidised to ferrous ion in the presence of light.

Identification Tests

- It gives reactions characteristic of ferrous salts.
- An aqueous solution of ferrous gluconate (0.75 g ferrous gluconate dissolved in 7.5 mL water) containing a little of glacial acetic acid (1 mL) and phenyl hydrazine (1 mL) is heated on water bath for 30 minutes. On cooling, the crystal of gluconic acid phenylhydrazide crystallises. It is purified and its melting point is 200 to 202°C with decomposition.

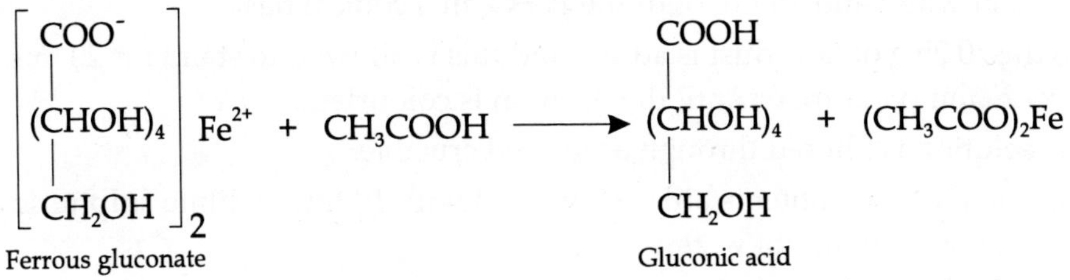

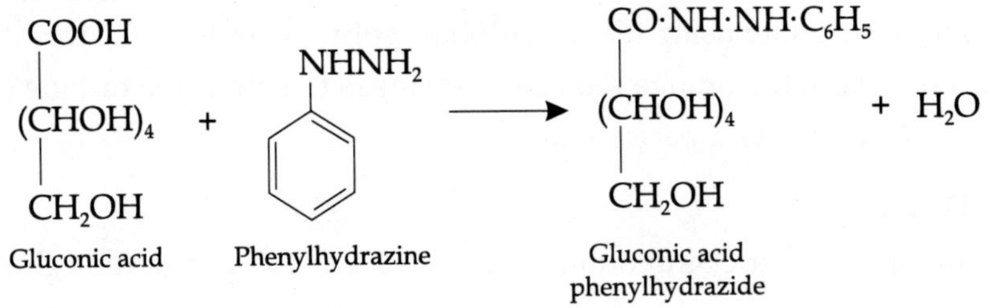

Tests for Purity

- It is tested for acidity, As, Ba, ferric iron, heavy metals, chlorides, sulphate, oxalic acid, dextrose and sucrose and loss on drying.
- Arsenic should not be more than 2 ppm.
- Heavy metals should not be more than 20 ppm.
- Other impurities, viz. barium, ferric ion, chloride, sulphate, oxalic acid and reducing sugars, should not be more than 10 ppm.
- Loss on drying should not be more than 7%.
- It is important to note that here ferrous gluconate has to be tested for ferric iron because a ferrous compound, if kept open, gets oxidised into ferric by the oxygen of air. It is for this reason that the tablets of ferrous salts are kept in a closed container.

$$Fe^{2+} \xrightarrow{\text{Air}} Fe^{3+}$$

Assay

Principle

- Based on oxidation-reduction titration technique by using ceric ammonium sulphate. Solution of ferroin sulphate solution is used as an indicator.

Procedure

- An accurately weighed, about 1.5 g of ferrous gluconate is dissolved in about 75 mL of water and 15 mL of dilute H_2SO_4 in a conical flask.
- To this, 0.25 g of zinc dust is added and this is allowed to stand for 20 minutes at room temperature or until the solution is colourless.
- The solution is filtered through a sintered crucible.
- The crucible and contents are first washed with 10 mL of dilute sulphuric acid and then with 10 mL of water.
- The combined filtrate and washings are immediately titrated with 0.1 N ceric ammonium sulphate using ferroin sulphate solution as an indicator.
- At the end-point, the orange red colour changes to pale green or blue colour.
- A blank titration is also performed.

Equivalence Factor

- Each mL of 0.1 N ceric ammonium sulphate Ξ 0.04461 g of ferrous gluconate.

Storage Condition

- It is stored in well-closed containers protected from light.

Dose

- 0.3 to 0.6 g.

Pharmaceutical Uses

- Used in the preparation of ferrous gluconate tablets.
- As haematinic, i.e., promotes formation of haemoglobin.
- It is regarded to cause fewer side effects than other ferrous salts, including ferrous sulphate.
- It is generally used in the form of tablets or as elixirs.

4.4 POISON

- A poison may be defined as any substance, administered in whatever way (either by mouth, injection, inhalation, skin, mucous membrane, etc.), producing ill health, disease or death.
- The diagnosis of poisoning is often difficult.

- But acute poisoning may be accidental, occupational, suicidal or criminal.
- Self-medication is also a major cause of drug poisoning.
- The poisoning, either accidental or intentional, requires immediate support and symptomatic management to avert any threat to life.
- The perfect management and treatment solely depends upon the identification of ingested poison or corrosive substance, so that specific antidote which can counteract the poison can be used.

4.4.1 Classification of Poisoning

Poisoning can be classified into three types:

(i) Intentional Poisoning

- In this type of poisoning, a person takes or gives a substance with the intention of causing harm to himself or some other person.
- Examples include suicide, assault, etc.

(ii) Unintentional Poisoning

- In this type of poisoning, a person takes or gives a substance without knowing its toxic effects.
- Examples include accidental poisoning.

(iii) Undetermined Poisoning

- It is a type of poisoning wherein the distinction between intentional and unintentional poisoning is not clear.
- Examples include pesticides or insecticides poisoning.

4.4.2 Reasons of Poisoning

Poisoning of body can be ascribed to various reasons:

- Because of heavy metals, as the environment is getting richer in heavy metals.
- Metallic contamination of food and water.
- Leaching of metals from utensils and cookware.
- Use of pesticides or insecticides.
- Excessive use of drug or drug overdose.
- Due to cyanide poisoning.

4.4.3 Signs and Symptoms of Poisoning

- Reducing breathing rate
- Nausea, vomiting and diarrhoea
- Dilated or shrunken pupils

- Increased or decreased heart rate
- Partial consciousness
- Muscle cramps

4.4.4 Heavy Metal Poisoning

- The most common heavy metals responsible for poisoning are the salts of arsenic, mercury, lead, iron and cadmium.
- It occurs because of their overdose or because of their incomplete metabolism in the body.
- Depending upon the content and type of heavy metal, their toxic effects can be seen.

4.4.4.1 Treatment of Heavy Metal Poisoning

- The most widely adopted method includes the usage of such heavy metal antagonist which is able to form specific chelate or complex with the heavy metals.
- The initial treatment includes the administration of activated charcoal for adsorbing heavy metal or poison.
- It is followed by administration of compounds which are able to produce emesis. This results in elimination of any poison left in the stomach being absorbed in circulation.
- Some inorganic compounds precipitate heavy metals and prevent their absorption.
- In case of poison being absorbed, some organic antidotes are used.
- Examples include activated charcoal, light kaolin, copper sulphate, magnesium sulphate, sodium phosphate, deferoxamine, dimercaprol, succimer, calcium disodium edentate, etc.

4.4.5 Cyanide Poisoning

- Cyanide poisoning either occurs accidently or intentionally to commit suicide.
- It may also occur by inhalation of fumes of hydrocyanic acid (HCN), ingestion of inorganic cyanide salt or cyanide releasing substances like cyanogens chloride, cyanamide, bitter almond, peach or apricot, photographic chemical or silver polishes as well.
- Even consumption of 300 mg of potassium cyanide may cause death.

4.4.5.1 Mechanism of Cyanide Poisoning

- Cyanide ions combine with ferric ion of cytochrome oxidase, an enzyme which is essential for electron transfer reactions.
- As a result of this, there is blockage in cellular respiration and metabolic reactions stop.

4.4.5.2 *Treatment of Cyanide Poisoning*

- Two inorganic antidotes, such as sodium nitrite and sodium thiosulphate, are used one by one in conjunction with each other.
- Initially, sodium nitrite is injected intravenously.
- This is followed by intravenous injection of sodium thiosulphate infusion.
- The sodium nitrite is able to convert haemoglobin to meth-haemoglobin, which binds to cyanide ions.
- As a result, the cyanide poisoning of cytochrome oxidase gets prevented.
- However, the cyanide-meth-haemoglobin complex slowly gets dissociated.
- Further, the sodium thiosulphate converts it immediately to non-toxic thiocyanate, which is excreted by the kidney.
- Besides, another compound named dicobalt edetate is more specific and directly reacts with cyanide ions to yield a stable non-toxic cobaltcyanoedetate complex.
- However, dicobalt edetate and sodium nitrite are toxic.

4.5 ANTIDOTES

- According to WHO, **antidote** may be defined as 'a therapeutic substance used to counteract the toxic action of a specific xenobiotic'.
- In other words, antidotes are the substances which react specifically with an ingested poison or toxic substance or an overdose of the potent drugs.
- They act either pharmacologically by neutralising the poison or its toxic effect (antagonistic action) or chemically by converting them to non-toxic or less toxic forms like chelates, acids or insoluble derivatives.

4.5.1 Classification of Antidotes

Based on the mechanism of action, antidotes are classified into the following four types:

(a) Physiological antidotes
(b) Chemical antidotes
(c) Mechanical antidotes
(d) Universal antidotes

(a) Physiological Antidotes

- They are also called antagonists.
- These antidotes are responsible for counteracting the toxic effect of a poison by bringing about physiological changes in the body.
- They are used after some of the poison is absorbed in the circulation.
- Example, sodium nitrite used in cyanide poisoning converts haemoglobin into methaemoglobin and binds to cyanide, thereby inactivating it.
- Atropine and physostigmine are antidotes for each other.

(b) Chemical Antidotes

- These antidotes are responsible for counteracting the toxic effect of a poison by changing the chemical nature of the poison and converting into inactive or harmless compound.
- Examples include sodium thiosulphate, which causes conversion of toxic cyanide into non-toxic thiocyanate; and EDTA, which acts as a chelating agent for heavy metal poisoning.

(c) Mechanical Antidotes

- These antidotes act by inhibiting the absorption of poison or toxin from the GIT into the blood or expel the poison by emesis or eliminating through the urine.
- Examples include activated charcoal, light kaolin, etc., which adsorb the poison and prevent its absorption.
- Other examples include copper sulphate, magnesium sulphate, sodium monohydrogen phosphate, etc., which inactivate the poison prior to absorption and precipitate the toxic material as insoluble salt.

(d) Universal Antidotes

- These are combinations of mechanical antidotes and are useful when type of poison is not known or more than one poison is consumed.
- A universal antidote consists of combination of:

  Magnesium oxide - 1 part

  Tannic acid - 1 part

  Activated charcoal - 2 parts

Table 4.1 gives a list of antidotes for selected unabsorbed inorganic poisons and drug overdose.

Table 4.1: Antidotes for selected unabsorbed inorganic poisons and drug overdose

Poison or drug overdose	Antidote	Mechanism of action of antidote
Acid (corrosive)	Antacid or weak alkali; e.g., milk of magnesia. Note: Avoid induced vomiting.	Chemical antagonism Acid-base neutralisation
Alkalis (caustic)	Weak acid like lemon juice, diluted vinegar, etc.	Chemical antagonism Acid-base neutralisation
Copper and lead salts	Penicillamine	Chelation
Iron salts	Desferroxamine, sodium carbonate, 1% lavage	Chelation
Mercury salts	Dimercaprol (BAL)	Chelation

4.5.2 Sodium Thiosulphate

Synonyms : Sodium hyposulfite, anti-chlor
Molecular formula : $Na_2S_2O_3 \cdot 5H_2O$
Molecular weight : 248.18 g/mol
Dose : 3 to 10 mL of 2% solution by IV or IM route

Standards

It contains not less than 99.0% and not more than 101.0% $Na_2S_2O_3 \cdot 5H_2O$.

Methods of Preparation

- It is obtained by boiling sodium sulphite with sulphur.

$$Na_2SO_3 + S \xrightarrow{\Delta} Na_2S_2O_3$$

- It is also prepared by reacting sodium hydroxide with sulphur.

$$6NaOH + 4S \longrightarrow Na_2S_2O_3 + 2Na_2S + 3H_2O$$

- It is obtained by passing SO_2 gas in a mixture of sodium sulphide (8%) and sodium carbonate (6%).

$$2Na_2S + Na_2CO_3 + 4SO_2 \longrightarrow 3Na_2S_2O_3 + CO_2\uparrow$$

- It is also prepared by passing sulphur dioxide into sodium sulphide solution.

$$2Na_2S + 3SO_2 \longrightarrow Na_2S_2O_3 + S$$

Physical Properties

Colour : Colourless or white
State : Prismatic crystalline powder
Solubility : Soluble in water, insoluble in alcohol
Nature : Effloresces in dry air

Chemical Properties

- It starts melting at 50°C and at 100°C, it loses its all moles of water.
- Its aqueous solution decomposes slowly as follows:

$$4Na_2S_2O_3 \longrightarrow 3Na_2SO_4 + Na_2S_5 \longrightarrow Na_2S + 4S$$

- Barium chloride reacts with sodium thiosulphate solution to give white precipitates of barium thiosulphate.

$$Na_2S_2O_3 + BaCl_2 \longrightarrow BaS_2O_3 + 2NaCl$$

- Sodium thiosulphate is used to dissolve silver halide, hence used in photography and is also known as 'hypo'.

$$2Na_2S_2O_3 + AgBr \longrightarrow \underset{\text{Sodium argentothiosulphate}}{Na_3[Ag(S_2O_3)_2]} + NaBr$$

Identification Tests

- It gives reactions characteristic of sodium and thiosulphate ions.
- Addition of few drops of iodine solution to 10% sodium thiosulphate solution results in the formation of colourless solution.

Tests for Purity

It is tested for the presence of heavy metals, sulphide, sulphite, sulphates, etc.

- Heavy metals should not be more than 10 ppm.
- Sulphide and sulphite should be absent.
- Sulphates should not be more than 0.2%.
- The pH of aqueous solution of 10% w/v sodium thiosulphate is 6.0 to 8.4.

Assay

Principle

It is based on iodometric titrations. It is assayed by titration with standard iodine solution with starch as an indicator.

Procedure

- About 0.8 g accurately weighed sample of sodium thiosulphate is accurately weighed and dissolved in 30 mL of water in a conical flask.
- This is then titrated with 0.1 N standard iodine solution added from a burette.
- Towards the end-point, 3 mL of starch solution is added as an indicator.
- The approach of end-point can be recognised by the discharge of yellow colour of iodine by shaking for few seconds.

$$2Na_2S_2O_3 + I_2 \longrightarrow Na_2S_4O_6 + 2NaI$$

Equivalence Factor

- Each mL of 0.1 N iodine Ξ 0.02482 g of sodium thiosulphate.

Incompatibility

- It is incompatible with solutions containing other metal cations. This is due to precipitation of metal thiosulphate. In acidic medium, these precipitates may darken due to the formation of respective sulphides.

Storage

- It should be stored in tightly-closed containers and in single dose.

Pharmaceutical Uses

- As antioxidant, limited to solution containing iodides.
- As standard titrant in iodometric analysis.
- As antifungal agent topically.
- As antidote in cyanide poisoning intravenously after the injection of sodium nitrite.
- As an antidote in lead, bismuth, mercury and iodine poisoning.
- As a fixer in photographic work.
- As antichlor in bleaching process in textile industry.

Note: The IP recommended dose of injection which is equivalent of 0.3 to 1.0 g (3 to10 mL) and is administered by IV and IM route.

4.5.3 Activated Charcoal

It is a dark grey or black residue consisting of carbon and any remaining ash obtained by removing water and other volatile constituents from animal and vegetable substances.

Methods of Preparation

- Commercially, it is obtained as a residue during destructive distillation of various organic matters or from burning of organic materials in a special manner. The coarse material is crushed and powdered.
- It is also prepared by burning wood in the absence of air. The residue obtained is nearly pure carbon.
- Other sources include sucrose, lactose, rice, starch, coconut, bone, pericarp, blood and various industrial wastes, which can be used for preparing charcoal.

Activation of Charcoal

- The absorptive power of charcoal could be increased tremendously by treating it with substances like steam, air, carbon dioxide, oxygen, zinc chloride, sulphuric acid, phosphoric acid or a combination of these at a temperature ranging from 500°C to 9000°C.

- In this process, the activating substance presumably removes substances previously absorbed on charcoal and in some instances at least, breaking down the granules of carbon into smaller ones having greater total surface of approximately 100 m^2.

Physical Properties

Colour : Dark grey or black

Odour : Odourless

Taste : Tasteless

State : Powder

Solubility : Almost insoluble in water and other usual solvents

Nature : Fine powder having smooth touch and is free from gritty particles.

Chemical Property

- Provides more surface area for adsorbent properties.

Pharmaceutical Uses

- As protective and adsorbent.
- As an emergency antidote in various types of poisoning.
- It not only adsorbs heavy metals, but also adsorbs drugs like hypnotics, sedatives, alkaloids, etc., in addition to gases like carbon monoxide, carbon dioxide, nitrous oxide, etc. It is normally employed in the ratio of 5:1 or 10:1 (charcoal: poison).
- As a burning fuel.
- As a filter-aid due to its large surface area.
- As disinfectant in wounds.
- As a constituent for gun powder.
- To filter toxins from blood and kidney diseases.
- To purify blood transfusions.
- To treat overdose of aspirin.
- As an antidote in case of snake, spider and insect bite.

4.5.4 Sodium Nitrite

Molecular formula : $NaNO_2$

Molecular weight : 68.99 g/mol

Dose : 10 to 15 mL of 2% solution by IV route

Standards

It contains not less than 97.0% and not more than 101.0% $NaNO_2$ with reference to substance dried over silica gel.

Methods of Preparation

- It is obtained by passing nitrogen oxide (NO) gas obtained during the catalytic oxidation of ammonia and oxygen in sodium carbonate solution. The solution is concentrated to crystallise.

$$2Na_2CO_3 + 4NO + O_2 \longrightarrow 4NaNO_2 + 2CO_2\uparrow$$

- It is also prepared by strongly heating sodium nitrate.

$$2NaCO_3 \longrightarrow 2NaNO_2 + O_2\uparrow$$

- It is obtained by heating sodium nitrate with lead.

$$NaNO_3 + Pb \longrightarrow NaNO_2 + PbO$$

Physical Properties

Colour : White
Odour : Odourless
Taste : Saline
State : Granular powder or crystals
Solubility : Soluble in water, sparingly soluble in alcohol
Nature : Alkaline and deliquescent

Chemical Properties

- It gets slowly oxidised to sodium nitrate.
- It is easily decomposed by acidification with dilute sulphuric acid.
- It acts as reducing agent and gets oxidised in acidic medium.

Assay

Principle

- Based on permangnetometric titrations.

Procedure

- 1 g of sodium nitrite is dissolved in 100 mL water.
- Pipette out 10 mL of this solution and transfer to another solution containing $KMnO_4$, 100 mL water and 5 mL H_2SO_4.
- This solution is then warmed to 40°C and allowed to stand for 5 minutes.
- To this, 25 mL of 0.1 N oxalic acid is added and again heated to 80°C.

- The excess oxalic acid is titrated with 0.1 N potassium permanganate.
- At the end-point, colour changes from colourless to pink.

$$NaNO_2 + H_2SO_4 \longrightarrow NaHSO_4 + HNO_2$$

$$HNO_2 + [O] \longrightarrow HNO_3$$

Equivalence Factor

- Each 1 mL of 0.1 N $KMnO_4$ Ξ 3.450 g of $NaNO_2$.

Incompatibility

- It is incompatible with oxidising agents.

Storage

- It should be stored in tightly-closed containers, away from light and moisture.

Pharmaceutical Uses

- As antidote in cyanide poisoning.
- As antioxidant to prevent rusting of surgical instruments.
- As a food preservative.
- Acts as a muscle relaxant.
- Acts as vasodilator.
- As a hypotensive agent.
- As a reducing agent.

Note:

- This compound is not included in IP monographs but finds place in the appendix on reagents and solutions.
- In cyanide poisoning, viz., sodium or potassium cyanides or hydrocyanic acid or bitter almonds, a 3% solution of sodium nitrite is slowly infused intravenously, until 10 mL (300 mg) over a period of 3 minutes has been administered. This is then followed by 25 mL of a 50% solution of sodium thiosulphate (12.5 g) infused over a period of 10 minutes.

4.6 ASTRINGENTS

- The word 'astringent' derives from Latin word 'adstringere' which means 'to bind fast'.
- These substances bring about protein precipitation.
- They are usually applied to damaged skin topically or to the mucous membrane of the GIT, including the mouth.

- The precipitated protein and the astringent form a protective layer on the surface.
- They are available in a wide range of dosage forms, viz., dusting powders, mouthwashes, gargles, topical solutions, etc.
- Astringents are normally used in much diluted form and are used topically to:
  - Stop bleeding
  - Clean the face and prevent acne breakout
  - Treat haemorrhoids
  - Relieve the discomfort and itching of insect bites

4.6.1 Actions of Astringents

- They are able to reduce cell permeability due to their protein precipitant action.
- They also inhibit the transcapillary movement of plasma-proteins, which helps to reduce local oedema, exudation and inflammation.
- They are also capable of reducing mucous secretion.
- On topical application, in low concentration, they stimulate growth of new tissue; while at high concentration, they bring about corrosive effect on contact with the tissue.

4.6.2 Mechanism of Astringent Action

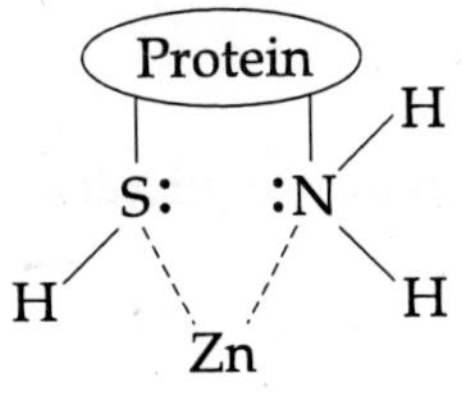

Figure 4.1: Mechanism of astringent action

- The protein precipitation brought about by an astringent may be ascribed to the presence of metallic ions having large charge/radius ratio or strong electrostatic fields **(Figure 4.1)**.
- Transition metal cations have protein precipitation action and if a very dilute solution of such metal cation is used over a tissue, a slight surface action specially leading to 'shrinkage' or 'firming up' of the skin takes place. This action is called 'astringent action'.
- The metal forms complex with various polar groups present on the protein or enzyme.
- This complexation results in a drastic change in the properties of protein.
- It hardens the epidermis and creates a barrier against infection.

4.6.3 Applications of Astringents

- They exhibit styptic action, i.e., stop bleeding by coagulation of blood and constriction of small capillaries.
- They exhibit anti-inflammatory action, by decreasing the supply of blood to the tissues.
- They act as antiperspirant, by decreasing secretion of perspiration by reducing the pore size of the skin.
- They exhibit antimicrobial action, by causing precipitation of proteins of microbes.
- They are used in the treatment of diarrhoea.
- They promote healing process.
- They also possess deodorant properties.
- They decrease sweating and make the skin tougher.

4.6.4 Potash Alum

Potash alum is potassium aluminium sulphate. It is a double salt.

Synonym : Alum

Molecular formula : $KAl(SO_4)_2 \cdot 12H_2O$

Molecular weight : 474.4 g/mol

Category : Astringent, antiseptic and pharmaceutical aid

Standards

It contains an amount of aluminium equivalent to not less than 99.5% of $KAl(SO_4)_2 \cdot 12H_2O$.

Method of Preparation

It is obtained by adding a concentrated solution of potassium sulphate to hot solution of an equimolecular proportion of aluminium sulphate. When the solution is concentrated and cooled, characteristic octahedral crystals precipate.

$$K_2SO_4 + Al_2(SO_4)_3 + 24H_2O \longrightarrow 2KAl(SO_4)_2 \cdot 12H_2O$$

Physical Properties

Colour : Colourless or transparent

Odour : Odourless

Taste : Sweet and astringent

State : Granular crystals

Solubility : Soluble in water but insoluble in alcohol

Chemical Properties

- When it is heated slowly on water bath temperature, it melts in its water of crystallisation.
- At 200°C, it loses its water of crystallisation and becomes anhydrous.

$$KAl(SO_4)_2{\cdot}12H_2O \xrightarrow{\Delta} KAl(SO_4)_2 + 12H_2O$$

Identification Tests

- It gives reactions characteristic of potassium, aluminium and sulphate.
- The aqueous solution (10 mL) is shaken with sodium bicarbonate (0.5 g) and filtered. The filtrate gives reaction of potassium and sulphate.

Tests for Purity

- It is tested for As, heavy metals, Fe and Zn.
- In addition, alum is also required to comply with a test for ammonium salts.

Assay

Principle

- It is based on gravimetric method.

Procedure

- An accurately weighed sample of about 2 g alum is dissolved in 300 mL of water.
- To this, 20 mL of ammonium chloride solution, 5 drops of methyl red and a sufficient quantity of ammonia solution are added to produce a distinct yellow colour.
- The solution is heated to the boiling point.
- Then it is filtered and the precipitate is washed with a 2.5% solution of ammonium nitrate until it becomes free from chloride.
- The precipitate of Al_2O_3 is dried to a constant weight at 120°C and weighed.

Equivalence Factor

Each gram of residue Ξ 9.307 g of $KAl(SO_4)_2 \cdot 12H_2O$.

Incompatibility

- It is incompatible with calcium, mercury and lead salts, in addition to borax, alkali hydroxides and carbonates, phosphates, phenols, tannins and salicylates.

Storage Condition

- It is stored in tightly-closed containers.

Pharmaceutical Uses

- As astringent.
- As antiperspirant (2% solution of alum).
- As a local styptic.
- As antiseptic.
- Finds use in the preparation of toxoids because of its protein precipitation property.
- In mouthwashes, gargles and dusting powders.
- Used by barbers for wetting and rubbing on the skin after shave because of its astringent and antiseptic action.
- As pharmaceutical aid.
- As a bladder irritant and for hyperhydrosis.
- Strong solution (5 to 10%) is used by athletes to harden the skin.

4.6.5 Zinc Sulphate

Synonym : White vitriol
Molecular formula : $ZnSO_4 \cdot 7H_2O$
Molecular weight : 287.6 g/mol
Category : Astringent and emetic
Dose : 0.6 to 2 g daily

Standards

It contains not less than 55.6% and not more than 61.0% of $ZnSO_4$, corresponding to not less than 99.5% and not more than the equivalent of 102.0% of hydrated zinc sulphate, $ZnSO_4 \cdot 7H_2O$.

Methods of Preparation

- It is prepared by digesting metallic zinc granules in dilute sulphuric acid. A slight excess of zinc metal is used and reaction is allowed to continue until hydrogen gas ceases to evolve. Excess of zinc metal is used so that all the sulphuric acid is consumed.

$$Zn + H_2SO_4 \longrightarrow ZnSO_4 + H_2\uparrow$$

- It is also obtained by the action of dilute sulphuric acid on zinc oxide.

$$ZnO + H_2SO_4 \longrightarrow ZnSO_4 + H_2O$$

- It is also prepared by heating zinc sulphide in the presence of air. The heated mass is dissolved in hot water, filtered and the solution is concentrated for crystallisation.

$$ZnS + 2O_2 \longrightarrow ZnSO_4$$

Physical Properties

Colour : Colourless or transparent

Odour : Odourless

Taste : Astringent and metallic taste

State : Prismatic or needle-shaped crystals or granular, crystalline powder

Solubility : Soluble in water and glycerine but insoluble in alcohol

Nature : (i) Effloresces in dry air

(ii) Aqueous solution is acidic to litmus

Chemical Properties

- Zinc sulphate reacts with hydrogen sulphide to yield white precipitate of zinc sulphide, which is soluble in HCl but insoluble in acetic acid.

$$ZnSO_4 + H_2S \longrightarrow ZnS + H_2SO_4$$

- Zinc sulphate reacts with NaOH to yield white precipitate of zinc hydroxide, which is soluble in excess NaOH.

$$ZnSO_4 + 2NaOH \longrightarrow Zn(OH)_2 + 2NaCl$$

$$Zn(OH)_2 + 2NaOH \longrightarrow \underset{\text{Sodium zincate}}{Na_2ZnO_2} + 2H_2O$$

- Zinc sulphate dehydrates by losing its water of crystallisation as follows:

$$ZnSO_4 \cdot 7H_2O \xrightarrow{50°C} ZnSO_4 \cdot 2H_2O \xrightarrow{100°C} ZnSO_4 \cdot H_2O$$

$$ZnSO_4 \cdot H_2O \xrightarrow{450°C} ZnSO_4$$

$$ZnO \xleftarrow{740°C} ZnSO_4$$

- Zinc sulphate is reported to form double salt with potassium and ammonium sulphate.

$$ZnSO_4 + (NH_4)_2SO_4 \longrightarrow ZnSO_4 \cdot (NH_4)_2SO_4 \cdot 6H_2O$$

- A white precipitate of zinc ferrocyanide is formed when zinc sulphate reacts with potassium ferrocyanide. The precipitate remains insoluble in dilute HCl solution.

$$2ZnSO_4 + K_4[Fe(CN)_6] \longrightarrow Zn_2[Fe(CN)_6] + 2K_2SO_4$$

Identification Tests

- It gives reaction characteristics of zinc and sulphate.
- 0.25 g zinc sulphate is dissolved in 5 mL water and 0.2 mL of sodium hydroxide (400 g/L) is added to it. A white precipitate is formed. Again, 2 mL of sodium hydroxide is added to the above solution. The precipitate will dissolve. Then, 10 mL of ammonium chloride (100 g/L) is added. The solution remains clear. Further, addition of 0.1 mL of sodium sulphide results in the formation of flocculent white precipitate.

Tests for Purity

- It is tested for reaction acidity, Al, Cu, Mg, Mn, Ni, As, Fe, chloride, alkalis and alkaline earths.
- In addition, alum is also required to comply with a test for ammonium salts.

Assay

Principle

- It is based on gravimetric method.
- Initially, zinc sulphate is converted to zinc carbonate by reaction with sodium carbonate.
- Then it is converted to zinc oxide by ignition.
- The residue, i.e., ZnO is weighed.

$$ZnSO_4 + Na_2CO_3 \longrightarrow ZnSO_3 \downarrow + Na_2SO_4$$

$$ZnCO_3 \xrightarrow{\Delta} ZnO + CO_2 \uparrow$$

Procedure

- An accurately weighed 1 g of sample is dissolved in 100 mL water and this solution is heated to about 90°C.
- To the hot solution, a solution of sodium carbonate is added with constant stirring, until complete precipitation of zinc carbonate occurs.
- Care should be taken to avoid excess addition of sodium carbonate.

- The precipitated zinc carbonate solution is boiled for a few minutes, filtered through tared Gooch crucible and washed with hot water until free from alkali.
- The residue is dried, ignited and weighed.

Equivalence Factor

Each gram of residue Ξ 1.984 g of $ZnSO_4$.

Incompatibility

- It is incompatible with alkali hydroxides and carbonates, borax, astringent infusion and decoctions.

Storage Condition

- It should be stored in tightly-closed containers in a cool place.

Pharmaceutical Uses

- As astringent in solution and powder form.
- As emetic in narcotic poisoning.
- As antiseptic lotion.
- As ophthalmic (0.25% solution is employed).
- Employed for protein precipitation as styptic.
- In topical preparations.
- As mild germicidal.
- In dermatological problems.
- As pharmaceutical aid in wound healing.

MULTIPLE-CHOICE QUESTIONS

1. Productive mucus produces
   (a) Mucus (b) Amalgam
   (c) Vomiting (d) None of the above
2. Emetics act by
   (a) Stimulation of CTZ
   (b) Increasing the amount of fluid
   (c) Decreasing the viscosity of the bronchial secretion
   (d) None of the above
3. An important antidote in cyanide poisoning is
   (a) Ethanol (b) Atropine
   (c) Desferioxamine (d) Sodium thiosulphate

4. Which kind of antidote reduces the poison across the intestinal wall?
   (a) Mechanical antidote (b) Physiological antidote
   (c) Chemical antidote (d) None of the above
5. Cyanide poisoning kit does not contain
   (a) Sodium bicarbonate (b) Amyl nitrite
   (c) Sodium nitrite (d) Sodium thiosulphate
6. How does a mechanical antidote act?
   (a) By producing the effects opposite to that of poison
   (b) By preventing the absorption of poison into the body
   (c) By changing the chemical nature of poison
   (d) By changing the physical nature of the poison
7. Cyanide poisoning has a characteristic odour of
   (a) Bitter almonds (b) Wheat
   (c) Lemon (d) Caraway
8. Sodium nitrite is given in conjunction with
   (a) Sodium bicarbonate (b) Sodium calcium edetate
   (c) Dimercaprol (d) Sodium thiosulphate
9. What is the effect of astringents on tissues?
   (a) Contraction (b) Shrinkage
   (c) Both (a) and (b) (d) None of the above
10. How do astringents act?
    a) Lipid precipitant (b) Bacterial inhibition
    c) Protein precipitant (d) Both (b) and (c)
11. Zinc sulphate is known as
    (a) Blue vitriol (b) White vitriol
    (c) Red vitriol (d) Yellow vitriol
12. Which inorganic astringent is used in the treatment of narcotic poisoning?
    (a) Alum (b) Ammonium chloride
    (c) Zinc sulphate (d) Zirconium sulphate
13. Zinc sulphate is prepared by the action of .... on zinc oxide.
    (a) Conc. HCl (b) Conc. HNO_3
    (c) Conc. H_2SO_4 (d) None of the above
14. Which of the following are haematinics?
    (a) Iron (b) Vitamin B_{12}
    (c) Folate ions (d) All of the above

15. The main portion of the body iron occurs in
    (a) Haemoglobin (b) Myoglobin
    (c) Both (a) and (b) (d) None of the above
16. Ferrous sulphate is also called
    (a) White vitriol (b) Yellow vitriol
    (c) Green vitriol (d) None of the above

FILL IN THE BLANKS

1. Cough is a .... reflux.
2. Emetics are used to produce ....
3. Ammonium chloride is prepared by ....
4. The Latin word 'expectorate' means ....
5. Productive cough produces ....
6. Expectorants are used to help in ....
7. .... inorganic compounds are used as saline expectorants.
8. Ammonium chloride is also known as ....
9. .... is used to counteract the poison.
10. .... therapy is used for lead poisoning.
11. Chemical antidote act by changing the .... of the poison.
12. Activated charcoal is used to .... the poison.
13. .... is an example of physiological antidote.
14. .... is the molecular formula of sodium thiosulphate.
15. Cyanide poisoning kit contains ...., ... and ....
16. An astringent is a drug which shrinks by .... from their surfaces.
17. Commercially, ... is prepared by heating metallic zinc to bright red in the presence of preheated air.
18. .... is used in narcotic poisoning and is also an inorganic astringent.
19. Astringents act as ....
20. Astringents cause .... of tissue.
21. Alum is prepared by adding a hot conc. solution of .... to a hot solution of .... and it gets separated.
22. .... is used as astringent.
23. Topical astringents are used to ....
24. Chemical formula of alum is ....
25. Chemical formula of zinc sulphate is ....
26. Zinc sulphate is used externally as ....

27. Chemical formula of ferrous sulphate is ....
28. The total body content of iron is estimated to be about ....

SHORT QUESTIONS

1. What are expectorants?
2. Define emetics.
3. What is the difference between irritant and stimulant emetics?
4. Which inorganic compound is used in the prevention and treatment of goitre?
5. Which expectorant is prepared by Solvay process?
6. Define haematinics.
7. Define poison and its classification.
8. What are antidotes? Classify them.

LONG QUESTIONS

1. What are expectorants? Classify expectorants with examples.
2. What is the mechanism of action of expectorants and emetics?
3. Define emetics. Classify them with examples.
4. What is the mechanism of action of emetics?
5. Give methods of preparation, properties, assay and applications of (a) ammonium chloride (b) potassium iodide, and (c) copper sulphate.
6. Give the official compounds, incompatibility, storage, action and uses of iron compounds.
7. Give a brief account of the preparation, properties, assay and uses of ferrous sulphate and ferrous gluconate.
8. Mention the reasons of poisoning.
9. Write a note on heavy metals and cyanide poisoning.
10. What is the mechanism of action of antidotes in poisoning?
11. Give a brief account of the preparation, properties, assay, and uses of sodium thiosulphate and sodium nitrite.
12. Write a note on activated charcoal.
13. Define astringents. What are the actions of astringents?
14. Explain in brief the mechanism of action of astringents.
15. Mention the applications of astringents.
16. Mention the chemical formula, method of preparation, physical and chemical properties, assay, applications and storage conditions of (a) alum and, (b) zinc sulphate.

ANSWERS

Multiple-Choice Questions

1. (a)	2. (a)	3. (d)	4. (a)	5. (a)	6. (b)	7. (a)	8. (d)
9. (c)	10. (d)	11. (b)	12. (c)	13. (c)	14. (d)	15. (c)	16. (c)

Fill in the Blanks

1.	Protective	2.	Vomiting
3.	Solvay process	4.	To drive from the chest
5.	Mucus	6.	Removal of secretions
7.	Potassium iodide/ammonium chloride	8.	Ammonium muriate/amchlor
9.	Antidote	10.	Chelation
11.	Chemical nature	12.	Absorb
13.	Sodium nitrite	14.	$Na_2S_2O_3.5H_2O$
15.	Amyl nitrite, sodium nitrite, sodium thiosulphate	16.	Protein precipitation
17.	$ZnSO_4$	18.	Zinc sulphate
19.	Protein precipitate	20.	Shrinkage or contraction
21.	Ammonium sulphate, aluminium sulphate	22.	Zinc sulphate, alum
23.	Firm up the skin	24.	$KAl(SO_4)_2.12H_2O$
25.	$ZnSO_4$	26.	Astringent
27.	$FeSO_4.7H_2O$	28.	3 to 4 g

5

Radio Pharmaceuticals

5.1 INTRODUCTION

- Radio pharmaceuticals are the radioisotopes or radionuclides which are employed in medicine for the diagnosis and treatment of certain diseases.
- These compounds are used in trace amounts to produce radioactivity that is essential for the pharmacological effect.
- It was discovered accidentally by the French Scientist, Henry Becquerel.
- Radioactive substances emit continuous rays or particles spontaneously by themselves to decompose to stable nuclei.
- However, they are also liable to produce hazardous effects when mishandled.

5.2 RADIOACTIVITY

- Radioactivity is defined as a spontaneous and continuous emission of radiations or rays, e.g., α, β and γ radiations from the substances.
- It is a natural and spontaneous process by which the unstable atom of one element emits or radiates excess energy in the form of particles or waves.
- After emission, the resulting daughter atom can either be a lower energy form of the same element or a completely different element.
- The emitted particles or waves are called ionising radiations because they have the ability to remove electrons from the atom of any matter they interact with.
- The emission of radiation is not influenced by temperature, pressure, concentration and catalyst.

5.3 RADIATIONS EMITTED BY RADIO PHARMACEUTICALS

- The most common radiations emitted have been classified traditionally as:

  (a) α-rays

  (b) β-rays

  (c) γ-rays

5.3.1 Alpha (α) Rays

- The alpha (α) rays are the heaviest as they are produced when the heaviest element undergoes decay.
- They are particulate in nature.
- These are not waves but exist as high-energy particles which are expelled from unstable nuclei.
- These particles carry two positive charges (charge = +2).
- These particles constitute two protons and two neutrons.
- Alpha-rays are similar to helium nuclei with mass of 4 amu, viz. ${}^{4}_{2}He$.
- They possess least penetrating power since they are large and heavy in nature.
- They can easily get absorbed and hence, possess greatest ionising capacity.
- They have low speed.
- α-rays are affected by strong magnetic and electric fields.
- The emission of α-particles from an element results in a daughter nucleus with atomic number less by 2 units, mass number less by 4 amu and 2 positive charges less than the original nucleus.
- For example, radioactive decay of radium yields radon nucleus by emitting α-particles.

$${}^{226}_{88}Ra \longrightarrow {}^{222}_{86}Rn + {}^{4}_{2}He$$

- They produce fluorescence and phosphorescence in some materials, such as zinc sulphide.
- Their energy is about 6 meV.
- Radioactive tracers emitting α-rays are used only for therapeutic purposes, as they liberate large amounts of energy over short distance, thereby destroying the local diseased tissues.
- They are intended not to be used as diagnostic agents due to their less penetrating capability.

5.3.2 Beta (β) Rays

- These are much lighter particles, about 8000 times smaller than α-rays in size.
- Beta rays exist as particles.
- These particles carry either a positive charge or a negative charge (charge = +1 or −1).

- These particles exist in two forms:
  (a) Positron or anti-particles of electron: a positive electron (β^+) or ${}^{0}_{1}\beta$
  (b) Negatron: a negative electron (β^{-1}) or (e^-)
- β-rays have negligible mass (about 1/1836th of the hydrogen ion) and are high speed electrons.
- The penetrating power of β-rays is greater, about 100 times more when compared to that of α-rays.
- They possess moderate ionising capacity, about 1/100th that of α-rays.
- They have more speed than α-rays.
- β-rays are affected by strong magnetic and electric fields.
- The emission of β-particles from an element results in a daughter nucleus with atomic number greater by 1 unit and no change in the mass when compared to the parent nucleus.
- For example, radioactive decay of carbon yields nitrogen with the emission of β-particles.

$$ {}^{14}_{6}C \longrightarrow {}^{14}_{7}N + {}^{0}_{-1}e $$

- They produce fluorescence and phosphorescence in some materials, such as zinc sulphide.
- Their energy ranges from 2 to 3 meV.
- Radioactive compounds emitting β-rays are usually employed as therapeutic agents, as they are more penetrating than α-rays, producing significant damage to the abnormal tissues.
- They are intended not to be used as diagnostic agents, as they can cause severe burns if exposed for an appreciable time.

5.3.2.1 Positrons

- It is a type of beta particle in which a proton inside a radionuclide nucleus is converted into a neutron.
- It is not common.
- Since they are short-lived, they do not find any application in biological field.
- Positron emission decreases proton number relative to neutron number.
- This kind of decay happens typically in large "proton-rich" radionuclide.
- Isotopes which undergo this decay and thereby emit positrons include Carbon-11 (C-11), Nitrogen-13 (N-13), Oxygen-15 (O-15), Aluminium-26 (Al-26), Sodium-22 (Na-22), Fluorine-18 (F-18) and Iodine-124 (I-124).

$$^{11}_{6}C \longrightarrow {}^{11}_{5}B + {}^{0}_{1}\beta$$

5.3.2.2 Negatrons

- These are emitted by those unstable nuclei in which neutrons are transformed into protons along with the emission of beta particles.

$$^{1}_{0}n \longrightarrow {}^{1}_{1}p + {}^{0}_{-1}\beta$$

- As a result, the released proton particle has the same mass as that of the original atom while the β-particle has charge as that of electron.

5.3.3 Gamma Rays

- Gamma rays exist as electromagnetic waves.
- These rays are uncharged (charge = 0).
- γ-rays are magnetic waves with shorter wavelength than X-rays and neutral due to the presence of photons.
- γ-rays have no mass, i.e., $^{0}_{0}\gamma$.
- They are highly penetrating into bones, organs and tissues. The relative penetration power of γ-rays is about 10,000 times greater as compared to α-rays.
- They move with a velocity equal to the speed of light.
- They are poorly ionising.
- They are not affected by strong magnetic or electric fields.
- The emission of γ-rays usually results in lowering of nuclear energy but no elemental change (i.e., no change or loss of atomic mass or number takes place).
- They produce fluorescence in some materials.
- They produce heat on the surface on which they fall and knout out electrons from it.
- They can produce nuclear reaction.
- Radio pharmaceuticals emitting γ-rays are preferably used for diagnostic purposes because of their high penetrating power.

5.4 SOME IMPORTANT TERMS

5.4.1. Isotopes

- These are the species which possess same atomic number 'Z' (number of protons) but different atomic mass number 'A' (number of protons plus neutrons). For example,

$$^{206}_{82}Pb\ ,\quad ^{207}_{82}Pb\ ,\quad ^{208}_{82}Pb$$

- They are also called nuclides.
- They have same number of protons but different number of neutrons.
- They have similar chemical but different physical properties due to different number of neutrons.
- They occupy the same place in the periodic table.
- Hydrogen has three isotopes as follows:

$^{1}_{1}H$	$^{2}_{1}H$	$^{3}_{1}H$
Protium	**Deuterium**	**Tritium**

- Isotopes are classified into two types:
  (a) Stable isotopes
  (b) Radioactive isotopes

(a) Stable Isotopes

- These isotopes are stable in nature.
- They do not emit any kind of radiation.
- For example, ^{13}C, ^{1}H (protium), ^{2}H (deuterium), etc.

(b) Radioactive Isotopes

- Radioactive isotopes are also called radioisotopes.
- These are natural or artificially created isotopes of a chemical element having an unstable nucleus that decays, resulting in emission of α-, β- and γ-rays until stability is reached.
- The stable end-product is a non-radioactive isotope of another element.
- The original nuclide is called the 'parent' while the product is called 'daughter nuclide'.
- This phenomenon of the nuclear changes is termed disintegration or radioactive decay.

- For example,

$$ {}_{a}^{b}X \xrightarrow{\text{Decay}} {}_{a-2}^{b-4}Y + \alpha\text{-rays} $$

Parent nuclei   Daughter nuclei

- Radioactive isotopes (radioisotopes) are further divided into two types:
  - **(i) Naturally occurring** for example, Potassium-40 (^{40}K), Rubidium-87 (^{87}Rb), Radium-226 (^{226}Ra), Uranium-235 (^{235}U), etc.
  - **(ii) Artificial radionuclides** are produced in nuclear reactions and are produced by bombarding atoms of a specific element with the radioactive particles, which results in the formation of new atoms from another type of element. For example, formation of radioactive isotope of phosphorus by bombarding aluminium with alpha particles.

$$ {}_{13}^{27}Al + {}_{2}^{4}He \longrightarrow {}_{15}^{30}P + {}_{0}^{1}n $$

5.4.2 Isobars

- These are the atoms of different species having different atomic number 'Z' (number of protons) but same atomic mass number 'A' (number of protons plus neutrons). For example,

$$ {}_{6}^{14}C, \; {}_{7}^{14}N $$

- They have different physical and chemical properties.
- They occupy different places in the periodic table.

5.4.3 Isotones

- These are the atomic species having same number of neutrons but different atomic mass numbers.

5.4.4 Nuclide

- It refers to the species of atoms characterised by the constitution of the nucleus, in particular, by the number of protons and neutrons in the nucleus.

5.4.5 Nuclear Isomers

- These refer to the atoms of the same species having same atomic number and same atomic mass number but differ in radioactive properties.

5.5 TYPES OF RADIOACTIVITY

Radioactivity is classified into two types:

(a) Natural radioactivity

(b) Artificial radioactivity

5.5.1 Natural Radioactivity

- It occurs spontaneously and continuously without any external efforts.
- For example, radium-226 (^{226}Ra), iodine-131 (^{131}I).
- These are further of two types:
  - (i) High atomic weight elements
  - (ii) Moderate atomic weight elements

(i) High Atomic Weight Elements

- There are about 40 elements emitting α-, β-, and γ-rays.
- For example, Uranium-238, Radium-226, etc.

(ii) Moderate Atomic Weight Elements

- Examples include Potassium-40, Rubidium-87.

5.5.2 Artificial Radioactivity

- It is also called **induced radioactivity**.
- It is produced by bombarding high velocity particles on an element.
- For example, bombardment of α-particles on nitrogen converts it into radioactive oxygen.

5.6 CHARACTERISTICS OF RADIOACTIVITY

5.6.1 Types of Decay or Activity

- Radioactivity may either be emission of α-, β- or γ-rays, accompanied by neutron particle or X-rays or only energy.
- This depends on the number of atoms of the radioisotope present.

5.6.2 Rate of Decay

- It is expressed as $t_{1/2}$ (half-life time).
- It is defined as the number of radioactive nuclei actually disintegrating or decaying or mutating to half of its original in a given time.

$$t_{1/2} = \frac{0.693}{\lambda}$$

where, λ = decay constant

- Each radioactive element has its own characteristic half-life ($t_{1/2}$), irrespective of quantity present.
- A radioisotope decays at the same time emitting same radiations or particles at any point of time or condition (viz., temperature, pressure and chemical environment).
- This is because radioactivity is a nuclear property and remains unaffected by changes in the outer electron environment.

Derivation of Equation

According to the Rate law,

$$N_t = N_0 . e^{-\lambda t} \qquad \text{Equation (1)}$$

where N_t = Number of nuclides at time 't'

N_0 = Number of nuclides at time '0'

λ = Rate constant

To calculate half-life, consider $N_t = N_0/2$ and $t = t_{1/2}$

Substituting these values in equation (1), we get

$$N_0/2 = N_0 . e^{-\lambda t_{1/2}}$$

or,

$$½ = e^{-\lambda t_{1/2}}$$

Taking natural log on both sides, we get

$$-\ln_e 2 = \ln_e e^{-\lambda t_{1/2}}$$

$$\lambda t_{1/2} = \ln_e 2 \text{ (Since } \ln_e e = 1)$$

$$\lambda t_{1/2} = 2.303 \log_{10} 2$$

$$\lambda t_{1/2} = 2.303 \log_{10} 2 \text{ (Since } \log_{10} 2 = 0.3010)$$

$$\text{Since } \log_{10} 2 = 0.3010, \text{ hence } \lambda t_{1/2} = 2.303 \times 0.3010$$

or,

$$\lambda t_{1/2} = 0.693$$

or,

$$t_{1/2} = 0.693/\lambda$$

5.6.3 Mode of Decay

- Radionuclide can undergo disintegration by different modes until a stable nucleus is formed.
- If the daughter element is unstable, it becomes a parent element and undergoes further decay till it is stable.
- This series is called radioactive series.
- Thus, the daughter nucleus formed from the parent nucleus will have different number of neutrons or atomic number.

α-Decay:

$$^{24}_{13}Al \longrightarrow\ ^{20}_{11}Na +\ ^{4}_{2}He$$ (Atomic number decreases by 2 units, n – 2)

α-particle

β-Decay:

$$^{14}_{6}C \longrightarrow\ ^{14}_{7}N +\ ^{0}_{-1}\beta$$ (Atomic number increases by 1 unit, n + 1)

β-particle

Electron capture:

$$^{7}_{4}Be +\ ^{0}_{-1}e \longrightarrow\ ^{7}_{3}Be$$ (Atomic number decreases by 1 unit, n – 1)

Electron

Positron emission:

$$^{11}_{6}C \longrightarrow\ ^{11}_{5}B +\ ^{0}_{+1}\beta$$ (Atomic number decreases by 1 unit, n – 1)

Positron

5.7 UNITS OF RADIOACTIVITY

Various units of radioactivity include the following:

(a) Curie (Ci)
(b) Roentgen (R)
(c) Becquerel (Bq)
(d) Radiation Absorbed Dose (RAD)
(e) Roentgen Equivalent in Man (REM)
(f) Grays (Gy)
(g) Exposure Rate Constant
(h) Relative Biological Effectiveness (RBE)

5.7.1 Curie (Ci)

- It may be defined as the quantity of any radioactive substance which undergoes the 3.7×10^{10} disintegrations in unit time.

$$1\ Ci = 3.7 \times 10^{10} \text{ disintegrations per second}$$

5.7.2 Roentgen (R)

- It is the unit of exposure.

$$1\ R = 2.58 \times 10^{-4} \text{ coulomb per kg}$$

5.7.3 Becquerel (Bq)

- Becquerel is the quantity of radioactive substance undergoing one disintegration per second.

1 Bq = 1 disintegration per second

5.7.4 Radiation Absorbed Dose (RAD)

- It indicates the actual dose of radiation absorbed by the body.

1 RAD = 100 ergs/g or 10^{-2} J/kg

- Pharmaceutical dosage forms are described in terms of RAD units.

5.7.5 Roentgen Equivalent in Man (REM)

- It refers to the unit of equivalent dose of the radiation.

REM = Dose in RADs × Quality Factor × Distribution Factor

5.7.6 Grays (Gy)

- It is the SI unit and equivalent to 100 RADs.

1 Gy = 100 RADs = 1 J/kg

5.7.7 Exposure Rate Constant

- It refers to the dose rate in roentgens per hour at 1 m distance from 1 curie.
- It is about 1/10th the dose at a distance of 1 foot from 1 curie.

5.7.8 Relative Biological Effectiveness (RBE)

It refers to the unit which determines the relative effects of different types of radiations emitted, such as α-, β- and γ-rays on the biological systems.

5.8 CHARACTERISTICS OF RADIOISOTOPES

- Should be capable of releasing high energy photon.
- Should decay without particle emission.
- Should be readily available.
- Should possess specific activity.
- Should possess the half-life of 1 hour to 1 year.

Example of an isotope that fulfils all the above properties is Technetium (^{99}Tc).

5.9 HAZARDS ASSOCIATED WITH RADIO PHARMACEUTICALS

The effects of radiation on living matter are called biological effects.

These are as follows:

5.9.1 Ionisation and Excitation

- Radiations cause abnormal chemical effects, such as inactivation of essential enzymes, coagulation of proteins, etc.
- Ionisation of nucleic acid like DNA and RNA damages the cell.

5.9.2 Skin Damage

- When skin is exposed to radiations, it may cause:
  (i) Reddening of skin
  (ii) Blackening of skin
  (iii) Loss of hair
  (iv) Dryness of skin
  (v) Burning of skin

5.9.3 Somatic Effects

- Effects of radiations on blood cells are called somatic effects.
- These are caused due to excessive exposure to radiation.
- These include:
  (i) Anaemia
  (ii) Leukaemia
  (iii) Cancer
- Somatic effects are observed after many years from exposure.
- The cancer is observed generally after 20 years from exposure.

5.9.4 Genetic Effects

- Genetic effects include:
  (i) Damage to chromosomes
  (ii) Change in frequency of gene mutation
  (iii) Due to genetic effects, abnormal effects are observed in future generations

5.10 PRODUCTION OF RADIOISOTOPES

- Radioisotopes can be produced by:
  (a) reactor irradiation, and
  (b) cyclotron irradiation.

5.10.1 Reactor Irradiation

- Also called neutron bombardment or activation.
- In this method, the reactor consists of a fissionable material in a moderator which slows down the fast neutrons to thermal energies.

- The fissionable material like uranium is taken in the form of rods which are arranged in a lattice pattern and hence, the neutron flux is maximum in the centre where there is maximum uranium.
- Heavy-water moderated reactor enriched uranium (Harwell reactor DIDO) is found to show a maximum flux of 10^{14} neutrons $cm^{-2}\ s^{-1}$.
- Examples of isotopes produced by this method includes:

$$^{59}_{27}Co + ^{1}_{0}n \longrightarrow ^{60}_{27}Co + \gamma$$

$$^{31}_{15}P + ^{1}_{0}n \longrightarrow ^{32}_{15}P + \gamma$$

5.10.2 Cyclotron Irradiation

- In this method, a particle accelerating equipment called cyclotron is used.
- The target nuclide is bombarded with high energy sub-atomic particles such as protons causing emission of fast moving electrons, resulting in the nuclear reaction.
- This leaves the target nuclides unstable. To attain stability, the unstable nuclides further dissociates into new radioisotopes or nuclides.
- Examples of isotopes produced by this method includes:

$$^{24}_{12}Mg + ^{2}_{1}H \longrightarrow ^{22}_{11}Na + ^{4}_{2}He$$

$$^{99}_{42}Mo + ^{2}_{1}H \longrightarrow ^{99}_{43}Tc + ^{1}_{0}n$$

5.11 MEASUREMENT OF RADIOACTIVITY

The instruments used to detect and measure various types of radiations are enlisted below:

(a) Mass spectrometer
(b) Gas ionisation devices
  (i) Pulse ionisation chambers
  (ii) Proportional counters
  (iii) Geiger-Muller counters
(c) Scintillation counters
(d) Autoradiography

(e) Solid state detectors
   (i) Semiconductor devices
   (ii) Photographic emulsion
   (iii) Cerenkov detectors
   (iv) Thermoluminescence dosimeters
   (v) Track-etch detectors

Principle

- All the detectors are based on the principle that the radiation deposits its energy through the formation of charge carriers, either directly or indirectly, which results in the flow of current or a voltage pulse.
- The ions created in the detector can be collected by applying the electric field within the detector and the current flowing through the detector can be measured using an electrometer.

5.11.1 Mass Spectrometer

- It detects and measures the mass of heavy particles like α-rays or neutrons.
- It is difficult to measure the masses of light particles, such as electrons or positrons (β-rays).
- Although γ-rays are not particulate in nature, they are detected from the mark of exposure left whenever they hit the photographic plates.

Limitations

- It is practically not useful in laboratories because of its bigger size and specific conditions are needed for its usage.

5.11.2 Gas Ionisation Devices

- These include:
   (i) Pulse ionisation chambers
   (ii) Proportional counters
   (iii) Geiger-Muller counters
- Selection of these instruments depends on the following two factors:
   (i) The extent of energy emitted
   (ii) Penetration ability of radiation

(i) Pulse Ionisation Chambers

- These indicate the electric current produced due to emission of electrons, following ionisation of the gas in the chamber by the radiation.
- It consists of an ionisation chamber which is filled with the ionising gases like argon, helium, air, etc.

- It also comprises of two electrodes kept at different electric potential (50 to 100 V for each cm of distance between two electrodes) and a measuring device to indicate the flow of current.
- Radiations bring about ionisation of gas molecules or ions which cause emission of electrons, which in turn, reveals the changes in electric current which are measured by measuring device.

Advantage

- These chambers are available in different shapes and sizes.

(ii) Proportional Counters

- These are used to detect both α- and β-rays.
- These are modified ionisation chambers which consist of ionising gas.
- The application of electric potential to the ionising gas causes production of primary electrons, which further leads to thunderous bursting of more free electrons, which are then carried to anode and current pulse through the electric circuit gets amplified.
- The voltage range over which ionisation occurs is called proportional region and the measuring devices are known as proportional counters.
- If the electric field gradient between the cathode and anode is increased by increasing the applied voltage, the electron produced in primary ionisation further ionises the gas molecule and the number of ion pairs is multiplied.
- For each primary electron liberated, a large number of additional electrons are liberated and the current pulse gets amplified.
- The total charge collected becomes proportional to the original number of ion pairs.
- It is operated at pulse ratio and used in the form of gas flow counter for α, β, and fission fragment counting.
- α-particles are detected and measured at low voltage, whereas β-particles are measured at high voltage.

(iii) Geiger-Muller Counters

- These are the most commonly used detectors of radiation and are capable of measuring α-, β- and γ-rays.

5.11.3 Scintillation Counters

- Scintillation counters can measure α-, β- and γ-rays.
- These counters use phosphorescent or fluorescent materials for the detection of radiation, which produce scintillations or flashes of visible light when the radiation (photon) falls on their surfaces.

- They consist of a series of photoelectric cells directly connected to photoelectron multipliers (multiplier tube) and coupled with solid state detectors, which make it superior to other counting instruments.
- Further, nowadays, a thallium activated crystal (sodium iodide) has been introduced which have resulted in advancement of this technique for γ-counting and energy detection.
- Thus, scintillation counters make use of sample cell, a sample chamber, a photomultiplier tube to amplify and convert scintillation or flash light produced into electric pulses, which are recorded using a scaler.
- Liquid scintillators are used in large volume detection for counting α- or β-rays with high efficiencies.
- The scintillation counters are used for detecting and measuring of Tritium (^3H) and Carbon-14 (^{14}C).

  Types of scintillation counters:

  (i) Inorganic scintillators – e.g., NaI(Tl), CsI(Na), LiI(Eu), BaF_2, etc.

  (ii) Organic scintillators – e.g., anthracene, stilbene, etc.

Limitations

- This method is tedious, slow and not sensitive.

5.11.4 Autoradiography

- This technique is used in case of physiological studies of plants and animals for detection and measurement of γ-rays.
- When a radioactive substance is administered to an animal and after sufficient time of lapse for localisation, the tissue is removed, embedded in paraffin, cut into thin section by microtome and section kept in contact with photographic emulsion in a dark room.
- After sufficient time of exposure, the radioactive substance emits particles which darken the photographic emulsion.
- These emitted particles are then detected and measured.

5.11.5 Solid State Detectors

- These are the most advanced detectors of radioactivity.
- They are of the following types:

  (i) Semiconductor devices

  (ii) Photographic emulsion

  (iii) Cerenkov detectors

  (iv) Thermoluminescence dosimeters

  (v) Track-etch detector

Advantages over conventional techniques

(a) High resolution.

(b) Compactness.

(c) Easy interpretation of output signal.

Limitations

(a) High cost.

(b) Requires low temperature to operate and maintain.

(i) Semiconductor Devices

- These devices are composed of semiconductors with a very small band gap of about 2 to 3 eV and thus produce huge quantities of electron pairs per incident radiation quantum.
- These conductors have high energy resolution.
- These are of two types:
  (a) N-type (electron-rich)
  (b) P-type (electron-deficient, consist of holes)
- When the incident radiation falls on semiconductors, it is absorbed forming electron-hole pairs, whose motion is influenced by the applied electric field, resulting in the generation of voltage pulse proportional to the energy of incident radiation.
- Examples include silicon detectors, Ge(Li), Si(Li), etc.

(ii) Photographic Emulsion

- These are commonly used to detect and determine γ-radiation in physiological studies of plants and animals.
- For example, radiographic films and nuclear emulsions.

(iii) Cerenkov Detectors

- These detectors are used for the light emitting fast-charged particles which are passed through an optically transparent medium with refractive index >1.

Advantages

- They possess high resolution.
- They have compact structure.
- Interpretation of output signal is easy.

Disadvantages

- They are very expensive.
- They require low temperature for their working and maintenance.

(iv) Thermo Luminescence Dosimeters

- These are made up of inorganic crystals in which electron-hole pairs have been formed due to radiation which can trap these pairs and on heating, results in emission of light.
- For example, $CaSO_4(Mn)$, LiF, $CaF_2(Mn)$, etc.

(v) Track-etch Detector

- Ionising radiations having higher linear energy transfer (LET) passing through a dielectric material create trail of damaged molecules along their path.
- In some materials, the tract can be visible upon etching in a strong acid or alkali solution.
- The damaged molecular tracks are etched faster than the bulk and look like pits in the surface.
- These tracks can be counted by viewing through a microscope.
- The commonly used track-etch materials are quartz, mica, silica glass, flint glass, lexan, polyethylene terephthalate, markrofol, cellulose nitrate, cellulose triacetate, etc.

5.12 GEIGER-MULLER (G-M) COUNTERS

G-M counter was developed by Geiger and Muller in Germany, in the year 1928. It is the oldest radiation detector in use due to its low cost, simplicity and in case of operation, it is the best detector amongst all.

It does not require any high gain amplifier.

5.12.1 Principle

- It consists of a G-M tube, sensing element which detects the radiation and processing electronics which display the result.
- The G-M tube is filled with an inert gas such as helium, neon or argon at low pressure, to which a high voltage of about 450 to 500 V is applied.
- The tube conducts an electrical discharge when a particle or photon of incident radiation makes the gas conductive by ionisation.
- The ionisation considerably amplified within the tube to produce easily measured detection pulse, which is fed to processing electronics which display the result.

5.12.2 Role of Quenching Vapours

- It functions:
  (a) to prevent the spurious pulses that may get produced due to positive ions reaching the cathode, and

(b) to absorb the photons emitted by excited atoms and molecules returning to ground state.

- Examples of quenching agents include chlorine, bromine and organic agents like ethanol and ethyl formate.
- The filling gas pressure has to be much below the atmospheric pressure for avoiding the use of high operating voltages.

5.12.3 Construction of G-M Counter

- It consists of stainless steel or glass cylinder coated with silver on the inner side, which acts as a cathode.
- A fine metal wire is mounted coaxially inside the cylinder which acts as an anode.
- The cylinder is filled with inert gases like helium, neon or argon at low pressure. A small amount of quenching vapours are also mixed.
- Radiations enter through the window.
- Due to radiation, gas is ionised.
- A high voltage of about 800 to 1300 V is maintained between the electrodes.
- Due to ionisation of gas, positively-charged ions are attracted towards cathode and negatively charged-ions are attracted towards anode.
- The passage of these ions through the tube constitutes flow of current.
- Each particle of radiation causes a brief flow or pulse of current, which is recorded by a device known as "scaler".
- Scaler shows the total number of pulses and results are analysed.

5.12.4 Types of G-M Counters

(a) Counting Solid Radioactive Sources

These consist of the following two types:

(i) End window-type G-M counter

(ii) Thin glass-walled counter

(i) End Window-Type G-M Counter

- It is the most commonly used type of G-M counter.
- Its construction is similar to the general structure but it contains a window which is made up of an aluminium alloy (7 mg cm^{-2}), mica or a thin glass bubble (about 15 mg cm^{-2}), as shown in Figure 5.1.

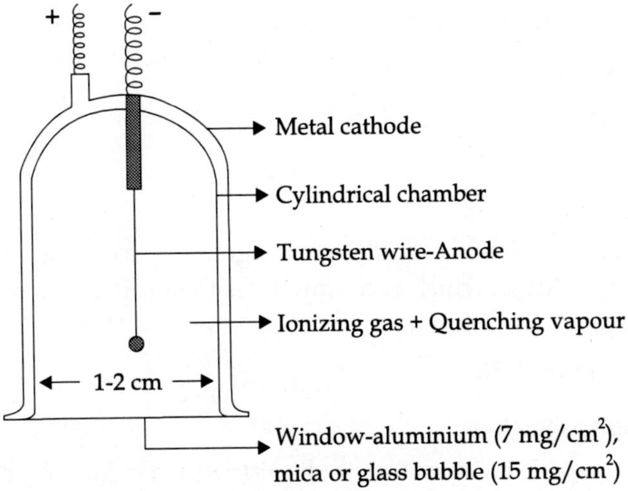

Figure 5.1: End window-type G-M counter

(ii) Thin Glass-Walled Counter

- It is used to detect and measure medium and high energy β-particles (above 0.5 MeV) and γ-rays.
- It is composed of thin glass-walled tube of 1 cm diameter.
- The thickness of the glass wall is generally about 20 to 40 mg cm^{-2} but the actual thickness varies with the length of the counter.
- Inner wall of the glass tube is coated with graphite that serves as cathode, as shown in Figure 5.2.

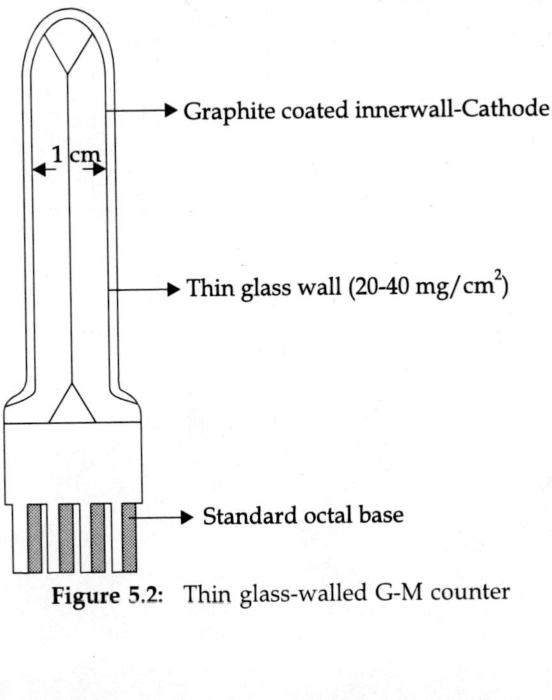

Figure 5.2: Thin glass-walled G-M counter

(b) Counting Liquid Radioactive Sources

These consist of the following two types:

(i) With spiral wire cathode

(ii) Connected by plug or socket

(i) With Spiral Wire Cathode

- This type of G-M counter is similar to the general structure with an annular space of 10 cm^3 volume, which accommodates the radioactive sample.
- It contains a spiral wire cathode.
- It is shown in Figure 5.3(a).

(ii) Connected by Plug or Socket

- This is another type of G-M counter for liquids which is composed of an annular space of 5 cm^3 volume and connected by a plug or socket and mainly consists of thin-walled tube, as shown in Figure 5.3(b).

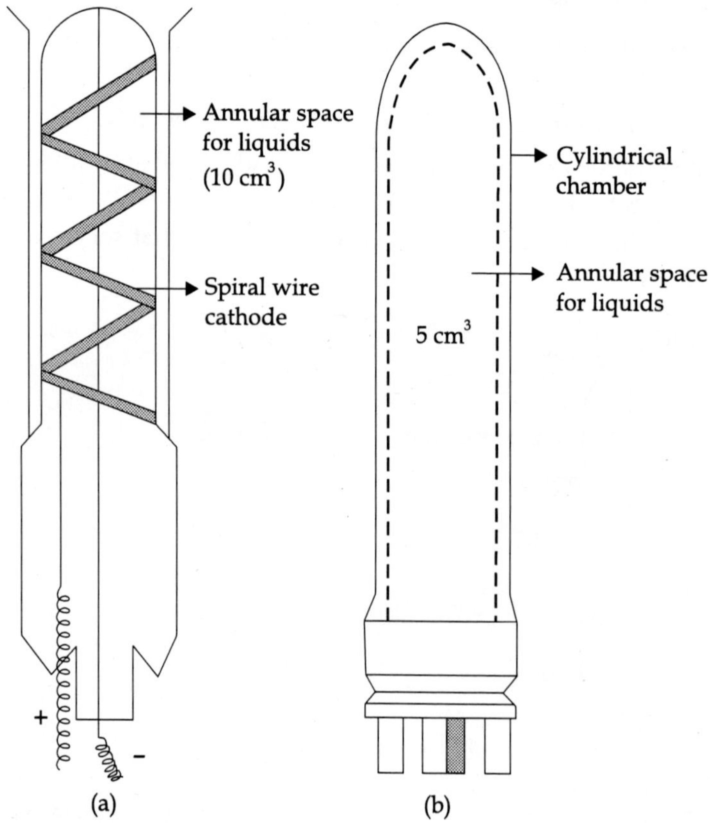

Figure 5.3: G-M counters for liquids (a) with spiral wire cathode, and (b) connected by plug or socket

(c) Counting Radioactive Gases

- This type of counter is used for counting gaseous radioactive sources.
- In this, radioactive gas and ionising gas are simultaneously introduced into the chamber.
- A lead or copper cathode makes the counter more efficient for detecting γ-rays (Figure 5.4).

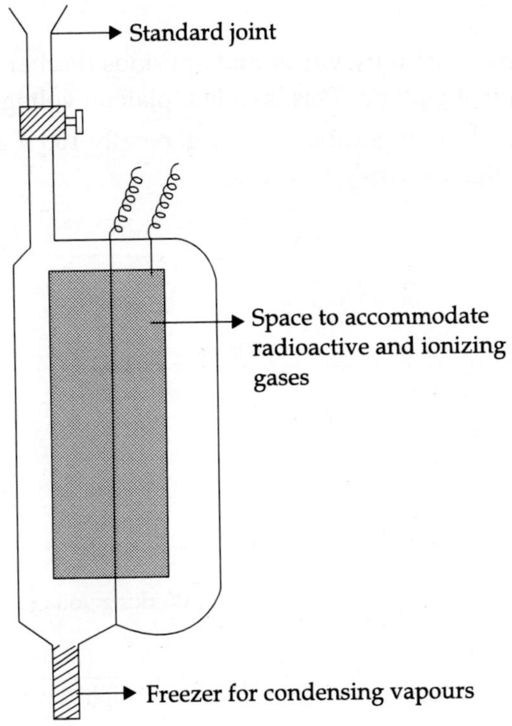

Figure 5.4: G-M counter for gases

5.12.5. Working of G-M Counters

- G-M counter requires a high voltage source, low gain amplifier and a sealing unit for its working.
- It also consists of a probe unit which serves as an electrical switch for recording the number of pulses.
- Each pulse directs the current to the scaler and then to the counting unit.
- G-M counter is placed on a lead shield which holds a source in one or more shelves and absorbers between the instrument and source.
- It helps in reducing the counting rate in the absence of a source known as background counting rate.

- The high voltage is to be adjusted so that the counter gets operated on the plateau of its characteristic curve, as shown in Figure 5.5.

The graph/curve represents the following voltages:

- When the voltage on the counter gets raised, no registration of pulses is observed until a certain voltage is reached. This is called 'starting voltage'.
- The counting rate increases rapidly to the threshold and at 150 to 200 V or more, the counting rate becomes sensibly constant. This is called 'threshold voltage'.
- At higher voltages, sensitivity varies and spurious discharge of pulses occurs, giving rise to slope of plateau. This is called 'plateau voltage'.
- The voltage selected for operating point is generally 100 V above the threshold voltage. This is called as 'working voltage'.

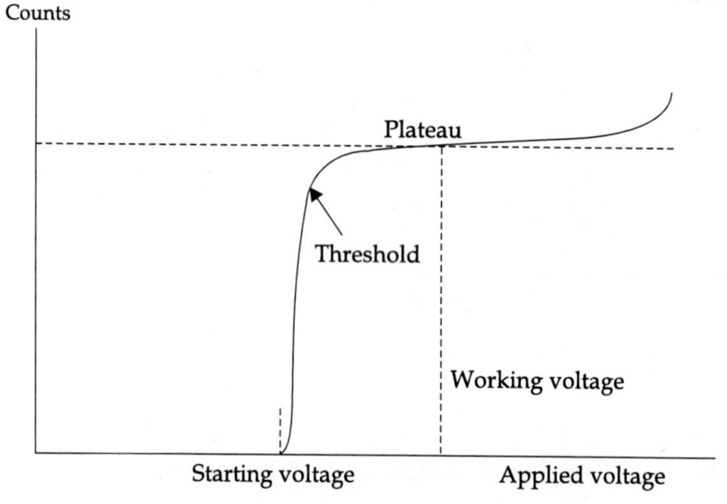

Figure 5.5: Characteristic curve of Geiger-Muller counter

5.13 STORAGE AND HANDLING OF RADIOACTIVE MATERIALS

Great care has to be taken in handling and storing radioactive materials. Stringent requirements are prescribed by the Department of Atomic Energy (DAE) for the establishment of a radioisotope facility in a hospital or pharmacy. These include specifications for premises, storage space, working area, disposal protocol, training of personnel, periodic checks on contamination or leakage, equipment, etc.

5.13.1 Storage of Radioactive Materials

- Radioactive materials must be stored in an area not frequently visited by people.

- Shielding may be required. Thick glass or perspex containers usually provide sufficient shielding.
- In order to protect from the gamma radiations, lead shielding is used.
- The storage area must be regularly checked for radioactivity.
- The radioactive material must be disposed of after complete discharge of its activity.
- The area where the radioactive substances or materials are placed should be checked for contamination.

5.13.2 Handling of Radioactive Materials

- Radioactive substances should never be touched with hand but handled with forceps.
- Activities like smoking, drinking, eating should be avoided in the area where radioactive substances are kept.
- Sufficient protective clothing should be used for handling of radioactive substances.
- Area where the radioactive materials are kept should be tested regularly for the presence of fluorescence.
- There should be proper disposal of radioactive materials.
- Radioactive materials should be kept in a suitable, labelled container.
- They should be kept in remote areas.
- All surfaces of the containers should be smooth, non-porous, non-wetting and heat-resistant.
- The wall finishing should be hard and smooth and should not easily get contaminated.
- The use of wood material should be minimum.
- The benches and cupboards should be made up of plastics.
- There should be minimum movement of workers.

5.13.3 Labelling on Radioactive Preparations

The label on the radiopharmaceutical preparations should be appropriate and bear the following details:

- Date of manufacture
- Date of expiry
- Date of calibration
- Dosage calculation
- A statement 'caution-radioactive material'
- The half-life of radioactive nuclei
- Correction to be made for radioactive decay

5.14 APPLICATIONS OF RADIO PHARMACEUTICALS

Radionuclides are widely used clinically or medicinally as described below:

5.14.1 Radioisotopes in Diagnosis

- Some pathophysiological conditions of the body are accurately diagnosed by employing certain radioisotopes.
- They are used to study their fate in the body or estimation of the amount in an organ by radioimmuno assays.
- For example:
  (a) Radiolabelled cyanocobalamin (^{57}Co) - Used for measuring glomerular filtration rate (GFR).
  (b) Ferric citrate (^{59}Fe) injection - Used for the diagnosis of haematological disorders.
  (c) Colloidal gold (^{198}Au) injection - Used for diagnostically studying the blood circulation in the liver.
  (d) Sodium iodide (^{131}I) injection - Used to diagnose the functioning of thyroid glands.
  (e) Iodinated (^{131}I) human serum albumin injection - Used to investigate cardiovascular functions.
  (f) Sodium iodohippurate I-131 injection - Used to study renal functions.
  (g) Sodium rose Bengal I-131 injection - Used as diagnostic agent to test liver functions.
  (h) Chromium (^{151}Cr) in the form of sodium chromate - Used to determine the blood flow through the heart.

5.14.2 Radioisotopes in Therapy

- The therapeutically used radioisotopes depend mainly on their ability to ionise atoms.
- The radioisotopes are administered either internally or externally.
- If the radioisotopes are used externally or used as implants in sealed capsules in a tissue, the dose could be terminated by the removal of the sources.
- If they are given internally, the dose cannot be stopped by removing the source.
- The total dose in therapeutic applications may be calculated on the basis of effective half-life of the isotope, concentration of the isotope and the type and the energy of radiation emitted.
- For example:
  (a) Gold (^{198}Au) - Used in the treatment of abdominal and pleural effusions associated with malignant tumours. It is also used in the treatment of carcinoma of uterus and urinary bladder.

(b) Sodium phosphate (^{32}P) - Used in the therapy of polycythemia vera to decrease the rate of formation of erythrocytes leukemia.

(c) Cobalt labelled cyanocobalamins (Vitamin B_{12}) - Used in the diagnosis of pernicious anaemia.

(d) Sodium iodide (^{131}I) - Used in the treatment of thyroid disorders.

(e) Yttrium-90 - Used in the treatment of cancer, particularly liver cancer and arthritis.

(f) Boron (^{10}B) - Used in the treatment of tumours.

5.14.3 Research

- Biological and medicinal research uses various radioisotopes as tracers for their study.
- These extensive studies have resulted in detailed knowledge of many biochemical processes.
- Carbon-14 and Tritium are the commonly used radioisotope tracers.
- For example, stable isotopes of carbon, calcium, hydrogen, chromium and iron are usually applied in research.
- Other isotopes of sodium, magnesium, calcium, copper and cerium have also been employed as radioisotope tracers.

5.14.4 Sterilization

- Surgical instruments in hospitals and most of the pharmaceuticals in their final packed containers are sterilized using constant radiations emitted from some strong radiation sources.
- The radiation does not destroy or harm most pharmaceuticals.
- No heat or chemicals get involved.
- Thermolabile substances such as vitamins, hormones, antibiotics, etc., can be safely sterilized.
- For example, Cobalt-60 or Cesium-137 may be used for sterilizing surgical instruments and pharmaceuticals.

5.14.5 Agricultural Use

- Gamma rays are used to kill pests.
- These are used to induce genetic mutations in a plant in order to produce a better strain which has higher resistance against pest and diseases.
- Radioisotopes used as tracers in the effectiveness of fertilizers are N-15 and P-32.

5.14.6 Industrial Use

- Americium-241 is used in many smoke detectors for homes and business in thickness gauges designed to measure and control thickness during manufacturing processes.
- Californium-252 is used for neutron activation analysis to inspect airline luggage for hidden explosives.

5.14.7 Analytical Applications

- Analytical procedures
- Radioisotope dilution analysis
- Recovery indication in analysis
- Radioimmuno assay
- Solubility determination
- Activation analysis
- Enzyme assays
- Receptor assays

5.14.8 Reaction Mechanism

- Several instances have been reported of information concerning reaction mechanisms obtained with the aid of artificial radio elements.

5.15 OFFICIAL PREPARATIONS OF RADIO PHARMACEUTICALS

Various official preparations of radio pharmaceuticals along with their applications are presented in Table 5.1.

Table 5.1: Official preparations of radio pharmaceuticals

Preparations	Application
Sodium iodide I-131 solution USP	Study of thyroid gland function.
Sodium iodide I-131 capsule USP	Study of thyroid gland function.
Sodium rose Bengal I-131	Study of liver functions.
Sodium iodohippurate I-131 injection USP	Study of kidney function.
Ammonium bromide Br-82 injection	Extracellular water measurement.
Calcium chloride Ca-45 solution	Study of calcium metabolism disorders.
Chromic chloride Cr-51 injection	Study of protein loss from the GIT and absorption.
Colloidal gold Au-198 injection	Treatment of cancers and study of reticuloendothelial system.
Ferric chloride Fe-59 solution	β- and γ-ray emitter, study of iron metabolism.

(Contd...)

Indium chloride I-113m	Diagnosis of diseases of placenta and study of cardiac blood pool.
Potassium chloride K-42 injection	Study of potassium exchange.
Rubidium chloride Rb-86 injection	Determination of myocardial blood flow.
Sodium chloride Na-24 injection	Study of sodium exchange.
Sodium orthophosphate P-32 solution	Treatment of polycythemia.
Sodium sulphate S-35 solution	Determination of extra-cellular fluid volume.
Cyanocobalamin Co-57 preparation	Diagnosis of pernicious anaemia.
Cyanocobalamin Co-58 preparation	Diagnosis of pernicious anaemia.
Calcium-44,45 (Ca-44, 45)	Study of bone structure and bone cancer.
Carbon-14 (C-14)	Emit β-radiations, used in medical and pharmaceutical research.
Strontium-90 (Sr-90)	Pure β-emitter, used in radiotherapy of superficial carcinoma.
Cobalt-60 (Co-60)	γ-emitter, used in radiotherapy, sterilization of heat labile substances, study of vitamin B_{12}.
Hydrogen-^2H,^3H	β-emitter, used to determine total body water content.
Nitrogen-13,15 (N-13, 15)	Investigation of amino acid and protein metabolism.
Oxygen-17,18 (O-17, 18)	Study of organic reactions and photosynthesis.
Sodium-22,24 (Na-22, 24)	In estimation of extracellular fluid, body circulation rate, excretion and distribution of water.
Sodium chromate (Cr-51) solution	In the measurement of red cell volume and its survival time.
Fluorine-18 (F-18)	Positron emitter, used in tumour imaging, bone imaging, myocardial imaging, etc.
Gallium-67 (Ga-67)	γ-emitter, used in tumour imaging and inflammation/ infections imaging.
Gallium-68 (Ga-68)	Positron emitter, prostate cancer imaging.
Krypton-81m	γ-emitter, lung ventilation and lung perfusion imaging.
Nitrogen-13 (N-13)	Positron emitter, used in myocardial blood flow imaging.
Phosphorous-32 (P-32)	In the treatment of polycythemia and related disorders.
Radium-223 (Ra-223)	α-emitter, in the treatment of metastatic cancer in bone.
Selenium-75 (Se-75)	γ-emitter, investigation of adrenal gland imaging and bile salt absorption.
Technetium-99m (Tc-99)	γ-emitter, investigation of stomach and salivary gland imaging, first pass blood flow imaging, bone marrow imaging, lachrymal imaging, gastric emptying imaging, etc.

5.16 SODIUM IODIDE (I-131 OR ^{131}I)

Out of all radioactive isotopes of iodine, ^{131}I is the most common isotope. It is used as an aqueous solution of sodium iodide having sodium thiosulphate in addition to as a reducing agent.

Synonym : Radioactive iodine

5.16.1 Standards

- It should contain not less than 90% and not more than 110% of labelled amount of I-131 as iodide, which is expressed in microcurie or millicurie at the time indicated in the labelling.

5.16.2 Methods of Preparation

- The first production of I-131 took place in France in 1949 at the *Fort de Chatillon,* the site of the first Zoe atomic reactor, before it was transferred to the nuclear research centre at Saclay. The isotope has been used since 1942, however, in the treatment of thyroid cancer.
- Most I-131 is prepared in nuclear reactor by neutron-irradiation of a natural tellurium target. Irradiation of natural tellurium produces almost entirely I-131 as the only radionuclide with a half-life longer than hours. Ultimately, in 8.02 days, it gets converted into Xenon-131 (Xe-131), a stable isotope.

$$^{130}\text{Te} \xrightarrow{(n,\,\gamma)} {}^{131}\text{Te} \xrightarrow{\beta^0} {}^{131}\text{I} \xrightarrow{(\beta^0,\,\gamma)} {}^{131}\text{Xe}$$

5.16.3 Properties

- It forms a colourless solution.
- I-131 has a half-life of 8.4 days and emits beta and gamma radiations.
- Its solution has a pH range of 7 to 10.

5.16.4 Hyperthyroidism Treatment by I-131

- Iodide inhibits the release of thyroid hormone and forms the basis for its use in hyperthyroidism.
- All the isotopes of iodide are rapidly taken up by thyroid follicles.
- Radioactive iodine I-131 is available as NaI-131 solution and is administered orally.
- The absorption of I-131 leads to highly localised destruction of thyroid follicles due to emission of β-particles.
- This property of I-131 has promoted radioactive iodine as a therapeutic alternative in surgical removal of the gland.
- The radioiodine therapy is considered advantageous over surgery because of the simplicity of its procedure, its applicability to patients, avoidance of surgical risks and complications.

5.16.5 Sodium Iodide-131 Solution and Capsule

- Sodium iodide (I-131) is suitable for both oral and IV administration.
- The solution is clear and colourless but as the time passes, both the solution and glass may get darken due to the effect of radiation.
- The pH of solutions varies between 7.5 and 9.
- Sodium iodide (I-131) capsules are prepared by evaporating an alcoholic solution of sodium radio-iodide directly on the walls of the capsule or on inert capsule filling material.

5.16.6 Sodium Iodide-131 Injection

- For injection, a suitable preservative such as benzyl alcohol is added.
- A reducing agent such as sodium thiosulphate is also added to the solution to prevent the oxidation of sodium iodide in aqueous solutions.
- Potassium salt, iodide and iodate have been acting as a carrier for iodide ions and for iodate ions present in the sodium iodide I-131 solution.

5.16.7 Radioactive Identification

- The spectrum of I-131 has been complex but the most abundant type of photon has energy of 0.364 MeV.
- It is possible to determine the energy in a spectrometer by detecting γ-radiation with a scintillation counter, which is having a thallium activated.
- The γ-ray scintillation spectrum of sodium iodide (I-131) solution has been found to be identical to that of specimen of I-131 of known purity, which exhibits major photoelectric peak, having energy of 0.365 MeV.

5.16.8 Assay

- It is possible to determine its activity, using suitable counting equipment by comparison with a standardised I-131 solution or by measuring an instrument calibrated with the aid of such solutions.
- Iodine-131 emits both beta and gamma particles in its decay process.
- Radioactivity has to be recorded on a counting assembly, which is having either a G-M counter or a scintillation detector used as a sensing unit and an electronic sealing device.

5.16.9 Packaging and Storage Conditions

- The solution has to be prepared in single-dose or multiple-dose containers that have been previously treated to prevent absorption.
- So as to avoid absorption of radionuclides on the wall of the container including laboratory vessels, it has been recommended that containers used to handle sodium iodide I-131 solution should be first of all rinsed with a solution having

approximately 0.8% of sodium bisulphate and 0.25% of sodium iodide and then water until the last rinsing has been neutral to litmus.

5.16.10 Uses

- Radioactive iodine is mainly used for the diagnosis of disorders of thyroid function.
- It is also used in the treatment of hyperthyroidism.
- It is also used in the treatment of Grave's disease (toxic diffused goiter).
- It is also used in radiotherapy of thyroid cancer.
- It is also used in the treatment of thyrotoxicosis.

5.17 RADIO-OPAQUE CONTRAST MEDIA (X-RAY CONTRAST MEDIA)

- **Radio-opaque substances** are the inorganic or organic compounds which have the property of casting a shadow on X-ray films. These substances have the ability to stop the passage of X-rays and hence, appear opaque on X-ray examination. Such compounds and their preparations are known as **X-ray contrast media**.
- They cannot be categorized as drugs because they are usually devoid of any pharmacological effects.
- However, all radio-opaque materials are not radiopharmaceuticals.
- Bones, cartilage and teeth are capable of blocking X-rays and whiteness is produced at their places in X-ray films. Phosphorus and calcium present in bones and teeth provide large electron density because blocking of X-rays or X-ray absorption depends upon the availability of electrons in the system.
- The various anatomical organs containing radio-opaque substances give a much clear and distinguished shadow on X-ray film/plate, which can be used for proper diagnosis and interpretation.

5.17.1 Examples of Radio-Opaque Contrast Media

(a) Inorganic Compounds

- Examples include barium sulphate and some bismuth compounds.

(b) Organic Compounds

- Iodinated compounds.

5.17.2 Routes of Administration

- These are administered either by:
  (i) Systemic, i.e., orally or intravenously
  (ii) Retrograde, i.e., by mechanical means backwardly

5.17.3 Uses

- These compounds are used for examining gastrointestinal tract, kidney (urography), liver (cholecystography), gall bladder and bile duct, blood vessels of heart (angiography and cardiography), bronchial tract (bronchography) and that of urethra, vagina, etc.

5.17.4 Requirements of a Radio-Opaque Substance

- It should prevent the passage of X-rays.
- It should have an adequate stability.
- It should have high solubility.
- It should not have any pharmacological effects.
- It should be non-toxic.
- It should be chemically and physiologically inert.
- Its stay in the body should be sufficient for X-ray visualisation.
- It should concentrate selectively in the concerned organs.
- It should have adequate radio-opacity, which usually requires an iodine content of at least 50%.
- It should be easily excreted from the body.

5.17.5 Types of Contrast Media

- The contrast media can be further subdivided into:
  (i) Water-soluble contrast media
  (ii) Water-insoluble contrast media

One of the pharmaceutical substances used as the X-ray contrast media is described as follows.

5.18 BARIUM SULPHATE

One of the pharmaceutical substances used as the X-ray contrast media is barium sulphate, which is described as follows:

Synonym : Barium meal, shadow meal
Molecular formula : $BaSO_4$
Molecular weight : 233.4 g/mol
Category : Radio pharmaceutical
Dose : 60 to 450 g orally and 200 to 600 g rectally

5.18.1 Standard

- It contains not less than 90% and not more than 110% of the labelled amount of barium sulphate.

5.18.2 Methods of Preparation

- It is prepared by the action of dilute H_2SO_4 on BaS.

$$\underset{\text{Barium sulphide}}{BaS} + \underset{\text{Sulphuric acid}}{H_2SO_4} \longrightarrow \underset{\text{Barium sulphate}}{BaSO_4} + \underset{\text{Hydrogen sulphide}}{H_2S}\uparrow$$

- It is also prepared from barium hydroxide and barium chloride by the action of sulphuric acid; the precipitates formed are filtered and dried.

$$\underset{\text{Barium chloride}}{BaCl_2} + \underset{\text{Sulphuric acid}}{H_2SO_4} \longrightarrow \underset{\text{Barium sulphate}}{BaSO_4} + \underset{\text{Hydrochloric acid}}{2HCl}$$

$$\underset{\text{Barium hydroxide}}{Ba(OH)_2} + \underset{\text{Sulphuric acid}}{H_2SO_4} \longrightarrow \underset{\text{Barium sulphate}}{BaSO_4} + 2H_2O$$

5.18.3 Physical Properties

Colour : White

Odour : Odourless

Taste : Tasteless

State : Heavy, fine, bulky and powder-free from grittiness

Solubility : (i) Insoluble in water, organic solvents and dilute acids and alkalis
(ii) It is soluble in concentrated H_2SO_4.

5.18.4 Chemical Properties

- It is soluble in concentrated H_2SO_4 due to the formation of barium bisulphate.

$$\underset{\text{Barium sulphate}}{BaSO_4} + \underset{\text{Sulphuric acid}}{H_2SO_4} \longrightarrow \underset{\text{Barium bisulphate}}{Ba(HSO_4)_2}$$

- Suspension of barium sulphate is susceptible to barium emitting micro-organisms and that is why its suspension is permitted to contain suitable preservatives.

5.18.5 Identification Tests

- 0.5 g of barium sulphate is fused with 2 g of anhydrous sodium carbonate and anhydrous potassium carbonate in a crucible and the resulting fused mass is treated with hot water and filtered. The filtrate is acidified with hydrochloric acid and used for reactions which are characteristic of sulphates.

- The residue obtained from the above is dissolved in hydrochloric acid and the solution is used for carrying out the characteristic flame test for barium.

5.18.6 Tests of Purity

- It has to be tested for arsenic, acid soluble substances, soluble barium salts, heavy metals, phosphate, sulphide, sulphite, bulkiness and loss of drying.
- pH 3.5 to 10.0 in 60% w/v aqueous suspension.
- Loss on drying: It loses not more than 2.0% of its weight when it is dried to a constant weight at 105°C for 4 hours.

5.18.7 Assay

As such there has been no assay for barium sulphate; the procedure presented here is for the assay of barium sulphate for suspension.

- Barium sulphate for suspension is assayed by fusing the known weight of compound with sodium carbonate and potassium carbonate at 1000°C for 15 minutes.
- It is cooled, suspended in water and decanted.
- The residue is made to wash with 2% sodium carbonate solution (until free from sulphate).
- Dilute hydrochloric acid is added, followed by ammonium acetate and potassium dichromate and urea.
- The suspension is digested at 80 to 85°C for 16 hours and then filtered through sintered glass crucible.
- The residue is washed with potassium dichromate solution, followed by water and the contents are weighed after drying at 105°C.

$$1.0 \text{ g of the residue} \equiv 0.213 \text{ g of } BaSO_4$$

5.18.8 Storage

- It should be stored in well-closed containers.

5.18.9 Pharmaceutical Uses

- Used for X-ray examination of the alimentary canal.
- Orally or by enema for examination of colon.
- Used for preparing barium sulphate compound powder.

5.19 BISMUTH COMPOUNDS

- Bismuthyl nitrate and bismuthyl carbonate in 30 to 60 g as suspension in water are used for examination of the alimentary canal.
- These compounds, however, have nowadays been replaced by other better compounds.

MULTIPLE-CHOICE QUESTIONS

1. Radioactivity was discovered
   (a) Henry Becquerel (b) Rutherford
   (c) J. J. Thomson (d) Madam Curie
2. The unit of radioactivity is
   (a) Curie (b) Rutherford
   (c) Ohm (d) Both (a) and (b)
3. A device used for the measurement of radioactivity is
   (a) Mass spectrometer (b) Cyclotron
   (c) Nuclear reactor (d) G. M. counter
4. Radioactivity is due to
   (a) Unstable nucleus (b) Stable electronic configuration
   (c) Unstable electronic configuration (d) Stable nucleus
5. When a radioactive nucleus emits an α-particle, the mass number of the atom
   (a) Decreases and its atomic number decreases
   (b) Increases and its atomic number decreases
   (c) Decreases and its atomic number increases
   (d) Remains the same
6. The decay of a radioactive element follows first order kinetics. As a result
   (a) The half-life period = a constant k, where k is the decay constant
   (b) The rate of decay is independent of temperature
   (c) The rate can be altered by changing chemical conditions
   (d) None of the above
7. Which of the following is correct?
   (a) Radioactivity is a statistical process
   (b) Radioactivity is a spontaneous process
   (c) Radioactivity is a characteristic of some elements
   (d) Both (b) and (c) are true
8. Radioactive decay is the reaction of
   (a) First order (b) Second order
   (c) Third order (d) Zero order
9. α-rays have
   (a) Positive charge
   (b) Negative charge
   (c) No charge
   (d) Sometimes positive and sometimes negative charge

10. Gamma rays have
    (a) High penetrating power than α and β
    (b) No penetrating power
    (c) Less penetrating power than α and β
    (d) None of the above
11. Alpha rays consist of a stream of
    (a) H^+ (b) He^{2+}
    (c) Only electrons (d) Only neutrons
12. The radiation which has the highest penetrating power is
    (a) α-rays (b) β-rays
    (c) γ-rays (d) None of the above
13. The atomic number of the element is equal to the
    (a) Sum of number of protons and neutrons
    (b) Number of neutrons
    (c) Number of protons
    (d) None of the above
14. The function of quenching vapours is
    (a) To ionise the ionising radiation
    (b) Produce amplitude for incident radiation
    (c) To prevent false pulses
    (d) All of the above
15. β-rays are
    (a) Positively charged (b) Negatively charged
    (c) Neutral (d) None of the above
16. Which is the commonly used quenching agent?
    (a) Chlorine and bromine (b) Methane
    (c) Argon (d) Alcohol
17) Which one of the following is not a gas-filled detector?
    (a) Scintillation detector (b) Geiger-Muller counter
    (c) Ionisation chamber (d) Proportional counter

FILL IN THE BLANKS

1. Radioactivity undergoes .... reaction.
2. An alpha particle carries .... charge.
3. A beta particle is .... charged.
4. Isotopes have the same .... but different ....

5. The order of reaction of radioactivity is ....
6. .... is used for the measurement of radioactivity.
7. .... is a gas filled detector.
8. The time required by the given amount of the element to decay to one-half of its initial value is known as ....

SHORT QUESTIONS

1. Define radio pharmaceuticals.
2. Define and classify radioactivity.
3. Define the following terms: (a) Isotopes, (b) Isobars, (c) Isotones, (d) Nuclide, and (e) Nuclear isomers
4. What is meant by half-life of radio element?
5. Define radio-opaque contrast media with examples.
6. Define Curie.
7. Give two examples of radioisotopes.

LONG QUESTIONS

1. Discuss the radiations emitted by radio pharmaceuticals.
2. Mention the characteristics of radioactivity.
3. What is meant by half-life of radio element? Discuss the various units of radioactivity.
4. Explain the biological effects of radiation.
5. Describe the methods for production of radioisotopes.
6. How can radioactivity be detected and measured?
7. Write short note on Geiger-Muller counters.
8. What precautions are to be taken in handling and storage of radioactive materials?
9. Discuss various applications of radio pharmaceuticals.
10. Mention the official preparations of radio pharmaceuticals and their applications.
11. Name the radio-nuclide present in the following commonly used radio pharmaceuticals: (a) cyanocobalamin injection, (b) sodium chloride injection, (c) sodium orthophosphate solution, (d) sodium iodide capsules, and (e) calcium chloride solution.
12. Mention the routes of administration and uses of radio-opaque contrast media.
13. Describe the requirements of radio-opaque substance.
14. Discuss the chemistry of sodium iodide-131 and barium sulphate.

ANSWERS

Multiple-Choice Questions

1. (a) 2. (d) 3. (d) 4. (a) 5. (a) 6. (b) 7. (d) 8. (a)
9. (a) 10. (a) 11. (b) 12. (c) 13. (c) 14. (c) 15. (b) 16. (a)
17. (a)

Fill in the Blanks

1. Spontaneous
2. Two unit positive
3. Negatively
4. Atomic number, mass number
5. First order
6. Geiger-Muller counter
7. Ionisation chamber, proportional counter
8. Half-life

Appendices

Appendix 1
Reagent Preparations

1. **Acetate Buffer pH 3.5:** Dissolve 25 g of ammonium acetate in 25 mL of water and add 38 mL of 7 M hydrochloric acid. Adjust the pH to 3.5 with either 2 M hydrochloric acid or 6 M ammonia and dilute with water to 100 mL.
2. **Acetic Acid, x M:** Solutions of any molarity x M may be prepared by diluting 57x mL (60x g) of glacial acetic acid to 1000 mL with water.
3. **Acetic Acid, 5 M:** Dilute 285 mL (300 g) of glacial acetic acid to 1000 mL with water.
4. **Acetic Acid, Dilute:** Contains approximately 6% w/w of CH_3COOH. Dilute 57 mL of glacial acetic acid to 1000 mL with water.
5. **Ammonia Solution, Dilute:** Contains approximately 10% w/w of NH_3. Dilute 425 mL of strong ammonia solution to 1000 mL. Store protected from moisture in a cool place.
6. **Ammonium Citrate Solution:** Dissolve, with cooling, 500 g of citric acid in a mixture of 200 mL of water and 200 mL of strong ammonia solution, filter and dilute to 1000 mL with water.
7. **Ammonium Cyanide Solution:** A 10.0% w/v solution of ammonium cyanide.
8. **Arsenic Standard Solution (10 ppm As):** Dissolve 0.330 g of arsenic trioxide in 5 mL of 2 M sodium hydroxide and dilute to 250 mL with water. Dilute 1 volume of this solution to 100 volumes with water.
9. **$BaCl_2$ Solution, 25% w/v:** Dissolve 25 g $BaCl_2$ in sufficient water and dilute to 100 mL with water.
10. **Chloride Standard Solution (25 ppm Cl):** Dilute 5 volumes of 0.0824% w/v solution of sodium chloride to 100 volumes with water.
11. **Citric Acid, Iron-Free, 20% w/v:** Dissolve 20 g iron-free citric acid in sufficient water and dilute to 100 mL with water.
12. **Dithizone Solution:** A 0.05% w/v solution of dithizone in chloroform. Prepare immediately before use.

13. **Dithizone Standard Solution:** Dissolve 10 mg dithizone in 1000 mL of chloroform. Store the solution in a glass-stoppered, lead-free, light-resistant bottle in a refrigerator.
14. **Dithizone Extraction Solution:** Dissolve 30 mg dithizone in 1000 mL of chloroform and add 5 mL of ethanol (95%). Store the solution in a refrigerator. Before use, shake a suitable volume of the solution with about half its volume of a 1% v/v solution of nitric acid and discard the acid.
15. **Hydrochloric Acid, x M:** Solutions of any molarity x M may be prepared by diluting 85x mL of hydrochloric acid to 1000 mL with water.

    Store in containers of polyethylene or other non-reacting material at a temperature not exceeding 30°C.
16. **Hydrochloric Acid, Dilute:** Contains approximately 10% w/w of hydrochloric acid.
17. **Hydrogen Sulphide (Gas):** Prepare the gas by the action of hydrochloric acid, diluted with an equal volume of water, on iron sulphide; wash the resulting gas by passing it through water.
18. **Hydrogen Sulphide Solution:** A recently prepared saturated solution of hydrogen sulphide in water.
19. **Hydroxylamine Hydrochloride Solution:** Dissolve 1 g of Hydroxylamine hydrochloride in 50 mL of water, add 50 mL of ethanol (95%) and 1 mL of bromophenol blue solution and then add 0.1 M sodium hydroxide until the solution is green.
20. **Iron Standard Solution (20 ppm Fe):** Dilute 1 volume of a 0.1726% w/v solution of ferric ammonium sulphate in 0.05 M sulphuric acid to 10 volumes with water. Contains iron in ferric state.
21. **Lead Standard Solution (0.1% Pb):** Dissolve 0.400 g of lead nitrate in water containing 2 mL of nitric acid and add sufficient water to produce 250.0 mL.
22. **Lead Standard Solution:** On the day of use, dilute 10 mL of lead nitrate stock solution with water to 100 mL. 1 mL of lead standard solution contains the equivalent of 10 µg of lead. A control comparison solution prepared with 2.0 mL of lead standard solution contains, when compared to a solution representing 1.0 g of the substance under examination, the equivalent of 20 ppm of lead.
23. **Lead Standard Solution (1 ppm Pb):** Dilute 1 volume of lead standard solution (10 ppm Pb) to 10 volumes with water.
24. **Lead Standard Solution (2 ppm Pb):** Dilute 1 volume of lead standard solution (10 ppm Pb) to 5 volumes with water.
25. **Lead Standard Solution (10 ppm Pb):** Dilute 1 volume of lead standard solution (100 ppm Pb) to 10 volumes with water.
26. **Lead Standard Solution (20 ppm Pb):** Dilute 1 volume of lead standard solution (100 ppm Pb) to 5 volumes with water.

27. **Lead Standard Solution (100 ppm Pb):** Dilute 1 volume of lead standard solution (0.1% Pb) to 10 volumes with water.
28. **Nitric Acid:** HNO_3 = 63.01. About 16 M in strength; wt. per mL, about 1.42 g; contains about 70% w/w of HNO_3. Store protected from light.
29. **Nitric Acid, x M:** Solutions of any molarity x M may be prepared by diluting 63x mL of nitric acid to 1000 mL with water.
30. **Nitric Acid, Dilute:** Contains approximately 10% w/w of HNO_3. Dilute 106 mL of nitric acid to 1000 mL with water.
31. **Nitric acid, Fuming:** HNO_3 = 63.01. About 22.5 M in strength; wt. per mL, about 1.5 g; contains about 95% w/w of HNO_3. Store protected from light.
32. **Phenol Red Solution:** Dissolve 0.1 g of phenol red in 2.82 mL of 0.1 M sodium hydroxide and 20 mL of ethanol (95%). After solution is affected, add sufficient water to produce 100 mL.
33. **Potassium Cyanide Solution:** A 10.0% w/v solution of potassium cyanide.
34. **Potassium Iodide, 1 M:** Dissolve 166.0 g of potassium iodide in sufficient water to produce 1000 mL.
35. **Silver Nitrate, 0.1 M:** Dissolve 17.0 g $AgNO_3$ in sufficient water to produce 1000 mL.

    Standardize the solution in the following manner.

    Weigh accurately about 0.1 g of sodium chloride, previously dried at 110°C for 2 hours and dissolve in 5 mL of water. Add 5 mL of acetic acid, 50 mL of methanol and 0.15 mL of eosin solution. Stir, preferably with magnetic stirrer and titrate with the silver nitrate solution.

    1 mL of 0.1 M silver nitrate is equivalent to 0.005844 g of NaCl.

    Store protected from light.
36. **Sodium Hydroxide, x M:** Solutions of any molarity x M may be prepared by dissolving 40x mL of sodium hydroxide in sufficient water to produce 1000 mL.
37. **Sodium Hydroxide Solution:** A 20.0% w/v solution of sodium hydroxide.
38. **Sodium Hydroxide Solution, Dilute:** A 5.0% w/v solution of sodium hydroxide.
39. **Stannous Chloride Solution:** May be prepared by either of the following two methods.
    (a) Dissolve 330 g of stannous chloride in 100 mL of hydrochloric acid and add sufficient water to produce 1000 mL.
    (b) Dilute 60 mL of hydrochloric acid with 20 mL of water, add 20 g of tin, heat gently until no more gas is evolved and add sufficient water to produce 100 mL. Store over a little of the undissolved tin remaining in the solution and protected from air.

40. **Stannous Chloride Solution AsT:** Stannous chloride solution, low in arsenic, commercially available or prepared from stannous chloride solution by adding an equal volume of hydrochloric acid AsT, reducing to the original volume by boiling and filtering through a fine-grain filter paper.

41. **Sulphate Standard Solution (10 ppm SO_4^{2-}):** Dilute 1 volume of a 0.181% w/v solution of potassium sulphate in distilled water to 100 volumes with the same solvent.

42. **Sulphate standard solution (10 ppm SO_4^{2-}), Ethanolic:** Dilute 1 volume of a 0.181% w/v solution of potassium sulphate in ethanol (30%) to 100 volumes with ethanol (30%).

43. **Sulphuric Acid:** H_2SO_4 = 98.07. About 18 M in strength; wt. per mL, about 1.84 g; contains about 98% w/w of sulphuric acid.

44. **Sulphuric Acid, x M:** Solutions of any molarity x M may be prepared by carefully adding 54x mL of sulphuric acid to an equal volume of water and diluting to 1000 mL with water.

45. **Sulphuric Acid, x%:** Mix x mL of sulphuric acid carefully with water, cool and adjust the volume to 100 mL to produce the specified percentage v/v of sulphuric acid.

46. **Sulphuric Acid, Dilute:** Contains approximately 10% w/w of H_2SO_4. Dilute 57 mL of sulphuric acid to 1000 mL with water.

47. **Thioacetamide Reagent:** Add 1 mL of a mixture of 15 mL of 1 M sodium hydroxide, 5 mL of water and 20 mL of glycerin (85%) to 0.2 mL of thioacetamide solution, heat in a water bath for 20 seconds, cool and use immediately.

48. **Thioacetamide Solution:** Contains approximately 4% w/v solution of thioacetamide.

Appendix 2
Buffer Solutions Used in Pharmacy and Research

1. **Acetate Buffer pH 2.8:** Dissolve 4 g of anhydrous sodium acetate in about 840 mL of water, add sufficient glacial acetic acid to adjust the pH to 2.8 (about 155 mL) and dilute with water to 1000 mL.
2. **Acetate Buffer pH 3.4:** Mix 50 mL of 0.1 M sodium acetate with 950 mL of 0.1 M acetic acid.
3. **Acetate Buffer pH 3.5:** Dissolve 25 g of ammonium acetate in 25 mL of water and add 38 mL of 7 M hydrochloric acid. Adjust the pH to 3.5 with either 2 M hydrochloric acid or 6 M ammonia and dilute with water to 100 mL.
4. **Acetate Buffer pH 3.7:** Dissolve 10 g of anhydrous sodium acetate in 300 mL of water, adjust to pH to 3.7 with glacial acetic acid and dilute with water to 1000 ml. Before use adjust to pH 3.7, if necessary, with glacial acetic acid or anhydrous sodium acetate, as required.
5. **Acetate Buffer pH 4.0:** Place 2.86 mL of glacial acetic acid and 1.0 mL of a 50% w/v solution of sodium hydroxide in a 1000 mL volumetric flask, add water to volume and mix. Adjust the pH, if necessary.
6. **Acetate Buffer pH 4.6:** Dissolve 5.4 g of sodium acetate in 50 mL of water, add 2.4 mL of glacial acetic acid and dilute with water to 100 mL. Adjust the pH, if necessary.
7. **Acetate Buffer pH 4.7:** Dissolve 8.4 g of sodium acetate and 3.35 mL of glacial acetic acid in sufficient water to produce 1000 mL. Adjust the pH, if necessary.
8. **Acetate Buffer pH 5.0:** Dissolve 13.6 g of sodium acetate and 6 mL of glacial acetic acid in sufficient water to produce 1000 mL. Adjust the pH, if necessary.
9. **Acetate Buffer pH 5.5:** Dissolve 272 g of sodium acetate in 500 mL of water by heating to 35°C, cool and add slowly 50 mL of glacial acetic acid and sufficient water to produce 1000 mL. Adjust the pH, if necessary.

10. **Acetate Buffer pH 6.0:** Dissolve 100 g of ammonium acetate in 300 mL of water, add 4.1 mL of glacial acetic acid, adjust the pH, if necessary, using 10 M ammonia or 5 M acetic acid and dilute with water to 500 mL.
11. **Acetate Buffer Solution:** Dissolve 14 g of potassium acetate and 20.5 mL of glacial acetic acid in sufficient water to produce 1000 mL.
12. **Acetic Acid-Ammonium Acetate Buffer:** Dissolve 77.1 g of ammonium acetate in water, add 57 mL of glacial acetic acid and dilute with water to 1000 mL.
13. **Acetic Ammonia Buffer pH 3.7, Ethanolic:** To 15 mL of 5 M acetic acid, add 60 mL of ethanol (95%) and 24 mL of water. Adjust the pH to 3.7 with 10 M ammonia and dilute with water to 100 mL.
14. **Acetone Solution, Buffered:** Dissolve 8.15 g of sodium acetate and 42 g of sodium chloride in water, add 68 mL of 0.1 M hydrochloric acid and 150 mL of acetone and dilute with water to 500 mL.
15. **Albumin Phosphate Buffer pH 7.2; Phosphate-Albumin Buffered Saline pH 7.2:** Dissolve 10.75 g of disodium hydrogen phosphate, 7.6 g of sodium chloride and 10 g of bovine albumin in sufficient water to produce 1000 mL. Before use adjust to pH 7.2 with 2 M sodium hydroxide or a 10% w/v solution of phosphoric acid as required.
16. **Ammonia-Ammonium Chloride Buffer:** Dissolve 67.5 g of ammonium chloride in about 200 mL of water, add 570 mL of strong ammonia solution and dilute with water to 1000 mL.
17. **Ammonia Buffer pH 9.5:** Dissolve 33.5 g of ammonium chloride in 150 mL of water, and 42 mL of 10 M ammonia and dilute with water to 250 mL.

    Store in polyethylene containers.
18. **Ammonia Buffer pH 10.0:** Dissolve 5.4 g of ammonium chloride in 20 mL of water, add 35 mL of 10 M ammonia and dilute with water to 100 mL.
19. **Ammonia Buffer pH 10.9:** Dissolve 67.5 g of ammonium chloride in sufficient 10 M ammonia to produce 1000 mL.
20. **Barbitone Buffer pH 7.4:** Mix 50 mL of solution containing 1.944% w/v of sodium acetate and 2.946% w/v of barbitone sodium with 50.5 mL of 0.1 M hydrochloric acid, add 20 mL of an 8.5% w/v solution of sodium chloride and dilute with water to 250 mL.
21. **Barbitone Buffer pH 8.6, Mixed; Barbitone Buffer pH 8.6:** Dissolve 1.38 g of barbitone, 8.76 g of barbitone sodium and 0.38 g of calcium lactate in sufficient water to produce 1000 mL.
22. **Boric Buffer pH 9.0; Borate Buffer pH 9.0:** Dissolve 6.20 g of boric acid in 500 mL of water, adjust to pH 9.0 with 1 M sodium hydroxide (about 41.5 mL) and dilute with water to 1000 mL.

23. **Buffer Solution pH 2.5:** To 25.0 mL of 0.2 M potassium hydrogen phthalate, add 37.0 mL of 0.1 M hydrochloric acid and dilute with sufficient water to produce 100.0 mL.
24. **Buffer (HEPES) Solution pH 7.5:** Dissolve 2.38 g of 2[4-(hydroxyethyl) piperazin-1-yl]ethanesulphonic acid in about 90 mL of water. Adjust the pH to 7.5 with sodium hydroxide solution. Dilute to 100 mL with water.
25. **Carbonate Buffer pH 9.7:** Dissolve 8.4 g of sodium bicarbonate and 10.6 g of sodium carbonate in sufficient water to produce 500 mL.
26. **Chloride Buffer pH 2.0:** Dissolve 6.57 g of potassium chloride in water, add 119.0 mL of 0.1 M hydrochloric acid and dilute with water to 1000 mL.
27. **Citro-phosphate Buffer pH 5.0:** Mix 48.5 mL of 0.1 M citric acid with sufficient 0.2 M disodium hydrogen phosphate to produce 100 mL.
28. **Citro-phosphate Buffer pH 6.0:** Mix 36.8 mL of a 2.1% w/v solution of citric acid with 63.2 mL of a 7.15% w/v solution of disodium hydrogen phosphate.
29. **Citro-Phosphate Buffer pH 7.0:** Mix 17.6 mL of a 2.1% w/v solution of citric acid with 82.4 mL of a 7.15% w/v solution of disodium hydrogen phosphate.
30. **Citro-Phosphate Buffer pH 7.2:** Mix 13.0 mL of a 2.1% w/v solution of citric acid with 87.0 mL of a 7.15% w/v solution of disodium hydrogen phosphate.
31. **Citro-Phosphate Buffer pH 7.6:** Dissolve 1.33 g of citric acid and 67.1 g of disodium hydrogen phosphate in sufficient water to produce 1000 mL.
32. **Cupric Sulphate Solution pH 2.0, Buffered:** Mix 5.3 mL of 0.2 M hydrochloric acid and 25 mL of 0.2 M potassium chloride, add 4 mL of a 0.393% w/v solution of cupric sulphate and dilute to 100 mL of water.
33. **Cupric Sulphate Solution pH 4.0, Buffered:** Dissolve 0.25 g cupric sulphate and 4.5 g of ammonium acetate in sufficient water to produce 100 mL.
34. **Cupric Sulphate Solution pH 5.2, Buffered:** Dissolve 1.522 g of anhydrous disodium hydrogen phosphate in sufficient water to produce 53.6 mL and add a 2.1% solution of citric acid until the pH of the solution is between 5.15 and 5.25 (about 46 mL). Mix 98.5 mL of the resulting solution with 1.5 mL of a 0.393% solution of cupric sulphate.
35. **Diethanolamine Buffer pH 10.0:** Dissolve 96.4 g of diethanolamine in sufficient water to produce 400 mL. Add 0.5 mL of an 18.6% w/v solution of magnesium chloride, adjust the pH to 10.0.with 1 M hydrochloric acid and dilute with water to 500 mL.
36. **Glycine Buffer pH 11.3:** Mix a solution containing 0.75% w/v of glycine and 0.58% w/v of sodium chloride with an equal volume of 0.1 M sodium hydroxide. Adjust the pH, if necessary.
37. **Glycine Buffer Solution:** Mix 42 g of sodium bicarbonate and 50 g of potassium bicarbonate with 180 mL of water and add a solution containing 37.5 g of

glycine and 15 mL of strong ammonia in 180 mL of water. Dilute with water to 500 mL and stir until the solution is complete.

38. **Imidazole Buffer pH 6.5:** Dissolve 6.81 g of imidazole and 1.23 g of magnesium sulphate in 752 mL of 0.1 M hydrochloric acid, adjust the pH, if necessary and dilute with water to produce 1000 mL.
39. **Imidazole Buffer pH 7.4:** Dissolve 3.40 g of imidazole and 5.84 g of sodium chloride in water and 18.6 mL of 1 M hydrochloric acid and dilute with water to produce 1000 mL.
40. **Palladium Chloride Solution, Buffered:** To 0.5 g of palladium chloride, add 5 mL of hydrochloric acid and warm on a water bath. Add 200 mL of hot water in small portions with continued heating until the solution is complete. Cool and dilute with sufficient water to produce 250.0 mL. To 50.0 mL of the resulting solution, add 10.0 mL of 1 M sodium acetate, 9.6 mL of 1 M hydrochloric acid and sufficient water to produce 100.0 mL.
41. **Phosphate-Albumin Buffered Saline pH 7.2:** Dissolve 10.75 g of disodium hydrogen phosphate, 7.6 g of sodium chloride and 10 g of bovin albumin in water and dilute to 1000.0 mL with the same solvent. Immediately before use, adjust the pH using dilute sodium hydrogen solution or dilute phosphoric acid.
42. **Phosphate Buffer pH 2.0:** Dissolve 0.136 g of potassium dihydrogen phosphate in 800 mL of water, adjust the pH to 2.0 with hydrochloric acid and add sufficient water to produce 1000 mL.
43. **Phosphate Buffer pH 2.5:** Dissolve 100 g of potassium dihydrogen phosphate in 800 mL of water, adjust the pH to 2.5 with hydrochloric acid and add sufficient water to produce 1000 mL.
44. **Phosphate Buffer pH 3.6:** Dissolve 0.900 g of anhydrous disodium hydrogen phosphate and 1.298 g of citric acid monohydrate in sufficient water to produce 1000 mL.
45. **Phosphate Buffer pH 4.0, Mixed:** Dissolve 5.04 g disodium hydrogen phosphate and 3.01 g of potassium dihydrogen phosphate in sufficient water to produce 1000 mL. Adjust the pH with glacial acetic acid.
46. **Phosphate Buffer pH 4.9:** Dissolve 40 g of sodium dihydrogen phosphate and 1.2 g of sodium hydroxide in sufficient water to produce 100 mL. If necessary, adjust the pH with 1 M sulphuric acid or 1 M sodium hydroxide as required.
47. **Phosphate Buffer pH 5.0:** Dissolve 6.8 g of potassium dihydrogen phosphate in 1000 mL of water and adjust the pH to 5.0 with 10 M potassium hydroxide.
48. **Phosphate Buffer pH 5.5, Mixed**

    Solution I - Dissolve 13.61 g of potassium dihydrogen phosphate in sufficient water to produce 1000 mL.

Solution II - Dissolve 35.81 g of disodium hydrogen phosphate in sufficient water to produce 1000 mL.

Mix 96.4 mL of solution I with 3.6 mL of solution II.

49. **Phosphate Buffer pH 6.5:** Dissolve 60.5 g of disodium hydrogen phosphate and 46 g of potassium dihydrogen phosphate in water, add 100 mL of 0.02 M disodium edetate and 20 mg of mercuric chloride and dilute with water to produce 1000 mL.

50. **Phosphate Buffer pH 6.8, Mixed:** Dissolve 28.80 g of disodium hydrogen phosphate and 11.45 g of potassium dihydrogen phosphate in sufficient water to produce 1000 mL.

51. **Phosphate Buffer pH 6.8, 0.2 M Mixed:** Dissolve 13.872 g of potassium dihydrogen phosphate and 35.084 g of disodium hydrogen phosphate in sufficient water to produce 1000 mL. Store in a cold place.

52. **Phosphate Buffer pH 7.0, Mixed:** Dissolve 0.50 g of anhydrous disodium hydrogen phosphate 0.301 g of potassium dihydrogen phosphate in sufficient water to produce 1000 mL.

53. **Phosphate Buffer pH 7.0 with Azide, Mixed:** To 1000 mL of a solution containing 1.8% w/v of disodium hydrogen phosphate and 2.3% w/v of sodium chloride, add sufficient of a solution containing 0.78% w/v of sodium dihydrogen phosphate and 2.3% w/v of sodium chloride (about 280 mL) to produce a pH of 7.0. Dissolve sufficient sodium azide in the resulting solution to give a 0.02% w/v solution.

54. **Phosphate Buffer pH 7.0, 0.067 M Mixed:** Dissolve 3.532 g of potassium dihydrogen phosphate and 14.542 g of disodium hydrogen phosphate in sufficient water to produce 1000 mL.

55. **Phosphate Buffer pH 7.5, 0.33 M Mixed**

    Solution I - Dissolve 119.31 g of disodium hydrogen phosphate in sufficient water to produce 1000 mL.

    Solution II - Dissolve 45.36 g of potassium dihydrogen phosphate in sufficient water to produce 1000 mL.

    Mix 85 mL of solution I and 15 mL of solution II and adjust the pH, if necessary.

56. **Phosphate Buffer pH 8.0, 0.02 M:** Mix 50 mL of 0.2 M potassium dihydrogen phosphate with 46.8 mL of 0.2 M sodium hydroxide and add sufficient water to produce 500 mL.

57. **Phosphate Buffer, 0.025 M Standard:** Dissolve 3.40 g of potassium dihydrogen phosphate and 3.55 g of anhydrous disodium hydrogen phosphate, both previously dried at 110° to 130°C for 2 hours, in sufficient water to produce 1000 mL.

58. **Saline, Phosphate-Buffered:** Dissolve 2.5 g of sodium dihydrogen phosphate, 2.523 g of disodium hydrogen phosphate and 8.2 g of sodium chloride in sufficient water to produce 1000 mL.
59. **Saline pH 6.4, Phosphate-Buffered:** Dissolve 1.79 g of disodium hydrogen phosphate, 1.36 g of potassium dihydrogen phosphate and 7.02 g of sodium chloride in sufficient water to produce 1000 mL.
60. **Saline pH 7.4, Phosphate-Buffered:** Dissolve 2.38 g of disodium hydrogen phosphate, 0.19 g of potassium dihydrogen phosphate and 8.0 g of sodium chloride in sufficient water to produce 1000 mL. Adjust the pH, if necessary.
61. **Tris-acetate Buffer Solution pH 8.5:** Dissolve 0.294 g of calcium chloride of tris(hydroxymethyl)aminomethane in water. Adjust the pH with acetic acid. Dilute to 1000.0 mL with water.
62. **Tris(hydroxymethyl)aminomethane Buffer Solution pH 7.4:** Dissolve 30.3 g of tris(hydroxymethyl)aminimethane in approximately 200 mL of water. Add 183 ml of 1 M hydrochloric acid. Dilute to 500.0 mL with water.

    Note: The pH is 7.7 to 7.8 at room temperature and 7.4 at 37°C. This solution is stable for several months at 4°C.

Appendix 3
Definitions

Pharmaceutical Chemistry: It is a branch of science which makes use of the general laws of chemistry to study medicinal and pharmaceutical substances, including their preparation, chemical nature, composition, structure and influence on an organism.

Inorganic Pharmaceutical Chemistry: It is a branch of science which makes use of the laws of chemistry to study inorganic substances as drugs, viz., their preparation, chemical nature, composition, structure, influence on an organism, etc.

Pharmacopoeia: It is an official book of standards published by respective governments, containing list of drugs, pharmaceuticals, preparations, storage, uses, etc.

Monograph: It is a document which defines pharmaceutical substances and provides information that allows for its proper identification.

Assay: It represents a step-by-step description of chemical analytical method for the active substance.

Impurity: It is the undesirable matter which may or may not be toxic but is present in the pharmaceutical substances.

Impure Chemical Compound: A compound is said to be impure if it has the presence of foreign matter, i.e., impurities.

Pure Chemical Compound: It refers to that compound which is free from foreign matter, i.e., impurities.

Tests for Purity: These are those tests which are used for detecting impurities in the pharmaceutical substances.

Ash: It represents the residue after complete ignition of the drug.

Loss on Drying: It is the classic laboratory method of measuring high-level moisture in solid or semisolid materials.

Loss on Ignition: It is a test used in inorganic analytical chemistry, particularly in the analysis of minerals.

Limit Tests: These are quantitative or semi-quantitative tests designed to identify and control small quantities of impurity, which are likely to be present in the substance.

Acid: As per the Arrhenius theory, an acid may be defined as any compound which produces hydrogen (H^+) ions in aqueous solution. As per the Lowry-Bronsted theory, it may be defined as a substance which donates protons. According to Lewis Theory, it may be defined as species (molecules, radical or ion) that can accept an electron pair to form a coordinate bond.

Base: As per the Arrhenius theory, base may be defined as any compound which produces hydroxide (OH^-) ions in an aqueous solution. As per the Lowry-Bronsted theory, it may be defined as a substance which accepts protons. According to this theory, it may be defined as species (molecules, radical or ion) that can donate an electron pair to form a coordinate bond.

Buffer Solution: The solution which resists the changes in pH values upon the addition of small amount of acid or alkali is termed a buffer solution.

Acidic Buffer: The solution consisting of a mixture of weak acid (e.g., acetic acid) and its salt (e.g., sodium acetate) is called acidic buffer.

Basic Buffer: The solution consisting of a mixture of weak base (e.g., ammonia) and its salt (e.g., ammonium chloride) is called basic buffer.

pH: The term pH is defined as the negative logarithm (to the base 10) of hydrogen ion concentration.

Buffer Capacity (β)**:** It is defined as the amount of acid or base that must be added to the buffer to produce a unit change of pH. Practically, it is defined as the number of moles of an acid or base required to be added to 1 L of buffer solution so as to change its pH by 1 unit.

Osmotic Pressure: It is the minimum pressure which needs to be applied to a solution to prevent the inward flow of water across a cell semi-permeable membrane.

Osmosis: It refers to the movement of water or other solvent through a plasma membrane (semi-permeable membrane) from a region of low solute concentration to a region of high solute concentration.

Tonicity: The ability of an extracellular solution to make water move into or out of a cell by osmosis is known as its tonicity.

Isotonic Solutions: It refers to two solutions having the same osmotic pressure across a semi-permeable membrane.

Isosmotic Solution: It refers to the solution having the same osmotic pressure as blood.

Electrolytes: These are the inorganic ions carrying a positive or a negative charge and their aqueous solutions are responsible for conducting electricity.

Intracellular Fluid: It refers to the fluid which is present inside a cell.

Interstitial Fluid: It refers to the fluid which is present between the cells.

Plasma or Vascular Fluid: It refers to the fluid which is present within the blood vascular system.

Extracellular Fluid: The fluids present in the interstitial and vascular compartments are collectively referred to as the extracellular fluid.

Hyponatremia: It means decreased level of sodium in the blood.

Hypernatremia: It means increased level of sodium in the blood.

Hypocalcaemia: It means decreased level of calcium in the blood.

Hypercalcaemia: It means increased level of calcium in the blood.

Hypochloremia: It means decreased level of chloride in the blood.

Hyperchloremia: It means increased level of chloride in the blood.

Hypokalemia: It means decreased level of potassium in the blood.

Hyperkalemia: It means increased level of potassium in the blood.

Hypomagnesemia: It means decreased level of magnesium in the blood.

Hypermagnesemia: It means increased level of magnesium in the blood.

Hypophosphatemia: It means decreased level of phosphate in the blood.

Hyperphosphatemia: It means increased level of phosphate in the blood.

Replacement Therapy: It refers to the external administration of electrolytes in the body to restore and maintain electrolyte balance of the body.

Metabolic Acidosis: It refers to the disturbed acid-base balance of the body and physiological fluids become acidic in nature.

Metabolic Alkalosis: It refers to the disturbed acid-base balance of the body and physiological fluids become more alkaline in nature.

Respiratory Acidosis: It refers to the state in which carbon dioxide is retained in the body due to reduced ventilation.

Respiratory Alkalosis: It refers to the state in which excess of carbon dioxide is lost from the body due to hyperventilation.

Electrolyte Replenishers: The substances which are used to restore body fluid electrolyte balance are called electrolyte replenishers.

Oral Rehydration Salts (ORS) or Oral Rehydration Therapy (ORT): The preparations which are given orally to correct electrolyte balance of the body are called oral rehydration salts and the therapy is called oral rehydration therapy.

Dental Products: These may be defined as inorganic compounds and their preparations meant for local application in the oral cavity for maintenance of dental hygiene.

Anticaries Agents: These are the agents that are used in the treatment of dental caries or tooth decay.

Dentifrices or Cleaning Agents or Abrasives: These are the agents that are used to clean the accessible surfaces of teeth and adjacent gums and remove the stain from the teeth.

Desensitizing Agents: Dentifrices when used in the treatment of dental hyperaesthesia caused by any dental irritant like physical effects (heat or cold contact), physiological effects (abrasion) and chemical agents (acid erosion) are known as desensitizing agents.

Oral Antiseptics and Astringents: These are the inorganic substances which show antiseptic and astringent action in the oral cavity.

Mouthwashes: These are the non-sterile aqueous preparations usually used after brushing and mainly intended to provide fresh breath and to kill the bacteria that are responsible for plaque formation.

Cements and Fillers: These are the inorganic agents used temporarily to cover and protect areas that have undergone operation.

Polishing Agents: These are the substances which provide whiteness to the teeth by their abrasive action.

Dental Fluorosis: When the concentration of fluoride exceeds 2 to 3 ppm, the condition is called dental fluorosis.

Gastrointestinal Agents: These are those drugs which are used in the treatment of various gastrointestinal disorders.

Acidifying Agents or Acidifiers: These are the inorganic chemicals or drugs that are used to increase the gastrointestinal acidity.

Antioxidants: These are the reducing agents which are added to drugs or pharmaceuticals to prevent their oxidation through oxidative processes, thereby reducing their decomposition and increase their shelf-life.

Protectives: These are the generally insoluble and chemically inert substances that are meant to be applied onto the skin or mucous membrane to provide protection against irritation, friction and inflammation due to allergy, which is generally of mechanical origin.

Adsorbents: These are those substances which are used to adsorb the gases, toxins and bacteria.

Achlorhydria: It represents absence of hydrochloric acid in the stomach.

Hypochlorhydria: It represents decreased secretion of dilute HCl in the stomach below the normal level.

Antacids: It may be defined as the inorganic substances or chemical agents which are used for neutralising excess acid in the stomach of patients suffering from hyperchlorhydria (hyperacidity).

Cathartics: These are the drugs which activate peristalsis and motility of the gut, thus enabling bowel evacuation.

Purgatives: These are the mild form of cathartics.

Laxatives: These are the mild type of purgatives.

Antimicrobial Agents: These are the chemicals and their preparations which help in reducing or preventing infection due to microbes.

Antiseptics: These are the substances which kill or prevent the growth of micro-organisms and are meant to be applied to living objects only.

Disinfectants: These are the substances that prevent infection by the destruction of pathogenic micro-organisms and are meant to be applied to inanimate objects only.

Germicides: These are the substances which kill microorganisms.

Bactericide: These are the substances which kill bacteria.

Fungicide: These are the substances which kill fungi.

Virucide: These are the substances which kill viruses.

Amoebicide: These are the substances which kill amoebas.

Bacteriostatic: These are the substances which inhibit or arrest the growth of bacteria.

Sanitizers: These are the disinfectants that are used to maintain general public health standards.

Sterilization: It is a process of complete destruction of all living micro-organisms including bacterial spores.

Expectorants: These are the chemical agents that assist in removing sputum from the respiratory tract either by increasing the fluidity (or reducing the viscosity) of sputum or by increasing the volume of fluids that have to be expelled from the respiratory tract by coughing.

Emetics: These are the chemicals which give rise to forced regurgitation (emesis), thereby causing the contents of the stomach to be expelled through the oral cavity (mouth).

Haematinics: These are the substances which increase the amount of haemoglobin content in the blood.

Antidote: It may be defined as 'a therapeutic substance used to counteract the toxic action of a specific xenobiotic'.

Astringents: These are the substances which bring about protein precipitation, thereby forming a protective layer on the surface.

Topical Agents: The agents which are applied topically or locally to the skin or mucous membranes are called topical agents.

Radio Pharmaceuticals: These are the radioisotopes or radionuclides which are employed in medicine for the diagnosis and treatment of certain diseases.

Radioactivity: It is defined as a spontaneous and continuous emission of radiations or rays, e.g., α-, β- and γ-radiations from the substances.

Isotopes: These are the species which possess same atomic number 'Z' (number of protons) but different atomic mass number 'A' (number of protons plus neutrons).

Isobars: These are the atoms of different species having different atomic number 'Z' (number of protons) and same atomic mass number 'A' (number of protons plus neutrons).

Isotones: These are the atomic species having same number of neutrons but different atomic mass numbers.

Nuclide: It refers to the species of atom characterised by the constitution of the nucleus, in particular by the number of protons and neutrons in the nucleus.

Nuclear Isomers: These refer to the atoms of the same species having same atomic number and same atomic mass number but differ in radioactive properties.

Half-Life Time: It is defined as the number of radioactive nuclei actually disintegrating or decaying or mutating to half of its original in a given time.

Curie (Ci): It may be defined as the quantity of any radioactive substance which undergoes the 3.7×10^{10} disintegrations in unit time.

Roentgen (R): It is the unit of exposure.

Becquerel (Bq): Becquerel is the quantity of radioactive substance undergoing one disintegration per second.

Radiation Absorbed Dose (RAD): It indicates the actual dose of radiation absorbed by the body.

Radiation Equivalent in Man (REM): It refers to the unit of equivalent dose of the radiation.

Grays (Gy): It is the SI unit and equivalent to 100 RADs.

Exposure Rate Constant: It refers to the dose rate in roentgens per hour at 1 m distance from 1 curie.

Relative Biological Effectiveness (RBE): It refers to the unit which determines the relative effects of different types of radiations emitted, such as α-, β-, and γ-rays on the biological systems.

Radio-Opaque Contrast Media (X-Ray Contrast Media): Radio-opaque substances are the inorganic or organic compounds which have the property of casting a shadow on X-ray films. These substances have the ability to stop the passage of X-rays and hence, appear opaque on X-ray examination. Such compounds and their preparations are known as X-ray contrast media.

Index

H

I

K

L

M

N

O

P

Q

R

S